C O U R A G E &

M I S F O R T U N E

THE MOUNTAINEERS ANTHOLOGY S·E·R·I·E·S

VOLUME II

COURAGE & MISFORTUNE

THE MOUNTAINEERS BOOKS

Published by
The Mountaineers Books
1001 SW Klickitat Way, Suite 201
Seattle, WA 98134

Published simultaneously in Great Britain by Cordee, 3a DeMontfort Street, Leicester, England, LE1 7HD

Manufactured in the United States of America

Editors: Cassandra Conyers, Kathleen Cubley, and Donna DeShazo
Cover art, cover design, and book design: Ani Rucki
Layout: Ani Rucki

Library of Congress Cataloging-in-Publication Data
Courage and misfortune / compiled by the editors at the Mountaineers books.— 1st ed.
     p. cm. — (The Mountaineers anthology series ; 2)
   ISBN 0-89886-826-2
     1. Mountaineering. 2. Mountaineering expeditions. 3. Mountaineering accidents.
   4. Mountaineering—Environmental aspects. I. Mountaineers Books (Firm) II. Series.
GV200 .C68 2001
796.52'2—dc21

                                                              2001004523

Printed on recycled paper

CONTENTS

INTRODUCTION

The Mountaineers Anthologies of adventure and mountaineering writing reflect our longstanding role as publishing leaders in the worldwide climbing community. Many of the climbing world's most renowned authors publish through The Mountaineers Books, and it is from their work that we assemble these collections of exploits and expeditions.

Each volume is distinguished by a specific adventuring theme. Annotations to each selection provide the book title and pages where the original material can be found. Some original material may be out of print, making these anthologies the only source now available.

You are about to embark on a reading adventure filled with triumphs, daring feats, and heroics; disappointments, extreme challenges, and tragedies.

We hope you enjoy this journey through the best that mountaineering literature has to offer

The Editors
The Mountaineers Books

FOREWORD

As much as we may try to minimize the risks we face as climbers, the truth is that things can and often do go wrong. Many of our sport's best people have been lost in recent years, including my friend Alex Lowe, who was caught in an avalanche in 1999 on Shishapangma in Tibet. Alex, Jared Ogden, and I had recently completed a new route on the northwest face of Pakistan's Great Trango Tower. It was a climb on which he had more than his fair share of close scrapes. He was knocked unconscious by rockfall, developed a serious gastrointestinal illness at our last bivouac, and took a bouncing 50-foot fall on the second to last pitch. More than anyone I ever knew, Alex was a survivor, a James Bond-type character who would always dodge the bullet.

When we lose friends in the mountains, especially people who were as skilled and experienced as Alex, it brings home how much we are dependent on plain luck to survive these adventures. Objective hazards such as rockfall, icefall, avalanches, and weather are elements that, by their definition, are very difficult if not impossible to predict. Each time we walk up to the base of a climb, especially a long and committing one, we must face that inner voice that says: "You could die up there. Is it worth it?" The more times that we put ourselves in these situations, the greater the likelihood that one of those rocks or avalanches will eventually catch us in the wrong place at the wrong time.

Mountain climbing is a selfish pursuit—no one really gets a lot out of it other than the climber. But in reading this book, I was impressed time and time again by how selfless climbers become when one of their own is in trouble. The unwritten rule that you must always come to aid of a fellow climber—even when it means seriously risking your own life—is one of the most consistent themes I found in *Courage and Misfortune*. In his selection from *Storm and Sorrow in the High Pamirs*, Robert Craig recounts the events leading up to the deaths of a team of eight Russian women near the summit of Peak Lenin in 1974. As her teammates systematically freeze to death around her, expedition leader Elvira Shatayeva reports the grisly scene back to basecamp by radio. Although she is probably strong enough to fight her way down to safety, Shatayeva refuses to leave her dying comrades. After more than twenty-four hours of fighting for survival in the storm, there is finally no else left except Elvira. Her final message brings incredible sadness and frustration to her friends in basecamp who had pleaded desperately with her to abandon the others: "Please forgive us," she says. "We love you. Good-bye."

Reading this book may prompt you to ask: "Is the summit of a mountain ever worth the cost of even one human life?" Most would think not, but quite often this is exactly the price we pay to play in the mountains. What is it that compels perfectly intelligent, rational people to risk their lives for the abstract reward of standing on top of some distant, lonely peak? Cresting the summit ridge of a lofty Himalayan peak and staring over the back into a no man's land of glaciers and snow capped peaks, one can't help but feel an electric buzz of energy pulsing through the mind and body. There is a drama and beauty to be found in the world's most hard to reach places that far exceeds the intensity we experience in our normal everyday lives.

Dave Roberts is a climber and writer who has experienced this feeling, and he's one of those rare individuals with the ability to explain it in simple, understandable terms. In the conclusion to his classic essay, "Moments of Doubt," in which he recounts the tragic first ascent of the west face of Alaska's Mount Huntington, Roberts explains: " . . . nowhere else on earth, not even in the harbors of reciprocal love, have I felt pure happiness take hold of me and shake me like a puppy, compelling me, and the conspirators I had arrived there with, to stand on some perch of rock or snow, the uncertain struggle below us, and bawl our pagan vaunts to the very sky."

Perhaps there is a lesson to be learned from the fact that this pure happiness is usually only achieved after suffering some great hardship. In this mechanistic modern world, our primordial instincts for survival are often left untested, driving us to seek out those places where life is still hard. Huddled under overhangs as rocks and avalanches pour down from the sky, we peer over the edge of the abyss to confront our most primal fears. Regardless of why we seek out these trials, they emanate from too deep inside our psyches to be kept bottled up. In the classic book *Himalaya Alpine Style*, Stephen Venables sums it up perfectly: "We must channel, control, and ultimately feed our passion. To deny it is to dilute the experience of living. To let it run riot is to risk losing everything."

—Mark Synnott

FROM

NANDA DEVI:
THE TRAGIC EXPEDITION

BY JOHN ROSKELLEY

THE SEEDS FOR DISCORD ON THE 1976 NANDA DEVI EXPEDITION to the North Ridge were sown at the beginning. The co-leaders— philosophy/religion professor and mountain-mystic Willi Unsoeld and the legendary Ad Carter, a primary benefactor of the American Alpine Club— were men of different styles, and with different views of the goals of the expedition.

Carter had been with the team that made the first ascent of Nanda Devi in 1936, and he approached this expedition as if it were to be done in traditional style. Unsoeld, best known for his work on the Everest West Ridge route with Tom Hornbein in 1963, saw the trip as something of a pilgrimage for his daughter, Nanda Devi Unsoeld. Even with years of Himalayan experience behind them, the co-leaders adopted a laissez faire approach with the climbers, who were an uneasy mix of skilled, motivated mountaineers and optimistic neophytes.

Author John Roskelley had completed a new route on Dhaulagiri in 1973 and, with Lou Reichardt, would summit on K2 in 1978. Strong, single-minded, and plain spoken, Roskelley made his position clear when expedition members put themselves and the group in danger by pushing weaker, inexperienced climbers up the route.

In the end, three men reached the summit: Roskelley, Reichardt, and Jim States. And Unsoeld had to undergo one of the most painful experiences a father could face—watching his beloved daughter die, high on the peak for which she was named. The expedition itself went down in history as one of the most acrimonious in the annals of mountaineering.

Two years later Unsoeld and one of his Evergreen College students would die at Cadaver Gap on Mount Rainier. Perhaps tempting fate, Willi had been leading the students through treacherous winter conditions when the group was struck by an avalanche.

This selection, Chapter 13 from Roskelley's book *Nanda Devi: The Tragic Expedition*, pages 201-217, begins on a high point with the summit success. Then, as the second team readies for an attempt, there is a growing sense of dread as Devi becomes increasingly ill . . .

Liquids were the first priority at Camp IV. We boiled pot after pot of water and drank deeply to rehydrate. Shadows deepened in the valleys while we savored a dinner of beef and vegetables. Lou [Reichardt]reached Camp III on the radio at 5:30. "Devi! We took a rest day and climbed the nearest peak!"

"You went to the summit?"

"Yep, we were on top at two o'clock."

"Fantastic!" she cheered. "Congratulations on a wonderful job!" The rest of the team was returning from jumaring practice on the Buttress, so we agreed to talk with Willi at seven o'clock.

"Congratulations on your ascent," Willi's voice boomed over the radio. "We'll be sending a team up tomorrow to take your place—probably Devi, Peter [Lev], and Andy [Harvard]. Leave your sleeping bags at Camp IV and you can use theirs down here."

"John [Evans] wants to know, what if they don't make it this far?" Lou asked. I didn't like the idea of being separated from my sleeping bag, but Lou later shamed me into agreement.

Andy's voice broke in: "Don't worry: We'll get there."

Hoping to get a good night's rest, Jim [States], Lou, and I slipped into our bags early. The altitude and crowded conditions, however, prevented us from sleeping very well. It was a long cold night after the summit.

➤   ➤   ➤

We were awake at 6:00 A.M. It was too cold and too early to descend. Jim leaned forward, still in his bag, and lit the stove. After a small breakfast with several cups of steaming tea, we dressed and left the tent to pack. Jim and I were gloveless; our Dachsteins (preshrunk woolen mittens made in Austria) were frozen solid, having become wet the day before. We held them against our bodies, straightened our gear, and waited for the sun to warm our tiny perch. The weather was beautiful.

I was too cold to wait very long, so I hooked my rappel system to the first rope, snapped a few pictures, and descended. Jim followed as soon as the rope went slack. I made it a point to wait at the end of each rope to take pictures of Jim rappeling and to make sure he was all right. Lou descended close behind. At Sugar Delight, I waited for half an hour for Jim to appear. He was coming down slowly, carefully. I stuffed an extra three-hundred-foot nine-millimeter rope and a rack of hardware I found at the anchor into my pack to take to Camp III, then, after seeing Jim round the corner, descended the rest of the Buttress.

Jim and I were at the base of the Buttress two hours after leaving Camp IV. "We're down!" We clasped each other's arms. "I couldn't feel my feet or hands on the first rappels—I thought I was going to lose them," he said. We relaxed in the snow and warm air and waited for Lou.

"I wonder where Devi, Andy, and Peter are?" Jim asked.

I was puzzled too. "On Dhaulagiri, someone would have broken trail out here to meet us. Usually someone's there . . . "

"They asked us to leave our gear at IV because they said they would be going up. And no one's gotten even this far. I can't understand why someone didn't meet us here at least—they know we're tired."

Lou descended the last rope to where we were sitting and removed his crampons. He, too, was disappointed not to see the second team. He was the one who had argued for us to leave our gear when the others insisted, and now he felt responsible. There was a single track fifty yards from Camp III where someone had ventured out that morning, but then decided against it and returned to camp. Jim had tears in his eyes. We stopped just behind a rise outside of camp to collect ourselves.

Kiran and Nirmal ran out of their tent to greet us warmly. John Evans and Peter came over and congratulated us. The others were more reserved, however. Although the proper words were spoken, it was a very cool welcome. By contrast, the air was quite warm; everyone gathered outside in the sun to discuss the route and the next few days. Devi passed around a pot of pink lemonade.

"Why didn't anyone go up today?" I asked after sitting down with the others.

"It looked like the weather would turn bad," Andy said.

"But it's been perfect all morning!"

"It looked bad earlier this morning. A large black cloud hung over Nanda Devi," he insisted. Andy later confided to Lou that Devi had not been feeling well, further influencing their decision not to go. Willi and the others began talking about going to Camp IV the next day.

"Who's on the second team, Willi?" I asked, hoping the team had been changed.

"Devi, Andy, and Peter."

I had great misgivings. "Willi, I'm going to say my piece."

"Yes John, I thought you would," he said, laughing gently.

"I don't think Devi should go up, or Andy either, if he's still got that cough. Devi," I faced her, "you've got a hernia, which could give you problems, a bad cough you haven't shaken off since the expedition began, and you've been ill every other day from some stomach ailment. I think there are stronger people to go up—like Nirmal, or Evans. Willi could go with Peter. But neither you nor Andy have acclimatized."

They all looked right through me as if I were a phantom and not a man. "That's it. I've said all I'm going to."

I expected to hear Jim or Lou back me up, but neither said a word. I was alone in voicing what I thought was a serious problem.

Devi showed her anger with calculated subtlety. Since Base Camp, Jim had asked everyone—for health reasons—to use a clean utensil or cracker to scoop out the peanut butter. Devi thought this was a ridiculous rule, but obliged. Now she asked for the pail of peanut butter and opened it. Jabbing her fingers deep into the pail, she scooped out a glob of peanut butter and waved it in the air toward me. "This is the way we do it at Camp III," she snapped, and ate from her fingers.

Several minutes later, Willi came over and we talked alone. "I just don't think she should go up, Willi."

"Well, John, what can a father do?"

"I don't know."

"What would you do if she were your daughter?"

"I don't know, Willi . . . she's not." Our conversation ended.

I finished unpacking while Willi went over to his tent to fix a jumar system for himself so that he could help on the Buttress the next day. The others had all disappeared into their tents. I was annoyed with Lou and Jim for not speaking up when I knew they believed in what I was saying, and I wanted to know why. Lou was in John Evans's tent. I went in and lay down beside him.

"Why didn't you back me up?"

"I guess I should have," Lou answered, but he had no explanation.

I found Jim in his tent, stretched out on a mat. As yet no one had offered us any sleeping bags for the night.

"Jim, why didn't you say something? You know Devi's got some health problems. They're not going to pay any attention to me."

"I don't think the hernia is that big a problem," he shrugged. "I haven't checked her out yet but I'll do that later this afternoon. Right now I don't have anything to go on."

Jim grew irritated with my questions, so I dropped the issue. No one wanted to argue with Willi. Dibrugheta and Marty's evacuation had been bad enough. [Marty Hoey had suffered suspected cerebral edema.]

Meanwhile, Peter appeared outside our tent and peeked in. "Say, you guys want my sleeping bag? I'll be glad to let you have it."

We just about cried at Peter's offer. He had certainly changed in my eyes. "No, Peter, you need the rest if you expect to make it tomorrow. We'll do all right in down pants and coats," Jim said. "Could you loan us those?"

"Sure, I'll bring 'em right over." He turned to go.

"Say, Peter," I called impulsively. "Here's a bicentennial flag for you . . . Make sure you get it to the summit, O.K.?"

"Thanks, John," he smiled. "It'll get there."

That afternoon Jim did a short examination of Devi's hernia with Willi in attendance. "If she goes up, there's a chance of a problem," Jim concluded. "If the hernia strangulates and she develops pain in her abdomen, it will take about two hours to kill the bowel and up to two days to kill the patient." Devi and Willi accepted this.

With neither his own authority nor backing from Willi, the expedition leader, Jim could only warn them. "I didn't feel it was necessary to yell and scream," Jim told me later. "I knew Willi wouldn't take my advice, even though I told him I felt Devi shouldn't go up. He refused to take my advice at Dibrugheta on Marty's problem, even on a clear-cut medical issue. Devi's hernia was not clear-cut; it was only problematic."

We spent the rest of the afternoon drinking and eating dinner that Devi prepared. That night, Jim and I dressed heavily in down coats and pants. Lou, having spilled his urine bottle inside his bag during our last night at Camp IV, had brought his sleeping bag down to dry out. It felt good not to have to trust those ropes again, and we dozed off.

         ˎ   ˎ   ˎ

September 3 was warmer than usual, and the weather looked promising. The powder snow squeaked under their boots as Andy and Devi left for the Buttress and Camp IV. Having left earlier, Peter was only a dot on the Ridge. Willi, Kiran, Nirmal, Evans, and Jatendra followed to practice jumaring behind the second summit team. Willi and the Indians were new to the technique; John Evans, who was already experienced with jumars, would give them some pointers.

Only Lou, Jim, and I stayed behind, asleep in our tent, relaxing for the first time in days. We didn't have to ascend the Buttress again. I was concerned, though, for the others, knowing the difficulties they faced and the poor state of the fixed lines. Even the idea of practicing on the lower ropes made me nervous. The Buttress and upper slopes of Nanda Devi were socked in by drifting clouds, but we could monitor the second team's progress by listening to them calling to one another. The two parties seemed to spend a lot of time communicating. Jim, Lou, and I spent a leisurely day eating, relaxing, and listening to the climbers.

Jatendra, the only IMF trainee to reach Camp III, returned to camp first, exhausted by the hike from the Buttress. Willi, Kiran, Nirmal, and Evans returned several hours later, cold and tired. Practice on the ropes had not gone well. Willi and John had taught them what they could, but both Kiran and Nirmal had been too slow to reach Sugar Delight Snowfield. Jim cooked hot drinks for the returning climbers while Lou and I started dinner.

"Where did you last see the second team, Willi?" Lou asked.

"Andy was just below Devi and they were about to the snowfield," Willi guessed. "They were moving slowly."

There was no radio contact at 6:00 P.M., our scheduled time. We tried again at seven without success. Speculation as to what had happened spread among the tents. No one mentioned the possibility of the ropes breaking, but we all thought of it.

At 8:30 P.M., Peter came in over the radio from Camp IV. He sounded weak and was probably hypothermic.

"O.K., Peter," Willi asked, "have you seen Devi or Andy?'"

"I haven't seen them since four-thirty on Sugar Delight Snowfield. They were still coming, but slowly. Since then I've been working to get to here. It was a bitch."

"We want half-hour radio contacts until they both arrive, understand?" Willi ordered. "Hold on—Jim wants to speak with you."

"Heat up some milk and sugar, Peter," Jim instructed. "We left some in the pan in the front vestibule."

Peter came on again at 9:00 P.M. No one else had shown up yet, but his stronger voice indicated a definite improvement in his condition.

Willi was worried. He left the tent to yodel to Devi, their private mode of communication. Bell-like, his voice rang through the cold air, to be met only with silence. Then we heard Devi's faint, high-pitched reply. Her voice had cracked slightly; she was still alive.

Frozen and covered with snow, Andy arrived at Camp IV at 11:00 P.M. and piled into the tent with Peter. He had stayed behind Devi until Sugar Delight—where he had suggested turning back—but Devi had not taken the idea seriously. Andy continued staying just in front of Devi to keep an eye on her. She had a slow but even pace. He left her just below the ridge at the top of the gully and had managed to reach the crest. Devi should have been close behind.

Just before midnight, Lou thought he heard someone yell from the Buttress. It sounded like "Camp III, Camp III!" but he wasn't sure. Jim stepped outside in the clear starlit night and shone his headlamp at the Buttress, but there was no answer.

"Camp III, Devi's here!" Peter finally reported.

Devi got the rope and jumars stuck fifteen feet below the crest, the place we all had had trouble. Unable to move up or down in her exhausted condition, she had yelled for help. We had heard her, but Peter and Andy, only thirty feet away and over the crest, hadn't heard a word. Worried about her taking so long, Andy returned to the crest, heard her calling, and helped her up. The three of them were finally together and safe. It was 2:00 A.M. when they turned in to sleep. "There were many ominous signs . . . a very desultory start, poor weather, and Devi's hernia popped out," Lou wrote of their ascent in his diary. They had been lucky to get so far.

⯈   ⯈   ⯈

The next day, September 4, I was to descend to Base Camp and send a porter out to Lata to summon the rest of the porters we would need to leave the mountain. One of us had to go and I was the logical choice. As the only doctor, Jim would stay with the main group until everyone was down. Lou was torn between staying to help the summit team and leaving for the U.S. to be with his wife for the birth of their next child. We felt that all the climbers would summit in the next three or four days if everything worked out well. Already the second team was in position and the Indians needed only to perfect their jumar technique to follow a day or two later.

"We're not moving today," Andy told us at the morning radio call. "All of us need a day's rest. We're pretty tired."

"How's Devi?" Willi asked.

"Exhausted, but fine. Her hat fell off during her ascent yesterday, but we'll work something out."

I cooked rice pudding for breakfast, filled my water bottle, and packed to leave. Willi gave me last-minute instructions on how many porters to send for and where the money was hidden at Camp I. It was one of the finest days of the expedition and already, at 8:30 A.M., the air temperature was warm. Evans and I floundered through deep snow down the Ridge a short distance from camp to photograph the Buttress and upper slopes of Nanda Devi. At one point on the Ridge we could see Nanda Devi East. After saying my good-byes, I started down alone for Base Camp. The ropes were buried deep under a heavy crust of snow. Each step down was a difficult tug-of-war with the rope as I tried to free it from the mountain's icy grip. The load I was carrying, heavy with personal gear and ice hardware, kept throwing me off balance. My progress was almost as slow as it had been when I came up.

Camp II was a shambles after only three days. One of the tents was crushed from snowfall, the other in an equally bad condition. I searched through several opened food bags to find only cornuts and crackers. The sun was now viciously hot, pounding the snowfield and me along with it. I stripped some clothing along with my crampons, which were balling up with snow, and continued down to Camp I, weaving and jerking from side to side on each rappel. The arm pulling the rope from the crust was drained of strength and almost useless, so I let my body weight pull the rope free.

Camp I was deserted, silent. Tent doors flapped in the slight breeze; food bags were torn open and scattered. No one had been there for some time. I found Jim's film but not the expedition's money bag. I continued descending through the same snow conditions. At the end of the fixed lines I slid and punched my way through avalanche debris until I was just above Advanced Base. None of the debris had been there three weeks ago and I was amazed at the accumulation.

Dropping over a small cliff above Advanced Base, I rounded the hillside, expecting to see a lively camp with several of the high-altitude porters, but I was wrong. Before me were the ghostly skeletons of three tents. Only the poles were standing; wisely, the nylon tents had been dropped in case of avalanche blasts while the camp was empty. Like a victim of war, I scavenged the dead camp for food and the rest of the belongings I had left there a month before. Everything was wet and filthy. Ravens were digging at the garbage and food sacks pecking apart the eight-man day units.

The mountain was silent, the camp ghostly. I never felt so insignificant. Rummaging through an open box, I found a two-month-old *Newsweek* and read it through. Later I searched my duffel for personal gear and the exposed film I had left, dumping the climbing hardware from my pack to make room. It was almost as good as Christmas, finding gear I had forgotten was there.

It was 2:00 P.M., but I decided to continue down and across the glacier for Base because Advanced Base was too depressing. My pack made me sink in the snow at the side of the glacier, which I dreaded crossing. As I reached the side, I hesitated, then followed some several-day-old tracks until they disappeared under tons of avalanche debris. I didn't hurry. It was now or never and I didn't want to breathe hard or suck air. After ten minutes I was across. I hoped I would never have to cross that area again.

I passed through Ridge Camp quickly. Only a few torn boxes remained to indicate we had been there weeks before. I stayed to the side of another avalanche debris slope, then crossed where the stream had once been, now a trough of avalanche snow. An hour later I crossed the Rishi on an immense snow bridge. There was no more danger. I was down.

Dharamsingh, Kesharsingh, and Balbirsingh met me at the stream near camp. They were smiling and eager to help me across. Tears welled in my eyes when I saw them.

"Up, Sahib?" Dharamsingh asked excitedly.

"Yes, yes, all the way up!" I answered, gesturing. They shook my hand and insisted on taking the pack from my weary shoulders. I knew in my heart they shared our success. It was good to be with them again. That night in their company was one of the most pleasant I spent in India.

⚑   ⚑   ⚑

Jim and Lou had enjoyed an easy day at Camp III. Willi, Evans, Kiran, and Nirmal also spent the day in camp resting because they planned to attempt Camp IV the next day. Willi was still unsure whether the Indians could jumar the ropes and decided to get an early start the next morning.

Lou continued to worry about his wife Kathy, so Jim persuaded him to leave for home the following day. There was no reason for Lou to stay; Jim would take his responsibilities.

No one had moved from Camp IV that day either. During the afternoon radio call Jim asked Devi about her hernia and about any symptoms of illness she may have had. Both Lou and Jim doubted she should go higher and Jim warned her about his concern.

"Willi, I only advised her to come down," Jim said. "I didn't order her."

"I'm glad you left it that way," Willi replied.

Before dawn on the fifth, Peter, Devi, and Andy at Camp IV were up and dressing. The weather was partly cloudy and a breeze was beginning to pick up. Devi was still lethargic and had some diarrhea. She decided to wait another day or until Willi could be with her to go for the summit. Andy complained of being tired and elected to stay with Devi. Peter wanted to go part way at least. He needed to make the attempt even if alone. His would be the expedition's last attempt for the summit.

Peter pushed hard, surmounting the major difficulties of the upper section, but turned back just below the rock band. The weather had worsened considerably as he climbed and snow began falling. He became exhausted in the deep snow and high altitude and, while descending, slipped and fell toward the abyss of the Northwest Face. Miraculously, he stopped after thirty feet, even though he had dropped his ice axe. After retrieving the axe, Peter descended more carefully and reached Camp IV in the afternoon. He retreated to the safety of the tent, where he, Devi, and Andy spent their third night at 24,000 feet.

At Camp III, Willi, Kiran, Nirmal, and Evans had gone through a similar day of hardship on the Buttress. The third summit team was awake at 6:00 A.M. and viewed the same storm clouds in the south, but decided to attempt the ascent of the Buttress anyway. After Jim fed them a hot breakfast, the four headed for the ropes and Camp IV. Jim and Lou descended: Jim for a food bag for Camp III, Lou for home. Jim returned to camp slowly, reaching the Ridge in a snowstorm. He relaxed the rest of the day, boiling liquids and listening to the climbers on the Buttress arguing whether to go up or down.

The four climbers straggled into camp at nine o'clock that night. Nirmal and Kiran had again been too slow; it was wiser to descend rather than try for Camp IV. John Evans, usually placid and introverted, was furious. "Willi purposely overextended the whole team," he told Jim. "We were in real danger."

The climbers were hypothermic, particularly Evans, and Jim forced foods and fluids into them. According to Evans, they were lucky to have made it back to camp alive.

⋆   ⋆   ⋆

For me, it was a peaceful September 5. I sent all the porters to Advanced Base except Dharamsingh, who was to run to Lata for more porters, and Tesh, a porter who was ill. I bathed early, long before the sun's warmth arrived in the deep valley, then walked through the meadows. The sounds and smells of the valley pleased my senses. It was another world.

Fall had come to the upper Sanctuary. Frost covered the vegetation along the spring that flowed through camp. The bright plants and flowers, predominant in August, had faded and withered. I thought about the expedition as I walked along a sheep trail above camp. The team had never been together in spirit in the U.S. or on the mountain. We had been divided by philosophy and opinion since the beginning. Success under such circumstances seemed even sweeter. Yet I was worried deeply about those still trying to summit. Kiran scared me because he was irrational when it came to "saving face." I knew he was not technically proficient and his tenacity could cause himself and others trouble on the Buttress.

Now that she had overcome the difficulties of the Buttress, Devi worried me less. But her illness and hernia made me think that she would only reach Camp IV. Willi had said that she was used to an unusual amount of stomach trouble and carried her own antacid. Perhaps she could mask her discomfort long enough to summit.

The day passed quickly for me at Base. I felt sure that someone had reached the top that afternoon because of the good weather, although it looked windy near the summit. I was hoping they would get up and down quickly so we could leave for home.

Early the next morning, on the sixth, I walked up the hill above Base to photograph Nanda Devi. Clouds sped past the summit and the winds looked fierce. Lou was at Base when I returned at noon. We briefly wished each other success and he continued to Pathal Khan, loaded with all the Gumperts drink mix and chapatis Tesh and I could give him. He hadn't heard anything from the others at Camp IV, but assumed they must have made the summit. I was entertained the rest of the day by two Japanese who were in the Sanctuary scouting a route on the northeast side that would eventually reach the North Ridge and ascend our Buttress. It would be a difficult, magnificent route if they could do it. Unfortunately, they didn't succeed.

➤   ➤   ➤

Both Camp III and IV were awake and busy at 6:30 A.M. Devi made the scheduled radio contact with Willi and Jim.

"I'm going alone to Camp IV," Willi announced. "Yesterday Kiran and

Nirmal were too slow on the ropes. Kiran even ended up upside down trying to jumar." Kiran and Nirmal couldn't decide what they would do. Kiran thought of soloing to Camp IV like Willi, but Nirmal wanted to go down. Later, under pressure from Kiran, Nirmal changed his mind.

Evans was ambivalent. He was feeling very lethargic and had been sleeping constantly for the past twenty-four hours. Jim thought this was due to exhaustion and hypothermia from the previous day. He couldn't know Evans was coming down with hepatitis. Evans later decided to descend because he didn't want to guide Kiran and Nirmal up the Buttress and to the top. Willi left for Camp IV shortly after breakfast.

That day the three climbers at Camp IV again remained in camp. Peter was exhausted from his solo attempt and needed the rest. Andy's desire to summit now depended solely on Devi; he'd do whatever she decided.

In the weeks on the upper slopes of Nanda Devi, Andy had asked for Devi's hand in marriage, and Willi had given his blessing. They would set a date when they returned home. The rest of us didn't know of their intended marriage. They didn't know what our reaction would be and, frankly, didn't care. The engagement was their secret and comfort during a very difficult time on the mountain.

In the meantime, the mountain had taken second place for Andy. His affection for Devi preempted his previous goals. Before he and Devi had gone up the Buttress, Andy had told her that no mountain was worth the risk, that instead he wanted to "wrap her in cotton wool." They both laughed at this and agreed that wasn't what Devi wanted or needed. She promised to tell him if she had the slightest inkling of trouble.

Andy retrieved the rope below Camp IV that morning. Devi felt lethargic, as she had since her arrival, so they performed a little test to see how strong she was. She climbed about thirty feet out of camp, stopped, rested, then returned. Devi was simply exhausted for no apparent reason. Although she still had diarrhea that morning, she seemed fine as long as she wasn't moving.

At the two o'clock radio call, Jim informed Camp IV that Willi was on his way up and that they should dig another tent platform. Jim knew Devi was a stoic about illness and pleaded with her, "Devi, what aren't you telling me?"

"I'm telling you everything," she answered. "I have no pain." Later in the day

Andy, Peter, and Devi decided she should descend. According to Andy: "Nothing suggested urgency, just her lassitude and diarrhea." Andy and Peter dug another tent site, but the wind prevented them from pitching a tent. Because Willi was on his way, they decided not to escort Devi down that afternoon.

Willi arrived around 7:00 P.M. He had never used a jumar in his life, yet had accomplished one of the most difficult jumar ascents a climber would ever encounter. Willi, Peter, and Andy decided to climb to the summit early the next morning. They would take Devi down upon their return. That night, Devi had terrible sulfur burps and complained of being cold and clammy.

High winds and snow pinned those at Camp IV down on September 7. The four had no choice but to sit out the storm. They made the best of a poor situation, cooking meals and boiling water to stay healthy. Devi's abdomen was tender and slightly distended, but the hernia appeared to be in place. She continued taking plenty of liquids and food. Toward evening, she again had severe sulfur burps and diarrhea. The others watched her carefully, although nothing suggested urgency to them.

"She ought to come down," Jim told Willi that evening. "Sounds to me as though she's getting some bowel obstruction."

"No, she has heartburn," Willi said. "Someone should bring up an antacid tomorrow."

Meanwhile, the climbers at Camp III sat out the bad day as well. Nirmal had complained of leg pains, acute chest pain, and shortness of breath, and Jim began to suspect a possible pulmonary embolism. His main concern now was Evans, who was revealing some real problems that Jim wasn't sure of. Jim evacuated both men with the help of Kiran and Jatendra the next morning.

Bad weather continued on September 8. The night at Camp IV had been difficult. The four occupants of the two-man tent had been cramped. Devi's condition was markedly worse.

Her sulfur burps were more frequent; she had to be helped into a sitting position, the only position she was able to assume with any degree of comfort. Andy had felt Devi's abdomen and it had become severely distended. The hernia was in place but she was in pain. They discussed the situation and decided, in spite of the bad weather, to help her down that morning.

Devi's burps became constant and her cheeks were puffy. Her face and lips took on a blue hue. At 10:00 A.M., according to Peter, she looked bad and everyone was concerned. Her face became puffier and puffier. The vicious storm, worse than any since we had arrived in the Sanctuary, delayed their departure until noon.

Willi went outside, leaving the others to put on their clothes and ready themselves to descend. Devi was sitting up in the back of the tent trying to drink some cocoa. Her stomach hurt terribly.

Devi suddenly became a ghostly white. "Take my pulse, Peter," she said. Then, calmly, "I'm going to die." Her eyes rolled as she pitched forward and vomited.

Andy grabbed her and started mouth-to-mouth resuscitation. Peter called Willi back into the tent. Willi immediately took over the mouth-to-mouth while all three tried cardiopulmonary resuscitation.

Willi would recall he knew they had lost her within fifteen minutes as he felt her lips grow cold against his. Despite this, they continued their efforts to revive her for another half hour without success. The three men were anguished. Devi was dead.

They clasped each other for comfort as their quiet moans filled the tent. What could they do with Devi's body? Leave her in the tent? Bury her?

"No," Willi decided. "We will commit her to the mountain. As if a burial at sea."

Stricken, Willi, Peter, and Andy finished dressing. Hugs and touches consumed their last moments with Devi. The sleeping bag was zipped shut and the drawstring closed around her face. Then into the raging storm they crawled.

They dragged her body up the ridge a short distance. It was to the uphill side of the fixed lines so that her remains would find their way into the most remote icy grave on Nanda Devi—the Northeast Face. They fell to their knees in the storm and linked their hands in a circle around her corpse. Each sobbed a broken farewell to the comrade who had filled such a vivid place in their lives. Willi said last rites:

"Thank you for the world we live in. Thank you for such beauty juxtaposed against such risk . . . Thank you."

The three men dragged Devi to the edge of the face. With a horrible shove, her corpse disappeared into the bowels of the storm, into the mountain of the Goddess Nanda Devi.

"We laid the body to rest in its icy tomb, at rest on the breast of the bliss-giving Goddess Nanda," Willi later pronounced.

Now cold and exhausted, their judgment distorted by grief, the climbers knew one thing: they had to leave Camp IV immediately.

An hour elapsed as they packed and readied to descend in the raging storm. Willi packed only those items of Devi's dearest to him. Peter and Andy descended first. Neither made the swing-over into the gully easily. Peter, already emotionally drained, felt as though the rope were strangling him. It eventually squeezed him so tight he thought he would die.

Willi drove himself beyond the limits of most men. Never have I met a man so determined. At times he asked himself if he even wanted to continue, yet each time he struggled on. The traverse from the gully to Sugar Delight almost made the decision for him. Because of the small ledge and unanchored section of rope, it was the most difficult section to descend. Each step of the traverse along the eight-inch ledge pushed the climber away from the wall. Balance was essential.

Willi slipped off the ledge and started to strangle. He knew he was in a struggle for his life. There was only one choice he could make to survive. He had to get rid of his pack and, with it, Devi's keepsakes. With extreme effort, Willi managed to hook the pack to the rope, hand-line to the anchor, and pull himself to safety. He wrenched himself away from the traverse and continued down. Once he dropped a glove and froze several fingers. Somehow he connected each rappel correctly, following Peter and Andy down the ropes in the black of night. Sometime during the night all three reached the base of the Buttress. Exhausted and close to the limit of survival, they arrived at 10:00 P.M.

The four sahibs and one porter there had descended to Advanced Base: Kiran and Jatendra escorted Nirmal, who had chest pains, while Jim stayed with Evans, now lethargic and slow. He was exhibiting symptoms of hepatitis and had to descend quickly.

There had been no radio contact between the two groups of climbers until late in the night, when Andy, Peter, and Willi finally called Jim at Advanced Base. Only then did the other team members learn of Devi's death.

"You had better stay at Camp III tomorrow and rest," Jim suggested. Lamely he added, "We're all terribly sorry, Willi."

"NOT A PRIVATE AFFAIR"

FROM
Everest: The Mountaineering History
BY WALT UNSWORTH

HISTORY DOES HAVE A WAY OF REPEATING ITSELF. EVEN WITH IN-
structive examples before them, when the goal happens to be Everest, mountaineers continue to delude themselves that tactics that failed before can be
made to work next time. Two cases in point are described by British mountain historian and author Walt Unsworth in this selection from his book *Everest:
The Mountaineering History*.

In 1970, a massive Japanese expedition (thirty-nine climbers) set out for
Everest with a split goal that almost immediately began to strain the group
in terms of logistics and leadership. Which effort should get the greatest
emphasis and hence party strength and support? A virtually certain but
unremarkable success via the South Col for a first Japanese ascent of the
mountain? Or the more challenging possibility of a place in mountaineering
history with a first ascent on the forbidding South West Face?

The leaders of the Japanese expedition hoped to repeat the success
of the American 1963 expedition, led by Norman Dyhrenfurth, that put
the first American on the summit via the regular (South Col) route while
simultaneously pioneering the remarkable West Ridge route. But the
Americans' luck didn't hold for the Japanese. Swayed by accidents, stonefall,
and weather, the Japanese leadership kept switching the emphasis from one
route to the other until, finally, they had to settle for simply getting four climbers
on the summit via the standard route. In terms of money and lives, the
results were hardly worth it.

A year later, an almost equally large expedition (thirty-three climbers) set
out for Everest with the same split goal that doomed the Japanese. The mix of
factors, however, was different. The 1970 Japanese expedition represented a
single country, and the leadership made all the decisions. The 1971 expedition
was international (thirteen different countries), and was cursed with all the nation-
alistic posturing, imagined conspiracies, and misunderstandings possible on
such a venture. Also, the leader of the international expedition, the same
Norman Dyhrenfurth as in 1963, kept putting everything to a vote. Yet the
results were remarkably the same for both expeditions—disastrous.

Author Unsworth presents some intriguing arguments for why both
expeditions failed, and has a good deal of fun recounting the almost farcical
events and squabbles that doomed the international effort.

This selection is a slightly abridged version of Chapter 17 of Everest: The Mountaineering History, pages 395-422.

I n 1963 the Japanese Alpine Club had been granted permission to attempt Everest during the pre-monsoon period of 1966. Unfortunately they, like everyone else, were prevented from fulfilling their ambition because of the Nepalese ban on expeditions, and it wasn't until 1969 that they could renew their hopes. However, they did gain a bonus—they were granted permission for three consecutive expeditions: spring and autumn 1969, and spring 1970.

During the post-war years, Japanese climbers had been very active in the Himalaya. They were skillful and tough, and had accounted for two top-class mountains, Himal Chuli and Manaslu, the latter being seventh highest in the world. In the number and frequency of their expeditions they outdid everyone else—even it is suggested, everyone else put together. Expense seemed no object: presented with three consecutive Everest expeditions most nations would have blanched at the cost. The Japanese took it in their inscrutable stride.

They were well aware of the modern trends in climbing (about this time they put up their own direct route on the Eiger) and realized that on Everest the next logical step would be to attempt the great South West Face whose crags loomed over the Western Cwm. Their three expeditions gave them a unique monopoly of the problem, enabling them fully to reconnoiter the face in 1969 in readiness for a full-scale assault the following year. Not since the British monopoly of Everest in the days before the war had anyone had such a continuous bite at the apple.

The great triangular shaped South West Face sweeps up from the Western Cwm for almost 8,000 ft. to the summit. The lower two thirds of this distance consists of steep snow slopes running up into a series of rocky towers and buttresses, the exploration of which could take a lifetime and the climbing of which might prove impossible. Fortunately, in the middle of the face, there is a wide break where the snow sweeps up to a higher point. This is known as the Central Gully, but it is wider than most gullies, so the name is a little misleading. It stretches up until, at a little more than 26,000 ft., it meets a steeper wall of rock known as the Rock Band, where it divides right and left, running below the band, but still ascending. On the right it is almost like a ramp, quite long and extending upwards another thousand feet or so, toward the South East Ridge. To the left it is shorter and steeper, arching up to meet a narrow gully cutting through the rock. Above the Rock Band there lies another snowfield, stretching across the face, and above that a steep triangle of summit rock.

The Japanese sent only a small reconnaissance party to the mountain in the pre-monsoon period of 1969. It made its way into the Cwm, but did little more than make a preliminary survey of the problem. In the autumn they returned in greater force, establishing Base Camp by September 16 and Advanced Base (Camp 2—in the Western Cwm) only twelve days later. The weather was exceptionally fine, with none of the high winds that can be such a demoralizing feature of post-monsoon climbing on Everest, and there was good, firm snow on the lower slopes of the face. Nevertheless, the Japanese concentrated on building up supplies in the Cwm before attacking the mountain, and it was a further two weeks before Camp 3 was set up, at 23,000 ft. Camp 4 was established at the mouth of the Central Gully (24,600 ft.) and Camp 5 at 25,600 ft. It was with these last two camps that the Japanese came across a problem nobody had foreseen—the snow in the higher reaches was not deep enough to allow proper tent platforms to be excavated. Henceforth portable platforms, adjusted to the angle of the slope, would be a necessary part of any expedition to the South West Face.

Spearheading the Japanese reconnaissance were Masatsugu Konishi and Naomi Uemura, the latter already building up a reputation as one of the world's most formidable mountaineers, despite his slight build and amiable, almost cherubic countenance. On October 31 they reached a point just below the Rock Band by working out to the left. The following day two of their companions, Hiroshi Nakajima and Shigeru Satoh, managed to climb even a little higher.

What the four Japanese climbers observed convinced them that it would be possible for a full-scale expedition to penetrate the Rock Band, the major difficulty, and climb the Face. For the moment they had gone far enough.

The Japanese reconnaissances of 1969 were in the time-honored mold of Everest exploration. Like the 1922 expedition, which showed that a way could be made via the North Col, and Shipton's expedition of 1951, which showed that entry to the Western Cwm was feasible, so they too had shown that there was a way to climb the South West Face. But was that enough? No doubt they thought it was, for they had another season in hand in which to prove it.

Yet once again the fact of Everest being Everest overshadowed the thinking and logistics of the final expedition, just as it had done for the Americans in 1963. Then, Dyhrenfurth's prime target was to get an American to the top so as to please his sponsors and satisfy the folks back home. Anything else was subsidiary, and it was only Tom Hornbein's determined individualism [in pushing the West Ridge route] which had converted an expensive exercise in public relations into an outstanding mountaineering achievement. And now here were the Japanese confronted with the same problem—the summit for national prestige, or a new and worthwhile route up the difficult South West Face? Hoping to repeat Dyhrenfurth's good luck, they opted for both.

It was a massive expedition—no fewer than thirty-nine climbers and seventy-seven Sherpas (including a woman climber, Miss Setuko Wanatabe) led by the seventy-year-old veteran Saburo Matsukata, who never went higher than Base Camp. The plan was that the combined resources of the expedition would be used to force the Icefall and establish Advanced Base (Camp 2), from where the two teams for the South West Face and South Col route would act independently.

The larger the expedition which has to traverse the Icefall, the greater the potential danger, because at any given moment there are likely to be more targets for the unpredictable ice to strike. The Japanese therefore stood a greater risk of accident, but to make things even more dangerous there was a *second* Japanese team on the mountain: a thirty-four-man ski expedition, completely independent of the climbers and separately financed. Altogether there must have been some 150 people passing through the Icefall, not counting the Icefall Sherpas who were going up and down in a constant daily stream, stocking the camps in the Cwm.

An accident was almost inevitable. On April 5, 1970, the day after Camp 1 was established at the lip of the Cwm, an Icefall avalanche hit a party of Sherpas from the ski expedition, killing six of them. A few days later another Sherpa was killed. Not since pre-war days had a wholesale disaster struck the little Sherpa community: they were appalled and distressed.

Nevertheless, despite these catastrophes, and the slowness of certain team members to acclimatize properly, Advanced Base was established in the Cwm by April 17. Or rather, *two* Advanced Base Camps, for it was decided that the Face team and Col team would live and work separately from now on. The camps were fairly near each other, with the Face team's camp situated a little closer to the South West Face itself.

Above base, responsibility for the expedition rested in the hands of Hiromi Ohtsuka, who, as he confessed in his diary, found himself facing all the problems of a large split-offensive expedition that had beset Dyhrenfurth, both in terms of logistics and in the philosophical realm of whether to place emphasis on virtually certain but unremarkable success via the well-tried South Col route or on the *possibility* of acquiring great prestige by a first ascent of the untried South West Face. Like Dyhrenfurth, he felt obliged to go for the former: logistically the South Col team was given an advantage, and the fact that Naomi Uemura was allocated to that route emphasizes the point. Unlike the Americans, the Japanese climbers do not seem to have had any option which route they would climb. The choice was made by the leader. The South West Face team consisted of nine men led by Masatsugu Konishi, who had led the autumn reconnaissance. Naturally enough, even among the Japanese, more accustomed than their Western contemporaries to accepting autocratic discipline, not everyone was pleased with their allocated climb. However, there was no Oriental Tom Hornbein to stir things up.

On April 21 another and totally unsuspected hammer blow fell on the expedition. During the evening meal at Camp 1, the youngest member of the expedition, twenty-eight-year-old Kujoshi Narita, suffered a sudden heart attack, and before his shocked companions could do anything to help, died. Earlier in the expedition, Narita had not been well but had spent a week recuperating at Lobuje, the staging post below the Khumbu Glacier, and had returned from there seemingly fit and strong—indeed, he was known as one of the strongest men on the expedition, which made the impact of his death all the more shocking. The expedition was halted while Narita's body was taken down the Icefall and from there down the Khumbu valley for cremation.

Narita's death, combined with the continual illnesses which seemed to dog the expedition, delayed matters to such an extent that Ohtsuka decided to abandon the South West Face altogether and put all his resources into climbing the ordinary route. This was too much, even for the disciplined Japanese, and four days later he changed his mind again—the Face climb would continue, but the South Col route would get priority (which it already had). Shades of Dyhrenfurth!

Suffice to say that progress via the South Col was now rapid, and on May 11 Naomi Uemura and Teruo Matsuura reached the summit of Everest. Next day Katsutoshi Hirabayashi and the Sherpa Chotare repeated the ascent, and took the opportunity, when near the South Summit, of descending a little way onto the South West Face to inspect the problems. Hirabayashi thought the route looked very difficult.

This was hardly surprising, for the winter of 1969 had been a particularly dry one. Hardly any snow had fallen and consequently the South West Face was stripped of much of its overmantle. The team now tackling it found that where during the reconnaissance there had been accommodating snow and ice slopes, there was now a good deal of bare rock. It made life difficult and dangerous, and progress very slow.

Ohtsuka's plan had been to establish Camp 4 just below the Rock Band by May12. This proved impracticable, and it was established much lower and sooner (May 6) on the slopes below the Central Gully, using special dural platforms for the tents. From there on May 8 Konishi and Akira Yoshikawa climbed up to 25,600 ft., following the left-hand branch of the gully previously reconnoitred. Two days later Katsuhiko Kano and Hiroshi Sagono, with two Sherpas, went higher still, but discovered that after a height of about 26,000 ft. the Face was so stripped of snow and ice that they had to remove their crampons and treat it as a rock climb. The rock was broken but unpleasant. Fortunately the weather was good and they were able to reach a height of 26,400 ft., where they could examine the narrow gully that cut through the Rock Band. Stripped of ice it looked formidable, but they thought it could be climbed.

However, they did not get a chance to put it to the test. While descending to Advanced Base for a rest, Kano was hit in the back by a falling stone and slightly injured. That same day Hiroshi Nakajima was also struck by a stone. Alarmed at these mishaps, Ohtsuka immediately withdrew all climbers from the South West Face, declaring that the stonefall hazard was too great and that, in any case, there wasn't time enough to complete the route before the monsoon.

Stonefall is a natural hazard on many face climbs, varying from mountain to mountain, season to season, and even hour to hour. Some faces are notorious for it—the Eigerwand, for example—but the South West Face of Everest has never been one of these. It could be that in 1970 the Japanese were particularly unfortunate in following such a dry winter, and that the blanket of snow and ice which holds most of the loose rock in place was largely absent. No other expedition has reported trouble with stonefall on this vast face.

Ohtsuka decided that the unfortunate Face team would now concentrate their efforts on making two more assaults on the South Col route. In this, however, they were frustrated by the weather, and by May 21 the expedition had withdrawn from the mountain.

Meanwhile, the Japanese ski expedition had accomplished its own peculiar achievement. Yuichiro Miura, a professional skier, skied down from the South Col to the foot of the Lhotse Face on May 6. When his speed reached 100 mph he opened a parachute brake. Unfortunately, a shift in the wind caught him off balance and he hit some rocks which threw him over. He slid some 600 ft. to the foot of the slope, stopping just short of a huge crevasse. He was unconscious but otherwise uninjured. The whole episode was dramatically recorded on film and eventually shown throughout the world on television.

Altogether, the Japanese had an unhappy time on Everest in 1970. In terms of cost, both in money and lives, the game hadn't been worth the candle. True, they had achieved their primary aim—to climb Everest—but in mountaineering terms they had achieved little that was worthwhile. Not for them the Dyhrenfurth luck! They had one small consolation prize—Miss Setuko Watanabe had reached the South Col. She was the first woman to do so, and she set a height record for her sex.

Summing up after the expedition the Deputy Leader Hiromi Ohtsuka said:

> *A 39 member expedition is too large to work as a cohesive*
> *unit. One leader should not have more than 12 to work with*
> *otherwise there will be a lack of common bond among the*
> *members. Furthermore, the pleasures of mountaineering will*
> *be stifled . . . the necessity of such a big expedition should be*
> *considered with restraint in the future.*

Ohtsuka's words were to prove prophetically wise, but unfortunately he was shouting against the prevailing wind. The fact is that in the 1970s mountaineering became a growth industry, and Everest itself was bound to be involved.

The world of 1970 was a very different world from that of half a century earlier when Mallory and his companions had first set out to find Mount Everest. Basically, mountaineering itself had not changed all that much, except in so far as technical advances had made life easier and safer in some respects: there is nothing to suggest that the climbers of 1970 were braver, stronger, or (as far as high-altitude climbing went) more skillful than those of 1920. Nor had their dedication changed: high-altitude mountaineering involved exhaustion, suffering, and nervous tension, with death riding on the climber's shoulder at every step. As technology makes things easier, the climber steps up the challenge as a counterbalance. The rewards are largely personal and private: fame is ephemeral and limited except in very few cases—a modestly successful pop star is better known to the general public than the most successful of climbers. The reasons for climbing are much the same as they were fifty years ago.

Nevertheless the external influences on the modern climber are very different from those on his predecessors. "The last innocent adventure" James Morris called the successful Everest expedition of 1953, and though he was perhaps a decade or so early in his judgment, there was little that was innocent about the late 1960s and the 1970s.

The prime cause of all this was the increasing wealth and leisure in the more advanced countries of the world. People had the time and money to do the sort of things their grandfathers would have considered suitable only for the squirearchy. Some of them turned to climbing mountains. In schools, too, "education for leisure" became a fashionable mode, some of it again directed toward mountain activities.

Easier travel helped: cheaper flying and long motorways took the average adventurer to places which were once almost inaccessible—even to the very foot of Everest itself. And over all this activity watched the pervasive eye of the television camera, recording, informing, ceaselessly turning out entertainment. Even if you couldn't afford to go to the mountains, you could at least live your adventures vicariously through the medium of the small screen. . . .

The trend was international. Every country produced its stars—Gaston Rebuffat in France, Carlo Mauri in Italy, Royal Robbins in the USA and many others. In Britain two Lancastrians had long dominated the scene: the wry, enigmatic Joe Brown and the pugnacious, sharp-witted Don Whillans. They were joined by others, but particularly by a young man of ascetic appearance, a Sandhurst voice and definite opinions called Christian Bonington.

➤   ➤   ➤

It was against this background of accelerating world interest that the International Expedition to Everest's South West Face was conceived. The midwife to this ill-starred child of the seventies was Norman Dyhrenfurth.

It all began innocuously enough as a simple expedition to Antarctica. Back in 1965 two teams had put up new routes on the immensely difficult Troll Wall in Romsdal, Norway. One was a British team from Manchester and the other a Norwegian team consisting of Leif Patterson, Jon Teigland and Odd Eliassen. They all became firm friends and it was not surprising, therefore, that a year or so later John Amatt of the British party should contact Patterson suggesting they combine on an expedition.

As luck would have it Patterson was planning a trip to the Antarctic with the other two Norwegians, so he invited Amatt to join them. However, this gave the expedition an international flavor and Patterson had the idea of extending this theme by inviting climbers of other nationalities to join in as well. Dave Isles of the USA, Dudzinski and Peterek (Argentinians of Polish descent) completed the team. All the members were personally known to Patterson.

Unfortunately the Antarctica project fell through, so they turned their attention to the Himalaya instead. Being of the new school of dedicated face climbers it was natural, if ambitious, that they should decide on the Rupal Flank of Nanga Parbat, regarded as the greatest single face in the Himalaya. Once again their plans were thwarted: a German expedition had already secured permission for Nanga Parbat. Their choice then turned to the South West Face of Everest.

And so, by a curious combination of circumstances, the friendly trip to Antarctica had become transformed into an attempt on the hardest route of the highest mountain in the world. Patterson and Amatt had not merely changed objectives, they had changed leagues and had elected themselves to the First Division. It was a daring promotion and they startled nobody more than themselves, for none of the team had any Himalayan experience whatsoever.

Recognizing that they were getting out of their depth they turned for help to Colonel Jimmy Roberts, the man whose organizational ability had played so large a part in the first ascent in 1953 and the American success ten years later. Roberts, a former Gurkha officer, had retired from the Army and was running a trekking organization in Kathmandu. His knowledge of the Himalaya and its peoples was extensive, perhaps greater than that of any other Westerner, and he had taken part in about a dozen major expeditions, often as leader, so he was ideal for the job.

Roberts became the new leader of the venture, but it is doubtful whether even he, with all his experience, realized the magnitude of the undertaking and the scale of resources that would be necessary to climb the formidable South West Face. At this time (1968) nobody had done more than look at the face from the Western Cwm. The Japanese had not begun their explorations, nor had Bonington's team climbed the South Face of Annapurna to demonstrate that big Himalayan faces were feasible. Roberts, Patterson, and Amatt were pushing out into unknown waters, with none of the resources which ultimately proved necessary.

They did, however, recognize that some Himalayan experience might be useful before tackling Everest and to this end made plans to attempt Dhaulagiri

II, an unclimbed Nepalese peak of 25,429 ft., in 1969. As a warm-up exercise this too was a little ambitious!

Meanwhile, the team had grown. Three Americans had joined—Gary Colliver, Barry Hagen and John Evans—as well as the Rhodesian climber Rusty Baillie. All were experienced climbers, but their addition simply exacerbated the organizational problems which were already becoming tiresome, owing to the fact that the team was scattered throughout the world. Communications were slow, especially with Roberts in Nepal and Patterson, who was now in Uganda, and the bulk of the work fell on Amatt. He bore it for some months until, in 1969, dismayed at the lack of progress, he decided to quit the venture.

Amatt's resignation was a serious blow and but for a curious twist of fate the expedition might have withered away and died stillborn for lack of progress. At this crucial time, however, Roberts received a letter from Norman Dyhrenfurth inviting him to take part in an expedition—to the South West Face of Everest! It transpired that Dyhrenfurth, unaware that others were interested, had been working on his own plans.

Roberts suggested a merger for an expedition in 1971. On the face of it this was a sensible move because it would revive the old Roberts–Dyhrenfurth partnership which had proved so successful for the Americans in 1963. The two men were complementary: Roberts for his logistical planning and knowledge of the Sherpas, Dyhrenfurth for his international connections and ability to raise the necessary money. However, it had one serious drawback. The comfortable little team originally envisaged by Patterson, in which everyone knew one another (despite their various nationalities), was on amalgamation to become a group of strangers, each jealous of his own reputation. There were serious misgivings in the Patterson team about the way in which their initial ideals were being radically altered, but the amalgamation was inevitable. Roberts and Dyhrenfurth became joint leaders, though Dyhrenfurth took the lion's share of the responsibility, including that of financing the venture.

Dyhrenfurth, in fact, assumed a staggering financial burden. As was the case with the earlier American expedition the costs escalated like a rocket; but this time, because there was no national prestige involved, there was no single national institution prepared to underwrite the expedition. It was the international nature of the enterprise which appealed to Dyhrenfurth. He wanted to demonstrate that men from different nationalities and backgrounds could work together harmoniously and to the common cause, even under conditions of extreme hardship. It was a feeling which ran deep in the Dyhrenfurth family background: his father Günter Dyhrenfurth, had organized international expeditions in the thirties and he himself had run an international expedition to Lhotse in 1955. What could be a better vehicle for international cooperation than Everest, the greatest prize of all?

Yet because it was international it had this built-in financial weakness. Each country, either through its media or some charitable body, was willing to contribute *something* toward the costs, but never enough, and Dyhrenfurth found himself in a situation in which he was inviting participants from different countries simply for the extra cash they could bring in, although every addition to the team pushed up the costs even further. By the time it was all over, Dyhrenfurth was facing a bill in excess of a quarter of a million dollars.

Each climber contributed 500 dollars to the expedition, but large sponsors were few and far between for the reasons mentioned—only Trans World Airlines, who gave 12,000 dollars, and the Mainichi Newspapers of Japan, who gave 25,000 dollars, were significant contributors. The countries of the so-called "Latins"—about whom much was to be heard—made very small contributions, and France, none at all. More surprisingly perhaps, Germany and Austria, countries with a strong Himalayan tradition, also contributed very little. The direct disadvantages of being international were summed up in NASA's refusal to help the expedition because it was "neither a corporation nor based in the USA" Dyhrenfurth had hoped for 30,000 dollars because of the work he was doing on oxygen equipment.

It was not until the BBC bought the TV and newspaper rights for 48,000 dollars that the finances looked healthier, though even that sum was less than Dyhrenfurth had hoped for. The BBC's total contribution jumped to 110,000 dollars, but the extra money paid for the seven-man film crew they attached to the already swollen expedition. In addition the BBC sold the newspaper rights to the *Sunday Times,* who sent a reporter, Murray Sayle.

Like Topsy, the expedition just growed. By the time it was in the field there were thirty-three members from thirteen different countries, including the media men—some of whom were good climbers in their own right. It was not, however, a *team*. Patterson's original ideals had disappeared under the crushing burden of financial expediency, and so, for that matter, had Patterson himself, along with Baillie, Hagen, and the two Argentinians. Of the innocent founder members, so to speak, only two remained: the Norwegians Teigland and Eliassen. Dave Isles was still there, and so were two of the other Americans who had joined Patterson before the link-up with Dyhrenfurth: Colliver and Evans. All the rest were newcomers, and they formed as disparate a bunch as one is ever likely to find on an expedition.

On paper it was a firmament of stars. Apart from those already mentioned the climbing team consisted of Wolfgang Axt and Leo Schlömmer of Austria; Duane Blume of the USA; Tony Hiebeler of West Germany; Carlo Mauri of Italy; Pierre Mazeaud of France: Harsh Bahuguna of India; Naomi Uemura and Reizo Ito of Japan; Dougal Haston and Don Whillans of Britain; and the husband and wife team of Michel and Yvette Vaucher of Switzerland. The two doctors (who were also climbers) were Peter Steele of Britain and David Peterson of the USA.

Few of them had climbed together and those who had tended to cleave together in a natural defense against the ambitions of the rest, anxious to protect their own reputations. Jealousy was rampant, being a much more cogent feeling than any superimposed international camaraderie. Islands of isolation grew up, not helped by the language barrier, for when the prevailing language is English it is easy for ancient Gallic fears to be revived and a plot suspected.

Ironically, the one thing which the members had in common—their skill as mountaineers—was one of the major causes. Put plainly: there were too many chiefs and not enough Indians.

Early in the planning, Chris Bonington was enrolled as climbing leader, but the experience he had gained from his Annapurna expedition, which took place while the Everest venture was being planned, gave him food for thought and he later wrote:

> *What worried me was whether I was going to be able to control a*
> *group of climbers of this caliber, all of whom would presumably*

want their turn out in front, and all of whom would have come with dreams—or the determination—of being in the summit party. My own authority would be tenuous, and I could even end up in an uncomfortable position as go-between for the expedition leadership and climbing members.

Shrewdly, Bonington had spotted the major flaw in advance, and he withdrew from the expedition. When he later rejoined it for a short time his initial doubts were reinforced, so he withdrew again. Not even a tempting offer from the BBC for him to go as a reporter could change his mind a second time.

It wasn't so much team selection as team collection: Dyhrenfurth was like a philatelist garnering the cream of the world's rare stamps—only to discover that they didn't make matched sets and some of the specimens were no longer in mint condition. But he could not afford to be too selective: some of those he would have liked to include simply couldn't get any backing and he was forced to take those who could. Only two nominees failed to bring in extra cash beyond the obligatory personal contribution of 500 dollars: the likeable Indian Army officer, Harsh Bahuguna, who had almost reached the summit of Everest in 1965, and the French politician Pierre Mazeaud, who took Dyhrenfurth's tentative inquiry as a definite offer and promptly accepted, ignoring the request for sponsorship. Whether it was because he did not wish to offend a member of the French Chamber of Deputies (and one, moreover, tipped to succeed to the plum job of Minister of Sport), or whether it was because Vaucher, Axt, and Hiebeler all recommended Mazeaud, Dyhrenfurth let the matter stand.

The hard core of the team were professionals to a greater or lesser degree. Uemura and Mauri earned their livelihoods directly from their worldwide adventures (Mauri had just returned from Thor Heyerdahl's *Ra* voyage); Hiebeler owned a prestigious climbing magazine, *Alpinismus;* Haston was director of a mountaineering school, and so on. Each, therefore, had a special motive for doing well, above and beyond the call of the mountain.

Had the team been able to meet in the Alps, as originally planned, some of the weaknesses and personality clashes might have been foreseen and action taken to eliminate them, but the financially stringent situation that

Dyhrenfurth found himself in prevented that. Indeed, finance—or the lack of it—dominated the preparations to a damaging extent. Quite apart from the difficulties already mentioned, Dyhrenfurth found himself once again tackling Everest when public interest in it was at its lowest. Not only the general public but the climbing fraternity too were disenchanted with the whole idea.

There were two possible explanations for this. One lay in the nature of the climb itself. The South West Face of Everest is not a particularly attractive-looking climb. It is a great triangular face whose main feature, the Rock Band runs across it horizontally. There is no natural line up: no challenging ridge or buttress that beckons to be conquered—just an awkward obstacle to be climbed or avoided as the case may be. Dyhrenfurth had countered this by announcing in the expedition newspaper that the climb was to be the *direttissima*—that is to say, straight up. Only the American members believed this way possible.

More cogent at the time, however, was the growing mood of revulsion that the climbing world was beginning to feel toward the whole concept of the huge super-marathon expedition. The Japanese Everest expedition of 1970 symbolized all that was going wrong. There was hostility toward the wheeler-dealer tactics necessary to raise the huge sums involved, the show-biz attitude of the media, the primadonna attitude of the climbers. *If this is expedition climbing,* the mood ran, *then we want no part of it.* Indifference turned to positive antagonism, and it is fair to say that a large section of the climbing public were looking forward to the failure of Dyhrenfurth's expedition with malicious glee.

Knives were out from the start, and one can't help but feel sorry for Dyhrenfurth, who was so wrapped up in the mechanics of the venture that he failed to see how the public mood had changed.

Why this should be so is difficult to see at this distance in time. After all, Bonington's Annapurna expedition had the full media treatment and yet was a popular success with climbers and public alike. But then, it wasn't international.

Bonington's part in the Everest story was to come to full fruition some years later, but suffice to say at this stage that his withdrawal from the International Expedition dealt a serious blow to its tactical strength. His undoubted ability to command from the front when necessary would have made him the ideal climbing leader for the South West Face. His absence left a gap which was never adequately filled, though Bonington did suggest a replacement.

The man he suggested was one of the post-war legends of British climbing, a stocky, sharp-witted, aggressive Lancastrian named Don Whillans. As we have seen, in 1970 Whillans, with Dougal Haston, reached the summit of Annapurna I by the South Face—a remarkable *tour de force* and one of the landmarks of mountaineering history. He was also an Alpinist of great repute, and it was because of an Alpine climb—the Central Pillar of Frêney, a difficult route on Mont Blanc—that he was disliked by Pierre Mazeaud. In 1961, Mazeaud and two others had survived a terrible ordeal on the Frêney Pillar while trying to make the first ascent. Four of their companions had died. Later that same year Bonington, Whillans, Clough, and Dlugosz snatched the first ascent, much to the disgust of Mazeaud. He thought the British were mere opportunists, trading on his own party's misfortunes. "Mazeaud can never forgive the British," wrote Whillans, "and me especially, for making the first ascent of the Central Pillar of Frêney."

Whether Dyhrenfurth was aware of Mazeaud's hatred of Whillans or not, he did know that the little Lancastrian had an outspoken nature whose very bluntness frequently upset people. Whillans seemed to move around in a perpetual aura of prickly controversy which fame and maturity (he was then thirty-seven) had done nothing to modify. On the one hand he was too good a climber to leave out, particularly since he would be teamed with Haston, his partner on the successful Annapurna climb, but on the other hand his forthright nature, in Dyhrenfurth's opinion, made him unfit to be in command. To solve this dilemma Dyhrenfurth once again sought refuge in compromise: Whillans joined the expedition, but the post of climbing leader was abolished. Instead, there was to be a "coordinator" between the active men on the mountain and the Base Camp gurus. John Evans, an American, was appointed to this task.

Bonington had taken part in the route-planning during his brief membership and had given it as his opinion that a team of twelve would be sufficient for the South West Face. More than that would lead to complications—which is exactly what Hiromi Ohtsuka, leader of the Japanese climbers, had discovered.

Dyhrenfurth therefore cast around for an alternative which would keep the rest of the climbers happy. He had a choice of two: first, and most obvious, the ordinary route up the South East Ridge by way of the South Col; second, the West Ridge climbed by his own party in 1963.

The first alternative was ruled out almost immediately. The predominantly Anglo-Saxon membership of the expedition in its early stages regarded the ordinary route with disdain. It had been climbed many times, and for the vast International Expedition, composed as it was of a galaxy of star performers, to climb it again was like using a steam hammer to crack a nut. Dyhrenfurth consulted his old buddies, Barry Corbet and Barry Bishop of the 1963 team, and they concurred.

Looking back, it seems as though this was a blinkered decision taken by men who thought only in terms of massive resources. In fact the resources of the expedition, particularly in terms of Sherpas, were scarcely adequate for the South West Face. The Sherpa force was fifty-five men compared with the seventy-five the Japanese had employed. This gave Dyhrenfurth a ratio of little more than one and a half Sherpas per team member. For the first ascent in 1953, John Hunt had needed double that ratio. Climbers were the only surplus, and as Ken Wilson, editor of *Mountain* magazine, later pointed out, a lightweight attempt via the South Col would have been a worthwhile objective. It might have been done without Sherpa support, or even without oxygen. In any case, a line of small camps leading to the South East Ridge could have been a valuable retreat route should anyone climb the South West Face and for some reason be unable to descend the same way. Nobody had ever descended the West Ridge.

Another point, and one that was to prove crucially important later on, was that the decision not to climb the ordinary route was made quite early in the planning by men whose nations had already climbed it. As more continental climbers were brought in, the relative importance of climbing Everest *by any route* grew. The latecomers were not, however, consulted. Perhaps they took it for granted that the summit was the prime objective if it came to a crunch— certainly Mazeaud did, as Whillans explained:

The attitude of Mazeaud on receiving the invitation seems to have been that he had been invited to climb *Everest, not that he had been invited to join a team attempting the difficult unclimbed South West Face.*

Dyhrenfurth opted for the West Ridge. Hornbein must have smiled at the irony of it when he heard, but this time it was to be the West Ridge Direct, not the alternative by the Hornbein Couloir, which the Americans had climbed in 1963. It was a formidable objective, guaranteed to stretch resources to the limit, but at the time it wasn't seen in that light. Only the advantages were seen—that it was more worthy of effort than the ordinary route, and that, should the South West Face attempt fail, the West Ridge was a nice consolation prize. It was also another hedge against the possible success of the Japanese in 1970.

Not everyone was happy with the dual role the expedition had now assumed. Rusty Baillie, at that time still a member, wrote:

Regarding the West Ridge and the West Ridge Direct: the former has been done and the latter is splitting hairs. To my way of thinking, the time will come in Himalayan history when variants will be climbed. But it is not now. Thus I would want to attempt the Face. Also I think that the Face will need the utmost, not only from every member, but also from the expedition as an entity. All expeditions are a strain on inter-relationships, an International one even more so . . . an international one with a divided aim may well spend its energy solving problems of personality rather than of mountaineering. I therefore respectfully submit that we all put our efforts into one route. I can appreciate that our sponsors and commercial interests may expect a route by any way, but hopefully we will not have to be ruled by them in mountaineering decisions.

Baillie was a prophet crying in the wilderness. He later resigned.

➤   ➤   ➤

The team was well equipped. For their high-altitude camps they had the rigid-framed Whillans Box, a tent that Don had designed after experiencing the trauma of a Patagonian gale. Its box shape gave the occupants greater freedom of movement than an ordinary tent—no small advantage in a high camp. The oxygen equipment, too, was excellent and a credit to its designer, physiologist Dr. Duane Blume.

As always, there were some faults. By a quirk of design the Austrian crampons didn't fit the German boots properly and gave trouble throughout the expedition. Then, too, Blume found that the oxygen masks didn't fit the Sherpas. This was because they were standard US Air Force issue, which came in two types discreetly marked *Caucasian* and *Oriental*—and the Oriental pattern was based on Vietnamese facial characteristics, which are quite different from those of Sherpas. Fortunately some masks of the 1963 pattern were available.

The radios were not always reliable either, particularly in the weather conditions the expedition was to encounter, and probably contributed to some of the misunderstanding that arose.

The only major drawback was the food, which arrived in Kathmandu in bulk instead of in the more easily organized man-day rations, and the subsequent labor involved in sorting it out was never satisfactorily accomplished. Tasty tidbits destined for the high camps would mysteriously vanish on their way up. Normally, this might have been something of a joke, but on this occasion the tidbits were eagerly sought after because the rest of the food was unpalatable. Dyhrenfurth had delegated the organization of the food to Wolfgang Axt, the thirty-five-year-old school teacher from Austria, not realizing that Axt was a vegetarian and health food fanatic. His choice of diet met with less than universal approval from his fellow team members.

In all there were some thirty-five tons of food and equipment, about half of which was flown to the STOL (Short Take Off and Landing) airstrip which had been built at Lukla in the Khumbu valley, about seven days' march below Everest Base Camp. The rest of the supplies were carried in by the expedition's 450 porters.

Base Camp was established on March 23, 1971, in the now traditional place below the Khumbu Icefall. During the march from Kathmandu relations between the various members of the expedition had been cordial. Both Whillans and Haston, however, were concerned at the holiday atmosphere of the trek; they had the uncomfortable feeling that some of the participants were not fully aware of the hardships that lay ahead, and they wondered how the camaraderie would stand up when it came to the crunch.

During this walk-in, the members were asked to choose the route they wished to take. In doing this, Dyhrenfurth was establishing democracy in the same way he had during the 1963 American expedition. It was the exact opposite to the dictatorial method used by the Japanese (Uemura must have been surprised) but there is nothing to indicate it was more successful.

After some changes of mind the teams settled down as follows:

For the South West Face: Evans (coordinator), Colliver, Peterson (all Americans); Ito and Uemura of Japan; Whillans and Haston from Britain; the German Hiebeler; and the Austrian Schlömmer.

For the West Ridge: Axt (coordinator); the Norwegians Teigland and Eliassen; the Vauchers, husband and wife; Bahuguna of India; Mauri of Italy; Isles of the USA; Mazeaud of France; and Steele, the British doctor.

Of the two leaders, Roberts intended to look after Base Camp, and Dyhrenfurth, Advanced Base in the Western Cwm. The Sherpas were to be divided equally between the two teams, once progress had been made beyond Advanced Base.

Hardly had Base Camp been established when there was a roar from the Khumbu Icefall and the startled climbers saw huge blocks of ice tumbling down, smashing everything in their path. It was an awesome warning to everyone that the holiday was over and there was grim work ahead.

The Icefall was in bad condition, very unstable and totally unpredictable as always. A great curving depression, which seemed to offer a quick way through it, proved illusory, and it was a fortnight before a relatively secure route was pioneered and Camp 1 set up on the lip of the Cwm. On April 5 Camp 2—Advanced Base—was established in the Cwm at 21,600 ft., and from there each team began to make its own way toward its objective. International relationships immediately began to wear thin.

On the Face route things began smoothly. There was a much better covering of snow than the Japanese had enjoyed the year before and the four lead climbers, Whillans, Haston, Uemura, and Ito, had little difficulty in fixing ropes up the fairly easy snow slopes and establishing Camp 3(F) on the same spot their predecessors had used.

Meanwhile the West Ridge team were encountering problems. The snow slopes leading to the West Shoulder were proving to be difficult—more so than in 1963 when the Americans climbed them. The two Norwegians, Eliassen and Teigland, together with the Indian climber Bahuguna, had at first tried to go straight up, but found this impossible. Later, in a savage article in *La Suisse,* Vaucher was to claim these three lacked experience and had poor ice-climbing technique. Be that as it may, nobody else was willing to try a direct route up the slope.

Vaucher and Axt now went to work to re-establish the original American route of 1963. They found that even this was difficult. Their way was blocked by an icefall which caused a circuitous detour, first downhill, then by a horizontal traverse, and finally up the slope again to rejoin the original line.

Axt then teamed up with Bahuguna. They managed to establish Camp 3(W) at 22,600 ft., then on April 17, after a night at this camp, they climbed up to the crest of the ridge, prospecting the way ahead and seeking a suitable place for Camp 4(W). In this they were successful: Camp 4(W) would be on the ridge itself, and so far as they could see the ascent of the rocky West Ridge would not be an insuperable task. Much heartened by this progress the two men descended.

It was at this point that chance threw the dice against them. The two men had worked hard and were due for a rest. They could have gone straight down to Advanced Base (and indeed Dyhrenfurth had wanted Bahuguna to go down to Base Camp itself for a recuperation period some days earlier but he had declined). Now, however, as they returned from the ridge they spotted a better site for Camp 3(W), which they had always thought was too low anyway. They decided to stay the night at 3(W), move it to its new site next day, then return to Advanced Base.

Meanwhile, their companions had not been idle. Their aim was to shorten the somewhat complicated route to Camp 3(W). Mauri and Mazeaud climbed up the slopes and dumped loads of ropes, stakes and pitons in readiness for this task, then Vaucher and Eliassen went to work, paying out the rope and fixing it in place with stakes and ice screws. It was a horizontal traverse about 400 ft. long, curling round a bulge of the mountain. The snow slope was some 40°—by no means excessive—and wherever the rope was pinned to the slope Vaucher and Eliassen cut a platform or large step, where a man could stand and rest in comparative safety. This was useful because if a climber was following the rope and was attached to it by a safety line he would have to stop and unhook himself whenever he came to a stake or piton, then hook on again beyond it. Laden porters in particular would appreciate this: under normal circumstances many of the climbers might not bother with a safety attachment because the traverse was not all that difficult. The new traverse was a valuable piece of work: it cut out the downhill bit of the route and shortened the time to Camp 3(W) by about an hour.

Up above, Axt and Bahuguna were told of these developments by radio and, they in turn informed the others of their plans for a new Camp 3(W).

Next day, April 18, Axt reported on the radio that the weather looked threatening: dark clouds were piling up to the northwest. Nevertheless, he and Bahuguna continued with their plan to move Camp 3(W).

At Advanced Base on this morning a different kind of storm was brewing. The two Vauchers, Carlo Mauri, and Pierre Mazeaud went to Dyhrenfurth with a strong complaint that their equipment for the West Ridge was not getting through, whereas the equipment for the Face team seemed to get through without difficulty. They had mentioned it before, but now they put it in stronger terms. They suspected bias: that preferential treatment was being given to the Face team because it was primarily an Anglo-American affair and therefore the only part of the expedition to interest the BBC, which had put so much money into the venture.

Dyhrenfurth explained that there was a hold-up at Camp 1. He suggested that to help matters out they should all go down the Cwm to Camp 1, pick up loads and bring them up. After all, during the American expedition he had led, characters like Unsoeld had cheerfully trudged uphill with loads of 60 pounds or more. But the Latins (as they had become known) refused to countenance this.

It was beneath their dignity, they said, to do work which was intended for Sherpas. Disgusted at their attitude, Dyhrenfurth decided to set an example by shouldering a pack frame himself and setting off for Camp 1.

Here was the chiefs and Indians syndrome showing its naked rawness! Throughout the expedition there had been (and continued to be) a reluctance on the part of many members to carry loads. In some instances the Latins had not even carried their own personal gear, but they were not alone in dodging heavy packs. Even where ostensibly heavy loads had been carried, on some occasions suspicious colleagues had surreptitiously "weighed" them and found them to be remarkably light. One-upmanship was rampant. Was it that load-carrying was really beneath their dignity, or was it that nobody wanted to burn himself out, thereby reducing his chance of the summit? The Sherpas, who were the silent butt-end of all this maneuvering, were not impressed.

At Camp 1 Dyhrenfurth met Peterson, Haston, Schlömmer, and Hiebeler and tried to sort out the logistic bottleneck. He then packed two oxygen cylinders ("One each for Face and Ridge, in fairness to both teams") and plodded back up the Cwm towards Advanced Base.

As he climbed the weather rapidly deteriorated and soon the Cwm was filled with a raging blizzard. Only the willow wands stuck in the snow at regular intervals showed Dyhrenfurth the way forward. A snow avalanche from the slopes of Nuptse struck him, but by bracing himself he was able to keep his stance, and fortunately it was only powder snow, not the wet, cloying, obliterating kind. He struggled on, and then out of the white darkness appeared the familiar figure of Ang Lakpa, his personal Sherpa, come to see that the sahib was all right.

Together they trudged back through the storm, losing their way momentarily, until they picked up the line of markers again. Suddenly, high above them they heard a fearful scream, then another and another. They shouted back but the wind whipped their voices away. They knew that the screams had come from Harsh Bahaguna.

While Dyhrenfurth and Ang Lakpa struggled up the Cwm a distraught and exhausted Wolfgang Axt staggered into Advanced Base Camp. He had descended from Camp 3(W) in the storm. "Bahuguna is still up there!" he gasped.

At once a rescue party scrambled into their gear and set off to rescue the Indian climber. Rivalries and national jealousies were put aside as Eliassen,

Vaucher, Whillans, Mazeaud, Mauri, Steele, and Ang Phurba faced the storm, in automatic response to the age-old climbers' code that help must be given at all costs. It was 5:15 P.M. Night in the Cwm wasn't far off.

They all climbed as rapidly as possible. It was a lung-tearing effort made worse by the storm. Perhaps because they knew the route better than the others, Eliassen and Vaucher were the first to reach the hapless victim.

Bahuguna's condition was bad. His chest harness was attached to the long fixed rope of the traverse and he just hung there, helpless with cold and exhaustion. A rime of ice covered his face. One glove was gone, and the harness had pulled up his clothes, exposing his bare midriff to the elements.

Eliassen, more to comfort him than anything else, asked him if he was O.K. and incredibly the Indian seemed to murmur that he was. The two men tried to move him across the traverse but were prevented by the force of the storm. They then decided to lower him on a rope and attempt to swing him across the slope to the shelter of a crevasse, where possibly the others could reach him. Hardly had they begun to lower him than he turned upside down, and Whillans, who had now arrived at the scene, climbed down and turned him right way up. Whillans then tried to move him sideways, at considerable risk to himself, but found it impossible. There was only one other option—to lower Bahuguna straight down the slope to another crevasse where it was hoped Steele, Mazeaud, and Ang Phurba could take charge of him.

Thirty-five feet above the sheltering crevasse the rope ran out. Whillans, teetering around on the steep slopes in the face of the storm and darkness, without ice axe or protective rope, took one last look at the Indian. He was unconscious, his face blue, his eyes staring. In half an hour he would be dead.

"Sorry, Harsh old son, you've had it," muttered Whillans.

The rescuers were themselves now in an unenviable position. Exhausted, battered by the storm, they had to fight their way back to camp.

It was a dejected group that met Dyhrenfurth in Advanced Base that night. Axt knew nothing of the final tragedy, for Steele had sent him to bed with sleeping pills before the rescue team set out, but the rest were there in a somber, angry mood. Harsh Bahuguna had been popular with everyone. Mazeaud accused Axt of murder through negligence, but Dyhrenfurth calmed him down, promising a full inquiry next day.

Next morning, as the team assembled in the mess tent, Axt was the last to enter.

"*Wie geht es Harsh?*" ("How is Harsh?") he demanded.

"*Weisst du es nocht nicht? Er ist tot!*" ("Don't you know? He is dead!") Dyhrenfurth replied.

Axt burst into tears.

The inquiry was set for 10 A.M. and Dyhrenfurth directed Bill Kurban of the BBC to tape-record the proceedings, in case there should be further inquiries or disputes. Asked what had happened, Axt said:

> *We were not roped during the descent, there was no need, there were no difficulties at all. Since I knew Michel (Vaucher) and Odd (Eliassen) had placed fixed ropes on all the steeper sections, I left my climbing rope and my harness and karabiner at the new camp. At first Harsh went ahead. Around 2 P.M. the weather turned bad. Soon we were caught in a raging storm. When we reached the long rope-traverse I took over the lead and got across it hand over hand. It was very long and tiring as hell. At the far end I waited for Harsh to follow. Voice communication was impossible, the storm was much too strong. I waited for a long time, perhaps as much as an hour. My hands and feet lost all feeling. Then I saw Harsh tied into a fixed rope with a harness and karabiner, groping his way round the last corner of the steep ice-slope that separated us. He waved with one hand. Everything seemed O.K., no indication of any serious difficulty. I was really worried about frostbite so I went down. Just before I got to the camp I heard his screams and alerted everybody. I couldn't have gone up as I was completely done in.*

When he was asked why he did not stay with Bahuguna he replied:

> *I had no idea how bad things were with him, and besides what could I have done without a rope or karabiner? Harsh had taken*

his gear but I would have had to go back hand over hand over that long traverse. I simply didn't have enough strength in me for that and my hands and feet felt like blocks of ice.

It was not the end of the affair for Axt. On his return to India some weeks later he was questioned closely by Brigadier Gyan Singh and Major H.P.S. Ahluwalia, who were the committee appointed by the Indian Mountaineering Federation to look into the causes of the tragedy. After considering various statements and a transcript of the BBC tape, they issued the following statement:

According to Axt, he did not go back to look for Bahuguna because he had no harness or carabiner without which he would have been of little help. Presumably for the same reason he crossed the rope traverse quickly without waiting for Bahuguna to follow close behind. But even before he started, Axt knew about the existence and nature of the traverse and as an "ice-specialist" he should also have known that the harness and the carabiner would be needed on this obstacle. However, he chose to leave this essential safety equipment, weighing no more than a few hundred grams, behind for "reasons of weight." The Committee, therefore, consider that Bahuguna may not have lost his life if Axt had brought his essential safety equipment and traveled close to his rope-mate.

The Committee find it difficult to agree that he did not realize that Bahuguna was in difficulty until he heard his shouts for help at 4:15 P.M.

The Committee rule out willful foul play on anyone's part.

The Committee are not certain if Bahuguna was, in fact, wearing silk or nylon gloves under his thick outer gloves. But, apart from that his clothing was appropriate for tackling the traverse, and in his rucksack he was carrying adequate insulated clothing. Unfortunately, after Bahuguna was incapacitated on the fixed rope, the clothing he was wearing was not sufficient to protect him from the elements and keep him warm.

This seems less than fair on poor Axt. It was precisely because he was an "ice-specialist" that he felt he did not need the safety harness—as events in his case proved. He did not expect to have to return along the rope to help Bahuguna. It was Harsh Bahuguna's enthusiasm and willingness that finally over-stretched him and led to his death.

The great storm lasted for ten days, marooning the climbers in their camps. Through rifts in the clouds the men at Advanced Base could see from time to time the body of Harsh Bahuguna dangling down the slopes of Everest like a puppet on a string. The sight contributed to the general mood of depression occasioned by the accident, the never-ending storm, and the food shortages the storm created.

Tony Hiebeler, editor of *Alpinismus,* had had enough. He had never acclimatized properly and had gone down to Base Camp on the first morning of the storm. When he heard of Bahuguna's death it was the last discouraging blow. He wrote a note for Dyhrenfurth: "I am a physical and mental wreck, I can't take a single step towards the mountain—forgive me." He packed his rucksack and left for home on April 25.

Hiebeler left for the best of motives—he genuinely felt he was no use to the expedition, and that he could do more to help the venture from his office in Munich. But of course, the media, realizing that things were going badly for the expedition and knowing that international tensions and squabbles make better news stories than the climbing of a mountain, boosted his "defection" out of all proportion. Had they but known it, they were shortly to have a field day.

Bahuguna's tragic death had particularly affected the spirit of the West Ridge team. Steele and Eliassen had lost all interest in it: all they wanted was to help the Face team to achieve their objective and then get off the mountain as quickly as possible. Mazeaud and Mauri, too, wanted no more to do with the West Ridge, but for a different reason. They felt it was too difficult and requested a switch to the South Col route, much to Dyhrenfurth's disgust:

> *I tried to convince them that Everest has already been climbed
> by five expeditions by way of the South Col. All told, 23 climbers*

*of six nations have reached the summit that way. I considered
this colossal investment in time, manpower and money
unjustifiable for a route which at this stage of Himalayan
mountaineering is of no further interest . . . All my pleas were
in vain. Against my better judgment I proposed a vote to be taken.*

The vote was among the West Ridgers only. Axt, Isles, and Surdel (a BBC cameraman assigned to the Ridge) voted to stick with the original plan; Steam and Eliassen voted to join the Face team in an all-out effort; Teigland voted to go with the majority. And the majority proved to be the four Latins: Mazeaud, Mauri, and the two Vauchers, all of whom voted for the South Col route.

It was as Dyhrenfurth had feared and he wrote:

*It is more and more obvious that Carlo Mauri and Pierre
Mazeaud are in no way interested in an all-out team effort. All
they want is personal glory by reaching the summit the easiest
way possible and to become national heroes in France and Italy.
Also the Vauchers' sole interest lies in the summit . . . Despite
serious misgivings and deep disappointment, I declared myself
ready and willing to lend support to their new project. . . .*

Man proposes, but the mountain disposes . . . The decision was taken on the fifth day of the storm at a time when nobody realized that it was going to last five more days, making it one of the worst storms in the history of the mountain. By the end of it morale and health were badly eroded. Most members went down to base to recuperate or to attend the funeral of Harsh Bahuguna, who was cremated at Gorak Shep and whose ashes were sent home to Dehra Dun.

Supplies once again began to move up into the Cwm from Base Camp, but Jimmy Roberts, who was in charge of the logistics, was not happy with the situation. There simply were not enough porters to supply two teams simultaneously, added to which the passage through the Icefall was changing daily owing to unusually frequent ice movements, which made the journey slower and more hazardous. He had put it to Dyhrenfurth that the South Col attempt should be scrapped and all resources concentrated on the Face, but Dyhrenfurth was reluctant to break his word to Mazeaud and the rest of the Latins.

Eventually, Roberts could stand it no longer. Unable to hold a full discussion of the situation with his co-leader at Advanced Base because of intermittent radio contact, he broadcast to all the expedition his thoughts on what needed to be done. Basically it was to scrap the South Col route and concentrate on the Face.

It seems that faulty radio transmission prevented Dyhrenfurth from hearing Roberts' message, but he had by this time come to the same conclusion. The South Col route would have to be abandoned—but, of course, not without a vote. He therefore went on the air, ignorant of Roberts' appeal, to ask members yet again to vote for which route they wanted.

The result was a foregone conclusion. Dyhrenfurth had caught the Latins divided: the two Vauchers were actually on their way down to Base Camp and therefore unable to vote, which left only Mazeaud and Mauri in favor of the South Col route. To make sure the decision was overwhelmingly democratic, Dyhrenfurth even included the leading Sherpas in the voting, much to the justified amazement of Mazeaud. The Sherpas voted for the Face route too—after all, their part in it was a simple straightforward snow slope which was both easier and safer than the long arduous flog up to the South Col!

Mazeaud was furious. The coincidence of the two broadcasts convinced him that he was the victim of background plotting. As his accusations grew wilder he inevitably included the arch-villain, Whillans, "that English working-man"(true) who "stood to gain millions from Karrimor for the climb" (untrue). Coming from a French Gaullist Deputy it is difficult to judge whether Mazeaud meant "English" or "working-man" to be the bigger insult. Perhaps fortunately for both (and certainly for Mazeaud), Whillans was at one of the advanced camps at the time.

Mazeaud and Mauri packed and descended to Base Camp. As he left Dyhrenfurth he gave one final histrionic outburst:

They expect me, Pierre Mazeaud, Member of the French Assembly, aged forty-two, to work as a sherpa for Anglo-Saxons and Japanese. Never! This is not me, but France they have insulted!

It was just what the popular press had been hoping for. Bang went international cooperation. Bang went *entente cordiale.* And bang went any chance Mazeaud had of becoming Minister of Sport.

At Base Camp Mazeaud and Mauri joined the two Vauchers, who were incensed at not being in on the vote. All were convinced that the affair was a typically devious Anglo-Saxon plot, engineered by the BBC to ensure that the two Britons, Whillans and Haston, got to the summit in preference to anyone else. The Americans and Japanese were in collusion with the British (though why this should be so remained unexplained). Meanwhile Whillans, up in the Cwm, had ordered the only camp established by the South Col party to be struck: a gesture of finality which enraged Mazeaud even more. Wild accusations flew in every direction and when the hapless Dyhrenfurth, a sick man, returned to Base Camp, Yvette Vaucher pelted him with snowballs, yelling *"Voici le salaud!"* ("Here's the bastard!")

The Latins were for leaving straight away, but even at this late juncture Dyhrenfurth procrastinated. He persuaded them to stay until Jimmy Roberts returned from Harsh Bahaguna's funeral next day. He was hoping for some mediation that would patch up the quarrel—by this time he himself was so ill that effective decision-taking was quite beyond him.

When Roberts returned and apprised himself of the situation his action was immediate. Tough as old boots and a hard whisky drinker, he had been brought up in a different world from Dyhrenfurth's. His school was that of the British Army, where to command meant just that. He called together the four dissidents and said: "No South Col. Face only—and if you don't like it you can go. There will be no discussion."

Roberts' attitude did nothing to ease the situation. Now more determined than ever to quit, the Latins threatened to crucify the leaders at press conferences in Europe, and there were wild innuendoes about reprisals. A Sherpa guard was mounted on the vulnerable and valuable oxygen supply.

Next day, as they made preparations for leaving, the Latins' anger still bubbled and, in the mess tent that night at dinner, it boiled over into one final, furious row. Peter Steele, the British doctor at Base Camp, has described what happened:

> At dinner one could predict a confrontation, and it came; yet I feel sure it might have been avoided. Instead of amicably forgetting our differences for the last night and all sitting together, the leaders and the predominantly Anglo-American members sat down at one end of the mess tent while opposite and separated by a short distance were the Vauchers, Mazeaud and Mauri with Jurec Surdel, Odd Eliassen, and myself.
>
> John Evans arrived late, having come down from the Hill and gave a first-hand account of events on the mountain. "Camp VI has been established and occupied this morning by Don and Dougal. The oxygen sets are working well and only minor troubles have been found with the rubber valves freezing up. Hopes are rising for the summit and morale is on the up."
>
> Yvette got up from the table to go to bed and upbraided John Evans in an emotional tirade, sarcastically thanking him for letting them down over the vote. John took it with characteristic calm and charity but the fuse was ignited and the charge exploded soon after. As Michel Vaucher, Carlo Mauri, and Pierre Mazeaud left the tent the latter threw some provocative taunts at Norman and the encounter began in earnest. The Latins were down one end of a long table, the leaders at the other end, and various members ranged on both sides.
>
> All the old arguments were produced, the old ground ploughed over and the tent took on the air of a courtroom. Pierre Mazeaud, magistrat, député, membre de L'Assemblée Nationale, was in his element holding the floor with a powerful command of language and rhetoric. He cut a fine figure leaning on the large teapot, his index finger pointed and wagging. Carlo and Michel

sat by and said little. I translated for them when they misun-
derstood the English.

Norman sat back at the end of the table and listened with
attention and dignity as Mazeaud's loquacious accusations
poured out: the Anglo-Saxon plot to oust the Latins, collusion
with the BBC to put a Briton on the top for the success of their
film, Whillans standing to make a million from his boxes if he
reached the summit, allegations of drunkenness and pot smok-
ing at Camp II, distorted radio messages over the vote. He
rounded off with a personal thrust, "Norman, tu es intelligent
mais tu es faible, pas comme ton pére."

One man, a BBC cameraman, had been sitting quietly; his
head was buried into his chest as he dozed off the effects of the
whisky that had been circulating freely. In the middle of
Mazeaud's most poignant plea for reconsideration of the deci-
sion on the South Col he stood up, lurched towards and fell
across the table, dislodging his spectacles.

"Look, another drunken Englishman," shouted Mazeaud. "You
are all drunkards and idiots."

Jimmy Roberts, who had remained notably silent in the face
of the onslaught, leaned forwards and slowly, deliberately, and
with power of feeling said: "Fuck off, Mazeaud."

Mazeaud's mouth drooped in horror. The bubble burst and a
peal of hysterical laughter rent the air, doing nothing to placate
the now furious Frenchman. Jimmy called for Sirdar Lakpa
and, speaking in Nepali, told him to muster a squad of Sherpas
outside the tent in case of trouble. But they were already there.
Eager faces stood back in the shadows hanging on every moment
of the action.

The next day the Latins left. If their conduct during the last few days had
been deplorable, it was also understandable. Human vanity had led them to
expect more than the expedition could give. They had seen it, wrongly, as a

way to achieve personal ambitions—Mazeaud would have been the first Frenchman to climb Everest, Mauri the first Italian, and Yvette Vaucher the first woman. As the Swiss had already climbed the mountain, no similar accolade was in store for Vaucher himself, though there was the possibility of man and wife climbing the mountain together, which would no doubt have been personally satisfying and publicly profitable. The pity was that Vaucher was one of the ablest climbers on the expedition and his rightful place was on the Face, with Whillans and the others.

Strangely enough, despite the fireworks and histrionics, the charges and counter-charges, there were some deep-lasting friendships formed, even between the Latins and the rest. Mauri, in particular, was unhappy at the way things had gone and he seems to have been dragged along by events against his will.

Needless to say, there was no deep-laid plot by the BBC or anyone else, to exclude the Latins or deny them their moments of glory. But had they been misled in the first place? Mazeaud certainly thought so and always maintained that the invitation was to climb Everest, not the South West Face. How he could have believed this, in view of the worldwide publicity that heralded the expedition and extolled the Face climb, is difficult to understand, but it is possible. The responsibility must rest with Dyhrenfurth, who acted from the start like a straw bending to accommodate every prevailing gust of wind.

The defection of the Latins was no serious loss to an expedition with as much manpower in reserve. Unfortunately, it was at this point that sickness swept like a scythe through the ranks and seriously reduced any chance of success.

Almost from the beginning the expedition had been dogged by minor illnesses, and there was some complaint from the hardier members that the doctors were molly-coddling their patients, sending them down to recuperate when it wasn't really necessary. But as time went on even the critics had to admit that the victims really were ill.

The earliest casually was Dyhrenfurth himself. Four days before he left home, a routine check by his doctor had revealed a thyroid complaint, but not wishing to jeopardize the expedition he had kept the news to himself.

Dyhrenfurth also seemed particularly prone to the fairly common high-altitude sore throat (he suffered badly both in 1963 and in 1971) and these two ailments, combined with the debilitating tensions of the previous few weeks, finally brought him down with glandular fever. Steele sent him home, and as the same illness swept through the team, Teigland, Howell, Colliver, Blume, Eliassen, and Evans left too, though Eliassen and Evans recovered and rejoined the expedition. Bronchitis, pneumonia, colds, and the inevitable headaches and sore throats all began to take a toll. Only four men remained unaffected throughout—Whillans, Haston, Ito, and Uemura, and they were the four who were out in front tackling the Face.

With all these upheavals Roberts was now the expedition leader and Whillans the climbing leader. Whillans, Haston, and the two Japanese had worked steadily on the Face, pushing the route up the great Central Couloir toward the Rock Band. Camps were established on the same sites as the former Japanese camps, using the alloy leveling platforms that the Japanese had left behind. Camp V was occupied on May 5 at 26,000 ft.

The problem from there was how to tackle the Rock Band, that immense fractured wall that ran across the mountain, barring access to the upper Face. The two Britons pushed out to the left to investigate the gullies that the Japanese had thought so promising, but they rejected them as being too steep. The center of the wall was impregnable (so much for the hoped-for Direct route!), so they explored out to the right along a broad but difficult ramp. At the far end of this, they established Camp VI (27,200 ft.).

For days at a time the weather was bad, preventing any progress. At times such as this the two Japanese retreated down the fixed ropes to Advanced Base where they waited out the storm. Whillans and Haston, however, remained in the high camp and because of this came in for criticism on the grounds that they were using up oxygen supplies to no good purpose, even though they were using it only for sleeping. During the bad weather days, said Whillans, "we considered it and just sat there feeling bloody miserable."

Apart from the two Japanese and the Sherpas, there was virtually no support for the two Britons. Whillans had asked Axt to help, but Axt was still visibly affected by the death of Bahuguna. He told Whillans that he could not go onto the Face because he had promised his wife that he would not—it was too dangerous. Schlömmer, the other Austrian, did volunteer to help, providing he could lead, but his request was refused. Shortly afterwards two Austrians returned to Kathmandu, where the media representatives were waiting like vultures to snap up the latest "international" controversy. They were delighted when Schlömmer accused the British of hogging the lead. It seemed to confirm everything the Latins had said earlier: that the whole thing was a typically devious British plot.

Certainly the rejection of Schlömmer's help seems curious until one learns the background. The truth is that the Austrian had gained a reputation among the Face team for dodging work. On one occasion, when he was due to go up to one of the high camps, he asked Whillans to send down a Sherpa to carry his personal gear, which the outraged Lancastrian indignantly refused to do. It was felt, therefore, that a climber who had avoided the hard and boring job of establishing the camps up the Central Gully had no right suddenly to slip into the lead when things got more interesting.

Nevertheless Schlömmer's accusation was hard to shake off. The fact is that Whillans and Haston were in the lead, and stayed there for three weeks. Yet who else was capable of taking over? Ito and Uemura had their chances, but didn't seem to have the tactical flair of the British: "I think they just lacked the Whillans cunning," said Haston. They seemed quite happy in the role they were playing, and both sides had great respect for the other's contribution.

Both parties too were deeply appreciative of the effort put in by the Sherpas, who tried their best to keep the camps supplied, often without any sahib support. Both they and Uemura managed to reach Camp VI carrying heavy loads and without using oxygen.

Above Camp VI, near the end of the big ramp, an 800-ft. buttress, black and formidable, reared up. It was split by a gully which, though climbable was a serious task at that altitude. The climbers were encumbered with oxygen gear, and the cold was intense, often more than 35° below freezing.

Whillans climbed up part of the way, then, rounding a corner, was astonished to see that it was a fairly simple matter to traverse to the right over some broken slabs and join the well-known ordinary route on the South East Ridge! The temptation must have been immense, but after all the trauma of the expedition how could he opt out in this fashion? He knew he would be accused of hypocrisy, of having planned it all from the start.

Turning his back on easy fame he faced the gully again. When Haston came up they looked at the obstacle and knew that they simply did not have the resources to tackle it.

"How about buggering off?" said Whillans. And the great international dream was over.

"MAKALU, TOO. WOULDN'T YOU?"

FROM
Stone Palaces
BY GEOF CHILDS

THIS IS THE TALE, IRONICALLY TOLD, OF A MISCONCEIVED AND mis-executed attempt on the unclimbed West Face of Makalu in Nepal, at 27,850 feet elevation the fifth highest mountain in the world. Starting off in hope and innocence, Childs is somewhat overwhelmed by the climbing resumes of his fellow adventurers. Soon, however, the elements, the mountain, and human foibles take their toll, and a number of the ill-assorted luminaries fall by the wayside. Childs finds himself rising to the surface to take his place among the hardiest, for one final, inglorious attempt . . .

Childs is a professional mountain guide and completely modern-day climber who can write of expeditionary disasters with the understated humor and self-mocking style of another era—sort of a latter-day Tilman but with more economy of words.

This essay is from his book *Stone Palaces*, a collection of writings on climbing and climbers, pages 49-61.

T he West Face of Makalu (27,850 feet) intimidates on sight. Pre-eminent among the climbing world's last great problems, it is 10,000 feet of frozen granite, bullet-hard ice, and falling debris. An alpine wall that, since its discovery, has remained among the least traveled of vertical spaces.

Our original plan had been to climb something else. Not another peak—from the beginning we knew we wanted to climb Makalu—just another route. Early on we had thought about repeating either its Northwest Ridge or the less technical Southeast Ridge. Each had the appeal of offering a direct shot at the summit and the strong likelihood of being able to put somebody on top. The more we talked about it, however, the clearer it became that few of us were really interested in going halfway around the world to follow in someone else's footsteps. Our attention then shifted to the unclimbed South Face, but that hope, too, was dashed when a Yugoslavian expedition succeeded on the route just prior to our arrival. So with tickets in hand, gear shipped, and permits in place, we changed plans. Based on a single photograph and the wildest of post-adolescent optimism we decided to head west and into the unknown.

We had hardly hired our porters before we found the full forces of the mountain turned against us. It was that kind of expedition. The trails were muddy, the locals ill-humored, and the critical bridges in poor repair. Rain fell upon us without mercy. Rain that translated to heavy snows up high that meant frostbitten feet for our porters and two days of trenching our way across slopes creaking with avalanche danger simply to establish our base camp. Then there was the wind. By setting up house in the shadow of the mountain's darkest architecture we found we had subjected ourselves to a micro-climate of hurricane downdrafts and piercing cold. Conditions that rattled the frames of our most stout tents and settled a chill over us for which even our state-of-the-art sleeping bags were no match. Our location hurt us in other ways, too. With the thin thread of our logistical resources already stretched taut by the exaggerated scale of the landscape, we found ourselves compelled to place base camp at 18,500 feet—too distant, as it turned out, to either resupply from the valley or allow adequate recovery from the rigors of the face.

In view of all this it is tempting to say that we never had a chance: Yet, in truth, our demise probably lay as much in mind as it did in matter. The difference between good intentions and a Himalayan summit is measured in will. Food, tools, and favorable weather carry you only so far. After that, the outcome is decided by desire. And although the idea of standing atop the world's fifth highest peak certainly had its appeal, if we were plump with want, we were perhaps somewhat slender in our passion.

Like members of all expeditions, the people on our team had been drawn together by a wide variety of ambitions. For some, the trip was the fulfillment of a long climbing career. For others, it was the next logical step. In a society of geographical morons, both groups knew that the segue from life as a big name among the lesser ranges to international credibility meant capping an 8,000-meter peak. Makalu was to be that stepping stone. But our largest contingent had no such ambitions. For them the trip was nothing more than an adventure. They had nothing to prove, no burden of reputation to defend. Only the pure and simple desire to ride the high as far as it went. They talked openly about the expedition as a kind of low-rent semester abroad, only funkier and with better drugs. They would carry loads and string ropes as long as the climbing was cool, but they had few hopes for the summit and no intentions whatsoever of giving up their lives in the process. Along with these bicameral camps came the usual collection of tag-alongs and money lenders. The temporary culture of mixed emotions, deep pockets, and love relationships that always accompanies an expedition in the field.

Subjecting this mix of personalities to three months of isolation and extremity resulted in just about as wide a play of human emotion as probably could have been predicted. On any given day lassitude and indifference rubbed shoulders with equal and opposite amounts of ambition and longing. Sex happened, egos clashed, friendships were made, messages misread, motives impugned, and feelings laid bare with the same regularity that meals were served and tea set to boil. Yet, even as base camp sank into malaise, so too did we press the route, slowly moving rope, food, gear, and fuel up the face. Camps were installed, problems solved, and the mind-numbing work of hauling loads accomplished. Enough that by the end of our first month on the mountain we had put the worst of the barriers below us and reached a point of decision.

All of which is to say that we were probably your normal, everyday, run-of-the-mill Himalayan expedition. A loose confederation of freelance adventurers who awaken one day to find themselves caught between daring and desire, half afraid of going on and half afraid of going back, overawed, underwhelmed, and grievously confused; an alpine Woodstock ten-day's walk from the nearest relief with nothing to do but roll the dice and nowhere to go but up.

⋆　　⋆　　⋆

It was a point I reached by accident. I had been sitting at home one night when the phone rang and I heard the voice of an old acquaintance on the other end of the line. We had climbed a wall in Yosemite together some years earlier but had been in only sporadic communication since. He had confused my phone number for someone else's. But, after exchanging pleasantries and correcting the mistake, he allowed as how he had recently acquired a permit for Makalu and was putting together a team. Would I care to go? Could I raise some money? Would I mind assembling some gear? Like Molly Bloom on creatine I was whispering "Yes, yes, God yes" before he'd even finished.

After that we discussed dates, possible routes, and an inventory of equipment, then said goodbye and that was pretty much it. No blood tests, no references, no résumé. In fact, I hardly heard another peep out of him for the next five months. Just a few phone calls, a couple postcards, and an airplane ticket. It wasn't until I arrived in Kathmandu three days late and $90 the poorer for having tried to bribe an Indian customs official that I started feeling like I was really going on an expedition. A point of view quickly corroborated by the fact that I was standing in the ninety-degree heat wearing double boots, a down parka, and toting an eighty-pound carry-on full of climbing gear.

Inauspicious beginnings are a specialty of mine, and I would not have imagined a big trip starting in any more appropriate fashion. If my previous visits to the Far East had taught me anything it was to stay open to omens. To pay attention to the little things. Indeed, the seventy-two hours of penance I had already spent in the departure lounge of the Delhi airport had amply demonstrated to me that in India even something as seemingly innocent as a smile can house many textures of meaning. Thus, having caught a cab into the city, I advanced upon the Kathmandu Guest House and the first meeting with my fellow expeditioners with catlike trepidation.

"Oh, Mr. Childs," shouted the clerk behind the reception desk the moment I entered, "We are so glad to be seeing you!" A jowl-stretching grin traversed his face and I stretched my mind to recall if we had ever met before. "Your friends, you know, they are already here!" he nodded enthusiastically, gesturing toward a door and spinning the registration book toward me. "Yes, yes, they are all out on the veranda," he continued. "Oh, they are going to be so happy to be seeing you!" He was still nodding as I picked up my bags and headed out through the door.

Now I confess that the reading I had done in preparation for this trip had, to some extent, seeded a number of unrealistic expectations in my mind. Dragging my gear down a long hallway I imagined turning a corner and finding a courtyard filled with the sepia-toned forms of gaunt faced Anglo-Saxons wearing pith helmets and jodhpurs, sipping tea and leaning over dog-eared maps marked "Terra Incognita." What I discovered, instead, was a dozen long-haired young men standing in an advanced state of undress among the strewn supplies of our impending siege and bobbing their heads to rock 'n' roll. Beer bottles lay everywhere. Sweating and vibrant with good health, muscles flexing every time they stooped to lift a bag or do pull-ups on the balcony railing, they were tall and loud and as American as Big Macs. Though nominally international—with members representing the United States, Britain, Scotland, Yugoslavia, and Mexico—only the two Yugoslavs stood out as "international." The rest were Yankee hardwood, our alpine elite, the superheroes of my sport.

We introduced ourselves, divided tasks, and as the day wore on I began to feel more at ease. For dinner, all eighteen of us gathered to hear our leader detail the strategy of our climb. The plan, as he explained it, would be to divide our assault into three tiers. The first would consist of the two Yugoslavs, both Himalayan veterans, and the two most experienced Americans. A second tier of six climbers would haul in support of the first team, and a third tier would haul in support of them. As weather, fitness, acclimatization, and luck staggered our ranks, he continued, we would mix the teams with the goal of keeping the strongest players closest to the front.

It all seemed very logical to me. But as the beer flowed and we stood around gabbing in the codified language of inquiry that climbers use to evaluate one another, it became increasingly clear to me that there was no one even amongst the third tier of climbers with a résumé weaker than my own. Other details also floated to the surface. There were not, for instance, enough wind suits and sleeping bags to go around. Same with packs. Furthermore, a second entourage of climbers were now slated to arrive three weeks into the trip. The hope was that their late arrival would turbo-charge our final push for the summit. In my desultory state of mind, however, they only threatened to push me further in the direction of latrine duty. By the time we adjourned for the night I was feeling about as welcome as a welfare mother at a Jessie Helms fundraiser. Though I was more absolutely certain than ever that we would climb the mountain, I was utterly resigned to the fact that my chances of getting anywhere on it were nil.

I shouldn't have worried.

We had hardly come together before we began falling apart. As the days and nights of our approach proceeded it became apparent that we were a whole composed of many parts that did not necessarily fit together well.

Along with our 175 porters there were among us ethno-cultists and cultural imperialists, tea drinkers and drug abusers, the funny and the foolish, those with whom any connection at all was impossible and those with whom it was impossible not to connect. We were a Noah's Ark of civilized quirks; a walking exploration of why, with all the reasons big expeditions fail represented in the pool of our talent and eccentricities.

On the other hand, the approach march itself was spectacular. With light packs and all day to kill, I would get up early, hike for two or three hours, and then stop at a tea house to read and eat or take photographs. Children and amber light accompanied me everywhere. The worst of the rains fell while I waited under thatched roofs. Monsoon clouds still gripped the high peaks but that only made it easier to focus on the scenery close at hand. Everywhere I looked there was something spectacular: shafts of smoking sunlight, the deep green of the jungle, the hand-tilled fields and mists swirling in the river bottoms. I felt immersed in magic. Even the languid gymnastics of the leeches held poetry.

But already things were beginning to go wrong. Gear was stolen and our medical supplies vandalized. A cow destroyed one of our tents. Porters quit or suffered injury. And then somewhere in between the last Hindu village and the first Sherpa settlement our physician went mad. His eccentricities had always been pronounced, but suddenly they seemed to take a turn into a darkness from which he never fully returned. When the two American members of our first team quit the expedition within one hour of each other it almost seemed anti-climactic. Our leader called a meeting complete with tears and accusations about personal space and intestinal problems, but in the end they had already made up their minds to leave and that was that. I got my sleeping bag and wind suit. Our liaison officer, who had been spending too much time with the doctor, threw stones and screamed Nepali obscenities at them as they walked away. By the time we reached the foot of the mountain three more of our key climbers had turned back from illness or a similar change of heart.

In any other circumstances the loss would have been a crippling blow. Having discovered that we had grossly underestimated our food stores, however, their departure actually improved our chances. "Besides," as our leader observed, "better they should leave now than later on when we were depending on them." I did not disagree. My name was now among the members of the second tier and I was feeling an unusual generosity of spirit. In fact, with the mountain in view and the worst of our approach behind us, we were all beginning to feel a lot better. The doctor was self-medicating, the weather was fair, and the team of Japanese climbers laying siege to Baruntse had welcomed us to the headwaters of the Arun with enough food and alcohol to dispel whatever acrimony existed between those who had decided to stay on. The last night before our push to base camp we stood outside under a full moon and gazed up at Makalu and joked that perhaps we would have the thing done before our reinforcements had even arrived. It was a horribly naive statement. But brought up in a world where our every hunger had always been fed we had no reason to believe that our dream would go unanswered. Hate us for our arrogance if you will, but forgive us our innocence.

➤   ➤   ➤

In legend, Makalu is a minor god with a reputation for being tough on good intentions. Over the years his granite counterpart has done its best to live up to that notoriety. Its easiest routes have turned back the strongest of climbers. Those who have aspired to ascend its more difficult features have been treated even worse. Perhaps because we aspired to climb its fiercest geography, and because it thought us weak, the West Face showed us no forgiveness at all. Our every indiscretion, every lapse of judgment was punished with inordinate severity. Crevasses opened beneath our feet. The snow fell relentlessly. Fevers, bronchitis, blood clots, and HAPE attacked us in our sleep. During the days our feet froze and an intestinal bug so ravaged our bowels that Lomotil outpaced Darvon as the after-dinner drug of choice. The higher we went, the worse it became. Camp II—our jumping-off point for moving food and equipment to the more technical terrain above—burned to the ground in a stove explosion. We ran out of toilet paper. Storms nailed us in place when we most needed to be moving, and attrition so savaged our ranks that even I was soon looking forward to the arrival of our second entourage. By the end of our sixth week on the hill only the two Yugoslavs were left climbing out front with me hauling in support. Camp III, a two-person tent into which the three of us now crammed ourselves, was re-christened the Death Box after all three of us were hit by rockfall during a single twenty-four-hour period while laying inside. We moved it twice but sleeping in that tent remained an experience akin to lying down beneath the executioner's blade. We knew the second ice field would offer better shelter, but after four days of climbing we arrived at the end of our rope supply 200 feet short of our objective. With tools too bent and dull for climbing we had no choice but to descend for replacements.

It was a much-dreaded decision. With momentum finally seeming to shift in our direction we did not want to go back. Reaching the second ice field marked our longest sustained advance. Yet we could not proceed without rope or better equipment. After a long discussion with our leader over the radio we decided we had no alternative but to descend.

The world to which we returned was much changed from the one we had left. Snow had melted out from around our base camp tent and lines of colorful prayer flags snapped in the wind. Smoke curled from the cook tent and we could hear the voices of our Sherpa kitchen staff shouting over the roar of their stoves. We had hardly sat down before they brought us cookies and cups of steaming tea. No one from the base camp tent even stuck his head out to offer a greeting.

Inside we found in place of our once proud and happy team the wounded and demoralized remains of an army in defeat. Whatever sense of community had once existed between those who climbed and those who waited was now gone. With nothing left to read, nothing left to say, and nothing left to do with their days, those who stood to serve in waiting had already given up on the climb. We argued that there was still a possibility of success, but all they had to do was step outside to gauge the folly of our petition. We were less than a third of the way up the route and so low on supplies that those at base camp had agreed to cut their rations in order to feed us. Our appeals for still more sacrifice struck them as nothing other than a selfish attempt to drag out the inevitable at the potential cost of someone's life. There was no screaming but there was no agreement, either. Eventually, a few of our colleagues volunteered for another carry to Camp I but only if it would help move things along. They had no enthusiasm for it. No hunger. It was the same dichotomy of desire that I have since learned every big expedition encounters at the moment when the decision to go on or to go back hangs in judgment.

In our case, the prospect of the arrival of a second band of healthy climbers tilted the balance in favor of one last try. The second entourage, our leader pointed out, was now acclimatizing at our South Face camp. In two days they would be in base, and in another forty-eight hours carrying supplies to Camp I. That meant we could have our shot. It was all the hope we needed. We began packing immediately. The plan was for the two Yugoslavs to start first. They would haul double loads to Camp III where I would meet them a day later. Then one of us would descend to Camp I to meet the new arrivals while the other two made a haul to the top of our fixed lines. Once Camp IV was in place we would make an alpine-style run for the summit.

My night in base camp after the Yugoslavs had gone up was less awkward. The decision had been made; there was an end in sight and people were happy. We smoked pot and played cards. I wrote some letters home and did some repair work on my gear. Then, after everyone else had gone to bed, I sat in the big tent and talked with our leader. He expressed his concern for us and then spoke at length about his family and children. It was the first time I understood how hard it was for him to find himself suspended between competing circumstance for which he felt responsibility but over which he had no power of control. But that's how it is on big trips. Some going up, some going down, some going nowhere at all.

⚬   ⚬   ⚬

The next day I carried a double load as far as Camp II. The following day I climbed alone to Camp III where I found our tent peppered with holes. The Yugoslavs had done their best to repair it with duct tape but the wind still whistled through and spindrift had half filled the end nearest the door. As darkness fell I watched the two Yugoslavs returning from their high point. One of them descended immediately for Camp II while the other burrowed in with me. The next morning we arose early and jumared to the top of our lines carrying more rope, ice screws, carabiners, food, and a tent. It was a gray, lusterless day and we exchanged few words.

What do you say about a falling rock, anyway? About being cold? About how hungry you are and how you can't stand the thought of eating? About the lyric that keeps circulating through your mind every time you take a step? Or about the things you left undone at home and what a waste it is hauling gear up a face where all you are accomplishing is increasing the likelihood of getting yourself killed? Hours pass. Lungs ache. The tedium and fear tangle around each other like snakes. Then suddenly you are there and done with it, pounding in an ice screw, hanging your gear, and watching your partner descend. Time to pull on my parka before the cold can seep into my chest cavity. I swing my gaze over to the South Face of Lhotse and the South Col on Everest. There is an Australian expedition on Everest this season. How are they doing over there today? I wonder. Then it occurs to me that maybe they're looking this way and asking themselves the same thing. There is a tug and I look down. My partner is on the second rope now and it's my turn to start descending. Okay, come on, Childs. You know how to do this. Don't go unclipping anything until you've had a good look at it. Check everything twice. Let's see, all those gates screwed closed? It's one thing to get killed; it's another to kill yourself. All right, then: time to weight the system. That's it, lean back a little. Now, look up and check the anchors one more time. Yep, all there. Easy does it, then just smooth and steady, no reason to hurry. Empty pack and going down sure makes a difference. There's that stupid lyric, again. Wish I could remember the rest of the words. Whew, first set of anchors. Just three more to go.

By the time I reach the end of the ropes my partner is already heading downhill in the direction of Camp II while his countryman slowly makes his way toward me with another load. I gaze for a moment at the gathering storm then crawl inside the tent and get the stove started. When my companion arrives I pass him a cup of soup. We talk a little and he dumps his gear. He has just shaken off the snow and started to scramble through the door when the first rocks impact a few meters to our right. We both scream at the same time.

It was not the first time we had heard rocks go by. Nor was it the only time they had landed nearby. It was just that this time they were bigger—much bigger—and they were landing closer. We could hear them rattling down the slope above us, rumbling and crackling, then buzzing through the air like incoming artillery. A sound that grew like the last yamp at the end of light and life, and which ended in an explosion of snow and rock and ice. We dodged around inside the tent like mice, never knowing which rock would end it all for one or both of us, waiting and screaming. By the time it was over we were completely broken. Neither of us was willing to spend another night up there. Taking our chances with the climb was one thing, but neither of us wanted to die in our sleep. We were in the process of packing when a flake the size of a dinner plate tore through the roof of the tent, incised my companion's jacket like a scalpel, and buried itself 15 inches into the floor.

It took us all night to descend. The storm had grown teeth by then with strong winds and heavy snow. So having worked hard all day to get up the mountain, we worked hard all night to get down. Fortunately, my companion's wound was not serious—a deep bruise, perhaps, but no broken bones or bleeding—and though dazed and sore, he was moving stoically. We both lost track of time and place. The snow made it nearly impossible to communicate or figure out where we were. In the absence of any other science we simply let gravity take us down. I have no idea how long we struggled or how long the storm raged. I do know that sometime toward morning the wind quit and the sky turned the color of chlorine and we could hear voices. Then we spotted the yellow domes of Camp II's half-buried tents beneath 3 feet of new snow. The people inside were cooking breakfast. We went to the larger tent, which I unzipped and shoved my friend inside. In that instant I saw three faces: the other Yugoslav and two of the late arrivals. Then I closed the door, shoveled out the ruins of our supply tent, and crawled inside. It was cozy enough with plenty of food and fuel. The rest of the day I spent eating and sleeping and doing sit-ups to stay warm. I counted the squares in the rip-stop and thought a lot about Ovaltine. The next morning I heard voices but slept until noon, anyway. It was still snowing when I finally stuck my head out. The day didn't look to hold much promise but I was suddenly eager for companionship, so I loaded my arms with sausage, brown sugar, and tea and groveled my way to the big tent. Only the two Yugoslavs were inside. The fresh troops were gone. Down, not up. The Yugoslavs just shrugged their shoulders. This time we all knew that it was over.

⁊   ⁊   ⁊

By the time we finally made it back up to Camp III there was nothing left, anyway. An avalanche had swept it all away. Tent, gear, and dreams—all gone. We collected what we could, shoved our garbage into a bergschrund, and started home.

That was pretty much it. Over, up, down, and back. Neither success nor failure; just an experience from which each of us is free to take and leave what he or she may have learned. Just like life, as someone once said, only more so.

Was it worth it? Well, personally, I got a lot out of it. I saw some amazing scenery. I made some good friends. We did some respectable climbing and we got back alive. Books have been written about much less. To our credit we pulled off a miracle of lowball financing, climbed without oxygen or Sherpa support, and when all was said and done we cleaned up our mess and went home without leaving the place any the worse for our having been there. I suppose that there are a lot of reasons why we didn't get further on the route. As it turns out we probably would have been better off on one of the ridges. Our disposition as a group was perhaps better suited to their elegant fluting and corniced architecture than the objective horrors of the West Face. Still, it was not so much the route as the timing that defeated us. We were simply there too soon. The West Face of Makalu belongs not just to climbers who are fitter, faster, and stronger than we were, but to a new generation. In the future some team of super-alpinists climbing without fixed lines or confused objectives, equipped with gear and eyes and ambitions that we just did not have, will climb the West Face of Makalu. They will come from the ranks of those to whom a new set of "last great problems" will fall until they, too, have consumed the possible and watch in amazement as what remains is redefined by their children. And in that age the West Face of Makalu, too, will be just another route, on just another mountain. And Lord I'd love to be there. Wouldn't you?

"STORM ON MANASLU: A CLASSIC HIMALAYA EXPEDITION"

FROM
To the Top of the World:
Alpine Challenges in the Himalaya and Karakorum
BY REINHOLD MESSNER

ONE OF THE MOST ACCOMPLISHED AND SUCCESSFUL CLIMBERS ever, especially among the high Himalayan peaks, is Reinhold Messner, born in the Tyrol in 1944. Messner climbed extensively in the Alps before he became the first person to climb all fourteen eight-thousand-meter peaks; he completed the roster with Lhotse in 1986. It was inevitable that, in amassing this record, Messner would encounter his share of disaster and sorrow at the deaths of climbers near to him. One of the most tragic events was the death of his brother Gunther on Nanga Parbat, in 1970, after the two had reached the summit and were descending.

All of the eight-thousanders had been conquered—by the "easiest" routes—between 1950 and 1964. So when Messner and his young fellow climbers looked toward the Himalaya in the 1970s, they took as their mission a different approach to these peaks: the hardest routes on the biggest unclimbed faces. Thus 1972 found Messner and a small South Tyrol team on the South Face of Manaslu, number eight in the list of highest peaks.

Once again, the almost magically fit Messner reaches the summit, alone, after his exhausted climbing partner, Franz Jäger, turns around and vows to return directly to their high camp and wait. A sudden storm turns Messner's descent into a race against death. Wandering, lost, despairing, he is finally led toward the tent and safety by a voice he is sure is that of Jäger—only to find the man isn't there. Two other members of the party come up from a lower camp; they, too, hear the voice of the missing climber and spend the night searching for him. But in the morning, only one of the searchers returns, alone . . .

This selection is from Messner's *To the Top of the World*, pages 13-30.

W e began the ascent to the summit of Manaslu on April 23, 1972 from Camp 3. Franz Jäger and I wanted to reach the highest point in two days and then return quickly to the lower camps. However, despite Sherpa assistance, on the first day we managed only about half of the ice ramp which leads to the summit plateau. The Sherpas went back to camp. Franz and I installed ourselves roughly in the tent. Nevertheless, we slept well and Franz declared enthusiastically the next morning that he was in cracking form.

On April 24 everything worked out according to plan. By the time the Sherpas arrived, we had taken down the tent and packed our rucksacks, except for the cooker which we had left out so that we could prepare tea for the porters. Shortly before midday, we gained the summit plateau after exiting from the South Face. The last rope lengths were over bare ice and, because the slope there was very steep, we had to help the Sherpas.

Just below the ridge, and still on the south side, we erected Camp 4, anchoring the tent to the ground with an 8mm rope. Ten meters above us was the divide between north and south. We had reached the ideal exit point for a summit push.

In good time, we lay down and I cooked the whole evening. Outside a strong wind was blowing. Over the radio we went through all the details of the summit plan once more: if we did not make contact at 6 A.M., we were already on the move and two people would at once ascend from below to give us back-up.

Our doctor, Dr. Oswald "Bulle" Oelz, recommended that we inhaled over the steaming kettle. The weather promised to remain fine. Franz and I ate as much as we could, drank tea and Ovomaltine, then placed our rucksacks under our legs, the better to rest. I slept until daybreak.

In the early morning, when all the others presumably were still asleep, I got up softly and got the cooker going. Inside my sleeping bag I put on my second inner boots, then I made the tea. During the night masses of snow had been driven into the tent and now lay hard pressed between our sleeping bags. I threw some lumps into the pot and rummaged at the head of the tent amongst clothes and snow for bread and jam.

Franz's sleeping bag was drawn right up to his nose. He had laid his curly head on his rucksack and was still asleep. I woke him up. From habit he undid the zip in the tent door but the wind blew a handful of ice crystals into his face, so he quickly shut it again.

"It'll stop soon," he said. "The weather is still fine. But the wind needs to die down."

The tent walls flapped and at regular intervals fine snow-dust flew through the triangular opening in the gable end which we had not covered sufficiently the evening before.

"We can't go in this wind," I said.

"It'll clear up soon," repeated Franz, "meanwhile we can get ready."

We slipped out of our sleeping bags and put on the things we had laid out the previous evening for the summit climb—an outer suit of coated Perlon fabric, our heavy outer boots and gaiters.

Franz had kept on his down jacket; his woollen cap had white spots, was full of snow and a little too big. As the day promised to be cold, he put a hood over it, and this made him look like a polar explorer. He tied his bivouac bag around his waist under his anorak rather than on the outside, so that the wind would not tear it away. He stuffed his spare gloves into the big thigh pockets in his long Loden breeches, which were full of odds and ends such as camera films, sun-cream, and goggles.

We drank the lukewarm water, which tasted of wool and tea, and tried to eat but we weren't hungry. I fetched my thin woollen gloves out of the inner pocket of my rucksack, pulled them on and opened the door of the tent. My grandmother had knitted these special gloves for me; I had asked her for them because there is nothing better to take to these high altitudes.

Outside it was already daytime and the wind had stopped raging across the plateau. The sun was peeping from behind the summit of Peak 29.

One after the other, we crept out into the open. Franz closed the zip while I tied our 15m rope on my back. We wanted to take it with us in case of unexpectedly difficult climbing on the summit ridge. We were both wearing down gloves now over our other pairs. As we stood face to face, all muffled up and clumsy, we had to laugh.

After the long hours in the tent our initial movements, awkward as they were, filled us with buoyancy, self-confidence, and a feeling of strength.

We made haste to get on so that we would not be delayed at the last moment. We dismantled the tent, tying it firmly to the ground so that the wind could not blow it away, picked up our ice axes and marched away.

On the faint ridge between the North and South Faces we stopped. Franz breathed deeply; it was windless, and the air was cold and pure. He looked around—there were no clouds in the sky and the world lay below us. It was the right day for the summit. Franz pointed over toward Himal Chuli, to Peak 29. The as yet invisible rising sun covered the sky with bright streaks.

Before us there extended a gigantic snow plateau, rising slightly eastwards; humpbacked sastrugi covered the white expanse. Only to the right of us, below the rock towers of the South-West Ridge, did a gentle hillock block the view. Once we had climbed up this ridge we would be able to see the summit, then after a few more hours' climbing we would be on top. Perhaps the summit was really behind this hill!

We moved fifty or a hundred meters at a time, past the delicate pointed edges of the sastrugi, then stopped for a breather. The storm had swept away the loose snow, so that our boot soles scarcely penetrated the surface. Only in the hollows and shadows of the sastrugi was there looser powder snow. Behind us, still recognizable, was the narrow, dark track back to our tent: it seemed to swim on the wavy surface.

The conditions were ideal. The weather had held for so long that the wind had been able to sweep bare all the ridges. There were no more obstacles in the way of our summit assault; we must use this opportunity.

On the ridge, far to the right above us, hung small, shining snow plumes. Filled with pleasure in anticipation of the summit as Himalayan climbers in particular feel, Franz came along behind me. During the rest stops, he often beamed at me as if he wanted to say "We'll soon be there!" His eyes raced far ahead, along the many waves of snow. Counting the hillocks and slopes in front of us, he said once: "The top must lie behind there!" Time and again he looked ahead. Behind the cold snow expanses the summit towers would rise up. For more than an hour we had been approaching—step by step and stop by stop—the hump from behind which they must emerge. Sharply drawn shadows now hung from the edges of the snow waves. Out of the valleys mist was rising, mixing with the white of the foothills. It was still not warm but in Butterfly Valley it must already have been unpleasantly hot.

Behind each ridge we expected to see the summit but each time fresh snow slopes and ridges lay ahead of us. As there were no technical climbing difficulties to overcome and the ground was free of crevasses, we proceeded unroped. To the north, above the mountains of Tibet, lay a cloudless sky. Gradually we became impatient: still no sign of the final rise!

With each ridge reached we were in despair. Franz suddenly abandoned his initial plans and decided to give up, to return to camp at once and to wait there for me.

"Reinhold," he said gently and stopped to draw breath. I turned round to him and saw renunciation in his eyes.

"I'm going back," he said resolutely, "we shan't make the top today."

"It can't be much farther," I tried to encourage him.

"That's what we thought three hours ago," he replied.

"Are you tired?'" I asked.

"No, it's not that, but I don't want to bivouac, I'd rather go back to the tent in good time." He persisted with his decision.

"I don't want to bivouac either. But we still have time, plenty of time before dark.'"

"You go on alone, you're faster, perhaps you at least can make it."

"And what about you?"

"I'm going back, I'll wait for you in the tent."

It was late morning. We were standing directly below the first two steep rises.

As there was only walking terrain between us and Camp 4, there was virtually no danger of falling and the weather promised to remain fine, so neither of us doubted for more than a moment that Franz would get back to camp alone. He was in good physical shape, was equipped with the best gear, and had a straightforward track which led easily downwards toward the tent.

"I'm going on, as far as I can. If I'm not up by early afternoon, I'll turn back. I'll be back in good time," I said.

"Good luck!"

"And you." I turned back to the slope.

"I'll make some tea for you," Franz called back after descending a few meters.

He went downwards, I went upwards, we could still see each other for a while. He followed the track which he had followed step by step on ascent and reached the gentle ridge with the resting place where, twenty minutes before, he had arrived full of hope, convinced he would see the summit.

This sudden abandoning of the summit, what was the reason for it?

In the winter, when Franz's participation in the expedition was in question, the thought of an eight-thousander had made him almost crazy. But now, despite the thin air, he had the strength to renounce it. Going down in good time meant so much time gained, safety. Franz crossed the ridge, sat down and gazed up at me. He waved. I had stopped to rest. How small he looked now!

I climbed on slowly and calculated how many hours were necessary for the return: two perhaps, three at the most. I wished I knew what the summit looked like, whether it were possible solo. But the slopes above blocked the view and I had difficulty keeping a regular pace.

Suddenly, however, there were rocks above me. I sat down and looked back along the slopes, wanted to call enthusiastically to Franz. I could still see him clearly, far off, very small, then he disappeared behind the ridge.

After four more breathers I reached the South-West Ridge. A rock tower stood before me but it was easy to imagine that there was another behind it. On the edge of the ridge a sharp wind was blowing, driving isolated shreds of mist before it. Very fine snow-dust adhered to the precipitous slabs. Beneath an overhang, I bore to the left on the northern side. Here there was no wind. The face fell steeply away below me and farther down stood a steep-sided rock tower—the Pinnacle. All the towers on the ridge—and there were very many of them—sloped and pointed eastwards.

After climbing for a while between rock and snow, I came to a notch. Again the wind blew hard from the south and the face there fell away almost vertically. A sharp snow edge led upwards to a rock rib. That must be the summit! I sat down in the notch. From here I could get a good view of the last part of the ridge. It was very steep, yet neither of the faces offered an easier climb.

I climbed slowly and carefully, resting more often than previously. Now I was standing, somewhat insecurely, on a rock ledge and saw once more a moderately inclined ridge in front of me. This short piece of ridge ought not to prevent me from reaching the highest point.

Meanwhile, the wind had strengthened, the air was icy and in the south there hung a bank of dark cloud. I would have liked to rest a while but here on the ridge I could neither sit down nor even stand comfortably.

I adjusted my speed to the difficulties and the thin air, going only ten paces without a breather. Then I saw beyond the ridge a rock tooth, five or six meters high, one half dark and the other bright, like a longitudinally-split pyramid.

This was the summit and never before in my life had I seen one so peculiar.

I climbed up the south side, with my feet on a rock ledge and my ice axe on the snow ridge. Perhaps because of the proximity of the summit, I felt no more tiredness now. At all events I felt safe and clear-headed. Then I discovered a notch so broad that it separated the ridge from the summit tower. As I climbed down into it I had to tread on some loose bits of rock and be doubly careful.

The final few meters to the summit were hard, as the rock was very splintered and steep. Then, in the middle of the summit pinnacle, I saw a bent and rusty piton about 15cm long. Further up was another, much firmer, with a ring. Some bits of material hung from it. I held it firmly for two or three steps, then I was on top.

As a change in the weather was coming in from the south, I stayed only a few minutes. I built a cairn, took some photographs, knocked out one of the pitons, and stuck it in my pocket.

I wasn't tired but the cloud bank in the south and the strong wind urged descent. I had to reach the tent before nightfall. I picked up a handful of pebbles for my comrades who were waiting for me below.

In the notch I turned around once more and looked back: a rock tooth, some wisps of mist, a little pile of stones—that was the summit. Just below, a piton and scraps of a one-time flag. The sky was all around, and to the south, heavy, bloated clouds were clinging to the summits. The wind hunted them on, closer, always northwards, away over the top of Manaslu.

The descent went smoothly and quickly to begin with, as I climbed back down my route of ascent. Suddenly and unexpectedly mist and a snow storm sprang up. Descent became a race against death. As I battled my way back, I imagined Franz safely in the tent at Camp 4.

So long as the route went down steeply, I could orientate myself excellently. Here a rock tower, there a glistening blue ice slope, and lower down I had to pass between some snow towers. I had every detail of the ascent in my head, so that I couldn't lose my way even without a track. I had ripped my windproof with my ice axe, so as not to slip if I fell. Soon the storm rose to hurricane force and it was impossible to see with goggles. My mouth and eyes iced up and the situation seemed hopeless.

The plateau was now flatter, and the storm threatened to hurl me to the ground. My eyes were stinging as I kept going straight ahead but the snow slope was endless. Where was the tent? I moved upwards, downwards, across the slope: I let myself drift with the wind, and came to a shining ice surface which had not been there in the morning. Everything was more or less altered—the snow waves and the ridges—and nowhere was a saving rock island. I moved against the storm, backwards, doubled up and fit to drop. In places the snow was already knee deep. When the storm came from the side, it overturned me.

I was reduced to crawling. I crawled across the plateau, no, not a plateau, rather a basin-shaped valley. Sharp ice crystals and snow-dust rushed toward me out of the mist. Occasionally they hit me in the face and pricked my eyes so that I could see nothing. I went on crawling and felt the weight of my body pressing me into the ground. At first I thought it was the storm which was pinning me down but it was tiredness—it was my legs which had become so heavy.

I felt my tired body and dragged it along, as if I were recovering from a bad illness. In this storm I thought I should never get on my feet again; yet it could not be much farther. The main thing now was not to give up, I must find the tent. I breathed deeply and recovered relatively quickly in the rest stops. Suddenly I was standing again, with my legs straight but with my body still doubled over.

I moved with my back to the wind, without hesitation, without thinking. I struggled on, straight ahead, to the left, to the right, staggered, groped with my feet in space, found firm ground again, stood still, took a breather . . . then I groaned and began to move in the other direction. The plateau had neither end nor beginning. The tent was nowhere to be seen.

Only as I kept coming to this same smooth-swept patch of ice did I realize that I was going round in circles. My despair grew. I didn't know where I was, imagined myself to be in close proximity to the tent, within a circle of at most 500m in diameter from it. Nevertheless, I didn't find it. I had been walking for hours but didn't know where I was going. The whole time the hurricane was chasing ice crystals ahead of itself, throwing them in my face until my skin stung. "Keep going," hammered through my brain. Things had never looked so hopeless. But the worst thing would be to stop and lie down here in this basin, without ever getting out again, to die here . . .

Suddenly I heard someone call my name. I stopped and listened. Nothing more. Was it an hallucination? No, there it was again, quite distinct: "Reinhold!" I was so excited that my voice shook.

It was Franz's voice, I recognized it exactly. He seemed to be calling to me from in front of the tent.

"Franz," I shouted, "I'm over here!" not that that told him anything.

"Franz!" I called again. He did not answer.

"Hello!" Again nothing. Only the storm howling and the shreds of cloth fluttering from my body.

I began to panic. Naturally, somewhere near here lay the tent. I must hurry, hurry . . . and I rushed forwards, curved around a 2m high wall of snow. My gaze hurried on ahead but my legs wouldn't follow. I was so tired, desperately tired!

Then I saw a dark heap in the snow. Immediately I thought: "That's it." I wanted to run to it but my legs refused and my chest threatened to burst. Exhausted, I let myself fall on the snow.

I had no breath left to shout out. Weak and coughing I lay there, not letting the tent out of my sight.

"Franz!" I shouted after a while. "Fra-anz!" And later: "Hello!" Why didn't he answer?

I crawled toward the tent—if only he would come out! . . . Nearer . . . nearer . . . and at last I was there. It was a pointed mound of snow!

I lay there and wanted to give up, to dig a snow hole and dig myself in. Nevertheless, I stood up and continued searching, driven by my survival instinct.

I was so cold that my whole body shook but, as I went back, I was amazed to notice that I was no longer so tired. The snow surface under my feet was now uncertain in an odd way, so that often I groped into space. Everything around me was indeterminate, and at most I could see only 8m.

I moved almost without thinking. Suddenly I was startled, believing I was hearing shouts again. I circled around, listening, in all directions. And then, more distinctly than before, I heard someone shout.

"Reinhold!" Again it was Franz.

"Hello," I screamed as loud as I could.

"Reinhold!"

"Franz," I begged him. "Stand still and call at regular intervals, otherwise I shan't find the tent." No answer. I heard him call once more. I never found him again.

Later on I began to call for help but no one heard me. I stayed in the same spot for a long time and shouted out regularly. However, the storm must have swallowed up my calls.

Now I was no longer despairing—for preference I would have lain down to sleep. Then it occurred to me where I had heard Franz's voice most distinctly: on the ridge, by the smooth-swept stretch of ice. I went quickly upward but couldn't find the place, recognized nothing again. There was no obvious upward slope any more, only an expanse of snow around me, the circumference of which was noticeably getting smaller. The storm increased, minute by minute . . .

Again I could hear Franz's voice; it must be coming from the tent. He's trying to direct me, I thought. Only in the lulls in the storm did I hear scraps of words, my name. Again I answered and called his. Again I waited for an answer, which never came. I wandered aimlessly around the great plateau, rested . . .

At that time I thought I would die. I sat in the snow which the storm tore away from under me. I was so tired that I had given up moving, given up looking for the tent. Snow and blood stuck to my cheeks and nose. I had partly torn out my beard, from which centimeter-long icicles hung, to be able to breathe.

Now and then I thought I would die of thirst. I opened my split lips and dreamed of a gulp of hot tea. Then, lost in thought, I looked at the tiny patch of snow which was still visible in the storm. Night was coming on, noticeable by the thick, gray mist which was mixed with snow. It surrounded me like a cage.

When the storm diminished a little, I rolled on my side, stuck a fist in the snow, stood up and carried on walking—to this day I don't know where.

During my next rest, I seized on a clear thought, to which I owe my life.

Again I was sitting on the edge of a sastrugi, blood dripping from my beard on the snow. There came to me the idea of moving against the storm, always against the storm. Only thus could I get out of this cage in which I was circling.

I thought to myself: "The wind is out of the south"; sudden changes of weather on Manaslu always came from the south. That had struck me during the expedition. Thus, if I walked against the wind, I reflected, I must come down to the South Face.

Naturally, I knew that in this snowstorm I would never have been able to climb down the South Face. I didn't want to do that. Our tent stood on the plateau just above the exit from the South Face. Vertical to the supposed wind direction, left and right of the tent, were rocks, the only ones on the broad slope. I remembered it. If I found them, I thought, the tent must lie in between. The storm might rage as much as it liked, but I would not give up before nightfall. I groped my way backwards, scanning the slope and got stuck in the snow again. For a long time I walked with my back to the storm, doubled over, gasping for air. Suddenly I came to the line of the South Face, turned back to the ridge, found the rocks, went along the stretch in between twice, three times—the fourth time I saw the tent. "Franz," I called, when I was still a few meters away. "I'm here." Something moved. There was the entrance. It really was the tent this time!

I was so glad that I wanted to run, yet my feet stuck in the snow and I fell over. Someone helped me to my feet and supported me. As I saw his face near mine, I asked: "Is that you, Horst?"

"Yes, it's me, Horst!" he replied.

I had not recognized him at once. He led me the last few steps to the tent and helped me inside. Head first, I crawled through the narrow slit. Andi greeted me. Snow covered the down bags.

Happy as I was to meet up with my comrades Horst Fankhauser and Andi Schlick, equally frightful was the discovery that Franz Jäger was not lying in the tent. I reckoned that he must be inside and must have been there since midday. I thought that he must have arrived at Camp 4 hours before the storm—he had been calling me!

Andi began to rub me down, to pick the snow from my face, then he held a mug of warm tea to my lips. I couldn't drink or speak, my whole body was shaking and I was breathing fast and irregularly.

"Isn't Franz here?" I uttered at last. Andi shook his head.

"I heard him calling, right around here!"

"When and where?" asked Horst, who was still standing by the tent door.

"Lots of times and only here on the plateau. I've been looking for the tent for hours."

"I'll go and have a look," called Horst from outside and went off. Shortly afterwards he returned.

"You're right," he said, "I heard him calling too."

"Where?" asked Andi.

"Up there, on the plateau, he's calling 'Reinhold,' I'm sure of it."

When I had arrived and told them about the shouts, Horst thought I could have been hallucinating. Now, however, he was convinced that Franz was out there calling in the snowstorm.

Andi and Horst immediately got themselves ready for a search. They didn't discuss it, for them it was a matter of course to go to Franz's aid—despite the dark and the snowstorm, and despite the cold and the altitude. They put on everything they had.

"Don't forget the bivy bag," I said to Andi before he went out.

"We'll be back soon," I heard one of them say, then nothing more. The storm howled.Shortly afterwards the crackle of the radio interrupted the icy silence in the tent.

"Camp 4, come in please!" It was Bulle [Oelz] from Camp 2.

"I got here alone about ten minutes ago, in a really bad way because I wandered at least five times around the tent before I found it. There's a terrible snowstorm up here, up on the big plateau it was impossible to orientate myself. During the last part of the descent I could hear Franz calling all the time. He came back down long before me because he gave up before the top. He must have got himself lost and apparently still hasn't found the tent. Horst went out and heard him shouting as well. Andi and Horst, who got here about an hour ago, have now climbed up to fetch him. Let's hope they find him soon. Over!"

"Reinhold, first of all, we hope Franz will be with you as soon as possible. Next, naturally we are terrifically bucked that you made the summit. How do you feel?"

"I'm a bit hypothermic because I've been searching for the tent for three hours. I didn't think I would find it. With a great deal of patience I finally discovered two rocks and got a fix from them, otherwise I wouldn't have made it here. It was hopeless working by compass because we have no maps. We set off relatively late because it was stormy early on. So I must have done more than 800m in six hours, to reach the summit. I was on top but it was misty, bad for photographs. Instead, I found a Japanese piton up there and photographed that, knocked out a second one and pocketed it as a summit proof. Then I came down. Franz turned back hours ago. I found one of his gloves and, as I kept hearing him call, I was certain he was already in the tent. But when I arrived, he wasn't here. It was a terrible shock. Five minutes later Horst, too, heard him calling again. Andi and he have climbed up to bring him down. I hope they can fetch him in about half an hour. I've hung a lamp outside the tent so that it's easier to find. Over!"

"Reinhold, how are your feet? Over."

"My feet are fine. I've checked there's no frostbite; hands are alright too. I was afraid that my nose was frozen but that is warm again as well. I've pulled out half my beard because icicles were stuck to it but that doesn't matter. I'm just rather cold but if I drink half a liter of tea, I shall be OK again. Now the main thing is for Franz to turn up, then all will be well. Then I'll call you at once."

After this radio conversation, my friends in Camp 2 were simultaneously happy and troubled—troubled and alarmed that Franz had not come back yet. Their worries were, nevertheless, not so great because Andi and Horst were in good form. We all believed that Franz would soon be found.

I waited in vain—thirty minutes, forty-five minutes, an hour. They didn't come. Time and again I crawled out of the tent, to call, to help guide them in. In doing so, I went no more than 5m away, so that I could still recognize the tent's outline.

I was in despair, exhausted and frozen. Inside the tent the snow already lay several inches deep. The lamp, which I had hung outside the entrance, had to be wiped clean every ten minutes because the light shone only dully through its coating of snow.

Every half hour our expedition leader Wolfgang Nairz came on the air from Camp 2. Still I could give him no positive answer. We weighed all the possibilities, hoped that the others had dug themselves a snow-hole, so that the three of them could warm each other up.

We considered why Franz had not been in the tent when I arrived at Camp 4 and came up with only two reasons. The first possibility was that Franz had reached the tent but quitted it later on account of the snowstorm in the hope of being able to lead me in. In so doing he must have lost direction and wandered aimlessly like I did around the big plateau. The second possibility was that, while descending, Franz had wanted to wait for me, as Otto Kempter had waited for Hermann Buhl on Nanga Parbat in 1953—and that he had been surprised by the storm.

Then Bulle's voice came over the radio from Camp 2.

"Of course, we don't know how things are with Franz and the others but if possible you must come down somehow to Camp 3 tomorrow. At all events, Wolfi and I are climbing up early again to Camp 3 to arrange everything there. How far you can get down from Camp 4 by yourself, I don't think one can decide right now, we must discuss it tomorrow. Over!"

"I can make it without the others, at least I think so. But how things will be with Franz I can't say. If things are really bad, we may well have to rope him down. For that we may need some Sherpas. Over!"

"We'll discuss that tomorrow early on the climb. There's also the following problem: Andi already complained up there that his feet were numb. If he spends the whole night outside, the consequences can be bad. I don't know about Horst. But we shall see. If possible, everybody should come down to Camp 3 for proper treatment."

Then Wolfi came on again.

"Reinhold, meanwhile you can sleep in peace again, I'll wake you with the squawk in half or three-quarters of an hour to see what's going on. Over!"

"Understood, I'll leave the radio on receive. Out."

I lay in the tent, troubled, head covered up, so that the snow, which would press in through the window, would not touch my face. In my thoughts I was with Franz, Andi, and Horst outside in the stormy night. Toward midnight, Wolfi called me again.

"Nothing new," was all I could say.

The whole night the storm raged across the high plateau, blew away rocks, excavated ice towers, filled hollows, and choked everything. So much snow fell that the plateau was completely changed in the morning and the tent scarcely still showed above it.

After Franz, Andi, and Horst had remained outside hour after hour, my friends in the lower camps and I had assumed that the three of them were sitting in bivy bags in a snow-hole. They would wait until morning, when they would find the way back to the tent more easily. Until 2 A.M. we were in hourly radio contact.

In the morning Horst came back. Alone. Our worst fears had come true!

As Horst stood alone in front of the tent, I could not work out what had happened during the night. The weather had seemed to improve. The storm had abated but it was still howling.

Horst let himself fall inside the tent. I shook him with all my strength, shouted in his ear, held a mug of hot tea for him but he was unable to drink. Shortly afterwards—Horst had closed the zip on the door—I noticed that he was very sad. Then he began to talk. His snow-covered face looked tired, his eyes were red . . .

After Andi and Horst had left the tent to look for Franz, they marched in the direction of Manaslu summit. The storm had briefly become bearable. Again they heard Franz's voice but could not find him. After a short while the storm increased anew, their faces were iced up but they did not think of returning to camp for the time being.

They felt afterwards that they had climbed for some hours. On account of the strengthening storm they had meanwhile lost Franz's calls and, when they wanted to return to Camp 4, this was impossible. The storm and the onset of night prevented it. Their only chance of surviving in this inferno was a snow-cave.

In order to protect themselves to some extent against the force of nature, they dug a hole in the snow. Inside, the biting cold was a little more bear-able. Horst massaged Andi to warm him up. Nevertheless, Andi pressed ever more strongly for finding the tent. In vain Horst attempted to dissuade him from this dangerous undertaking as Andi was already suffering rather from the cold conditions.

After a long time, in which Horst had tended to Andi and massaged him, Andi entreated him to look for Camp 4 with him. Andi was longing for tea and his warm sleeping bag. After much insistence, Horst gave in. They quit-ted the snow-cave and went out into the still-raging storm. In the meantime they had completely lost their sense of direction. In addition, there came sting-ing pain in the face, wind tearing at shreds of clothes, icy beards and gummed-up eyes which stayed open without seeing.

After a long and desperate wander around, Horst realized that searching further would mean their certain end. Once more Horst persuaded Andi to crawl into a snow-cave and to wait there until morning.

Andi stopped insisting and so they dug a second snow-cave, for they couldn't find the first one again. With the last of his strength, Horst burrowed in the snow. It was a superhuman exertion. They hid in the cave and again Horst tried to warm up Andi with his body. Andi was completely apathetic, exhausted by the horrors of the past hours.

They spent approximately two hours in the icy hole. Horst looked after Andi again, as before—he was still extremely weak and rather cold. Once Andi spoke of Hildegard, his wife, then again of the Sherpas. He was shaking. As in a dream he saw the Sherpas in front of the rising smoke in Base Camp, and heard their prayers which he had never understood. He remembered the stone, on which the sacrificial fire burned and the frequently recurring word in the prayer, "Manasuli." When Andi had recovered, after rather a long time, he said to Horst in a clear voice that he wanted to see what the weather was doing. Horst believed that Andi had recovered due to his massaging and was feeling better.

Andi went outside and did not return.

After a short while, Horst began to worry and left the snow-cave. Of Andi there was no trace. Horst's shout was lost in the raging storm. Andi had disappeared. Horst screamed, yet the storm tore the words from his mouth. His face was freshly iced up. He was close to losing his reason and wanted to run out into the night. With an iron will, he forced himself to go back into the snow-cave. Several times more he crawled out; still no trace, no sound, nothing.

He could stand only with difficulty. Now and then he fell at the edge of the snow-cave. "So this is the end," he thought, "I shall freeze."

There was nothing left for him to do but crawl back into the snow-cave. Only there had he a chance of surviving the night. Once more he left the hole to be on the look out for Andi. It was all in vain. If he had distanced himself from the cave in order to look for Andi, it would probably have meant death for both of them.

The rest of the night Horst fought for his own life. "Just don't fall asleep," he said to himself over and over again. He kept moving about. The night was endless, the storm howled on. He still didn't want to believe that Andi was no longer there.

Minutes became hours, became eternities. The inferno lasted until four o'clock in the morning and still there was no sign of his comrades.

At last day dawned, and the longest and hardest night of his life was over. He had triumphed over sleep and the cold which had never relented. In ever-greater circles, he moved around the cave, looking for a sign of life from Andi. Nothing.

Horst was in despair. The weather had improved so much that he could see enough to descend to Camp 4. He burrowed around in the fresh snow which had fallen during the night.

With the tiny glimmer of hope that Andi might perhaps have reached the tent, he got on with the descent, and after three hours' wading through very deep snow he reached the camp. Now also his last hope was gone, and the last chance was buried . . .

It was a miracle that Horst had survived the night. He warmed himself up a bit and drank some tea. Only because of his conscientious preparation and his fully developed abilities, as well as his clear and logical thinking in life-threatening situations, had he withstood this white hell.

Now he told me why he and not one of the others had come up to Camp 4, to cover our retreat.

Because of his cracking good form, Horst had come up from Camp 2 to Camp 3 on the morning of April 25. After a short rest, he continued climbing with Andi up the ice face to Camp 4. Only he could have done it. Hans Hofer and Hansjörg Hochfilzer didn't feel well on this particular day and gladly handed over to Horst. Later in the day the pair descended to Base Camp to recover.

"In Camp 3 I loaded up with another can of fuel," reported Horst. "We came up the ice face swiftly. Half-way up the weather suddenly deteriorated and the Sherpa turned back. We reached the tent in the late afternoon. The weather had deteriorated further, and the storm whistled and threatened to rip the tent to shreds. I secured the tent with a rope and ski sticks rammed deep into the snow. Then you arrived."

On this morning the Sherpas had prayed in all the camps and throughout the night they had chanted: "Manasuli, Manasuli . . . "

The cook in Base Camp knew nothing of the tragedy as he piled up the brushwood for the daily sacrificial fire on the stone in front of the kitchen. He did it as always and the kitchen boy repeated the prayers: "Manasuli, Manasuli . . . "

Horst then reported over the radio everything that had happened. All the expedition members, who had hoped so very much for a happy outcome, particularly Wolfi, were shocked.

Shortly after the radio conversation, the storm diminished. The wind abated, it became bright, cold and then even windless. Only on the western edge of the sky over the Annapurna range hung a narrow, dark streak.

Half an hour later, with Horst partially recovered, the sun was shining again in the valley. The mist had evaporated and I went once more around the tent. Then we began immediately with the search. The layer of snow with which the plateau was covered seemed to be bottomless. The wind-blown waves were often 2m high, the hillocks were swept clean and the hollows were filled.

"I came down from up there," said Horst, pointing eastwards.

I could see no track. It was cold. There were walls of snow standing on the plateau. No track. The tent was covered, everything was completely covered.

We walked and walked. In our down clothing we looked like astronauts. We searched but found no sign of our friends. So we continued searching. The sun shone, it was icy cold with clouds in the south and west again. We were tired by the time we found ourselves in the middle of the plateau. In this white desert we were the only dark points.

As we moved from north to south, the wind blew in our faces. We could not recognize the tent. Half-way through the snow field was a deep trench— our track. The snow was like fine sand.

We had been on the go for some hours and there was still no trace of the absentees. We had been around the search area twice but saw nothing except hollows and snow humps. Yet we knew they must lie there somewhere— so we trudged on in order to find them.

We did not find them.

And so we went on searching. We had been over every ridge twice, yet we said to ourselves, wherever they may be, we must find them. From where we had been poking about in a snow mound, we moved across vast flats. Still we saw nothing in particular and were dead tired.

Nevertheless, we climbed upwards a long way, as far as the South-West Ridge; we didn't find anything there either. Finally we gave up and went back down to camp.

I thought of Andi. He must have died toward the morning. Before anyone could help him, the storm and cold had worn him out. He must have been completely hypothermic and in a trance, like a sleep-walker. All his instincts were directed toward the search for Franz. He would first have been conscious of the approach of death when he no longer heard Franz. He had left the cave in the snow and the raging hurricane had swallowed him up.

Franz must have died hours before Andi did. He must have waited for me and frozen to death, even though he had given up the summit for worrying about exposure. Before we separated he had promised me he would make some tea and keep it warm for my return. Like Andi, he also died in the hope of being able to help a friend.

When the tent came in sight, I looked back once more. I didn't want to accept that the two of them had vanished forever. The snow gleamed brightly.

Then we noticed something which looked like a body and was buried under the snow. We went back again. As we approached, something dark rose out of the bright surface. Yet when we got there, only a sastrugi lay before us . . . We were very sad.

Laboriously we burrowed our way back. I had a frightful thirst and imagined I saw water. I saw it as a lake with neither beginning nor end; I saw it flowing from wells; I saw it in earthenware pots and jugs. We marched in the direction of the tent, making a deep trench in the snow and having to sit down frequently.

I lay in the snow getting my breath back. Then I stood up, took some more deep breaths and pressed forward once more. Two, three paces. We sat and moved, moved and sat. I pushed my legs in front of me and kept balance with my ice axe. I couldn't see my boots because they were swimming in the snow. My breeches were encrusted with it.

At midday—we were still searching—the weather worsened again and, as there was no question of assistance from Camp 3, we had to go down. At each rest stop I thought I would never make it to the tent. Time and again I stood up and we moved three paces, just three paces. When we sat down again, the tent was still endlessly far off.

At last we arrived back at Camp 4. I glanced inside and burrowed amongst the snow and bits of clothing, perhaps in order to find something important. But I found nothing, not even my second anorak. I crawled outside. The cloud bank in the south was coming ever nearer and there were many shadows on the great, white expanse. I looked for ski sticks but there was none. Again and again we looked across the snow slopes. One could have seen a person from miles away as the air was so clear and the snow so white.

A rope hung from the tent. I uncoiled it and we roped up for the descent. I heard the tent flapping in the wind.

When I thought about my time up here, it seemed long to me—about a month—as so much had happened.

The slope to Camp 3 was covered with new snow. We traversed it and were heartily glad that no avalanche came down. I felt all done in when I thought about our dead friends. We waded downwards, rested, waded on.

Carefully the others watched our progress through binoculars, as the weather got worse and worse.

On the one hand we were happy that the expedition leadership had ordered our descent. An even longer stay up above in this bad weather could have led to further tragedy. On the other hand, we were depressed because the search for our friends had been unsuccessful.

On the ice slope between Camps 3 and 4 there was a frightening amount of fresh snow and our companions were afraid that something else might happen.

After hours of wading through very deep snow, we finally approached Camp 3 and were welcomed there by Josl Knoll. He had kept constant watch on our descent. When he saw that we were well on the way down, he came toward us and helped break trail. We were grateful for this assistance. In Camp 3, he and Urkien took charge of us in a touching way. Urkien, our Sirdar, supplied us with drinks while Josl examined our frostbite. He massaged Horst's feet and managed to get them warm again.

Sitting on the air mattress, my frozen hand on my knees, I contemplated Urkien who, with hands full of items of clothing, fetched tea for us. In his haste to help he burned his fingers when he tried to lift the can from the cooker without a cloth. Although ultimately neither of us could drink, this selfless readiness to help left behind in me the deepest impression. It seemed to me as if I had become an old man in these few days.

After some hours when Horst and I were sufficiently recovered so that we could contemplate a further descent Josl accompanied us down to Camp 2. There Wolfi and Bulle were waiting for us. A few days later, Bulle wrote up his diary:

> *When one visualizes their long and hard route, the pair of*
> *them, although they were exhausted, were in astonishingly*
> *good shape. After they had recovered somewhat, I took care*

of their frostbite myself. Both had second-degree frostbite but the prognosis was favorable in that the damage only dated back about twelve to twenty-four hours, so that with intensive therapy much could be saved. I administered intravenous injections to Reinhold's and Horst's arms and legs for their condition.

Fortunately this led later to a complete healing of our injuries.

Horst and I lay next to Bulle in the tent. Although our doctor was sick himself, with high-altitude pulmonary edema, he exerted himself touchingly for us.

That night the storm began again and continued for ten days. . . .

THE TOTEM POLE: AND A WHOLE NEW ADVENTURE

BY PAUL PRITCHARD

YOUNG BRITISH CLIMBER PAUL PRITCHARD HAD EVERYTHING GOING for him. He was in a committed relationship with a woman who loved climbing as much as he did. His first book, *Deep Play,* had won the 1997 Boardman Tasker Award, and the prize money enabled him to start off on a world climbing tour. That tour started in Tasmania with the Totem Pole, a slender seastack 60 meters high and measuring only 3.5 meters square. And it was there that a chance rockfall shattered his skull and radically altered his life.

Immediately hospitalized, Pritchard was not expected to survive. But survive he did, through more than a year of hospitalization and rehabilitation, relearning basic thinking processes and muscle movements. Recovery gave Pritchard plenty of time to think about previous climbing accidents he'd survived—had he unconsciously caused them, to get away from pressures in his life?—and especially about how he'd live his life if he could never walk again, let alone climb. Pritchard writes movingly but without self-pity in recounting his recovery from this disastrous fall.

In this selection, a slightly abridged version of Chapters 4 and 5 of *The Totem Pole: And a Whole New Adventure*, pages 44-71, Pritchard tells of his injury and the immediate aftermath.

The rope danced in the updraft as if it were some uncontrollable serpent as we cast it loose. I put my descender on the rope and slid over the edge, watching Celia's face depart. Down the arête I went, quickly so as not to see anything. It is said to be a far better ascent when there is no prior knowledge of the climb. The more intimately you know each hand hold and foot hold, the less your ascent is rated by the cognoscenti. I arrived at a ledge, about twelve feet by three, which was to be used as our only belay, the climb being two pitches long. Putting a long sling on a carrot as a directional, to hold the rope where I wanted it, I carried on down the last 100 feet. I could look all I wanted now, as the existing climb goes around the other side of the stack. This was new rock, a line which I'd seen from above, a thin crack petering down to nothing. The start looked horrifying and smooth.

There was one arête out of the four that I had to swing around and it took me a couple of tries, down below the high water mark. I was aiming for a two-foot dry patch on a half-drowned boulder alongside the Totem Pole—dry meaning damp but not submerged. As soon as I landed I commenced fighting for my balance on the seaweed-greased rock, first sticking my crotch out and then my arse. All the while my arms behaved like the crazy cop in the silent movies who is trying to stop Harold Lloyd's motor car.

The next minute I was up to my waist in the sea that was flushing through the narrow channel. I couldn't believe my bad luck. We only had one try at this and I had just blown it. I would be hypothermic soon if I didn't get out of these soaking clothes and, besides, my boots and rope were wet and my chalk bag was full of water.

I shouted up to Celia at the top of my voice, "COME DOWN TO THE LEDGE AND TIE THE ROPE OFF." I figured that if we were to be denied the first pitch we might as well have a stab at the top one. But she couldn't hear me and I could just make out a distant "Wha-a-at?" carried away on the wind. The difficulty in hearing each other was due to the crashing waves which sounded like a whole pride of lions roaring. After screaming at each other for a while longer she understood and rappelled down to the halfway point, tying the rope off there. I fixed my jumar clamps onto the line and took in the slack, which is about two moves on the rope. I cut loose in a swing off the greasy seaweed-covered boulder. I had to tuck my knees up to avoid getting my feet in the water as I flew around the arête . . . And that is the last thing I remember—until I came around with an unearthly groan.

When I regained consciousness I was upside down, confused and there was blood pissing out of my head. I was immediately aware of the gravity of the situation. I needed to get back upright if I was to stem the flow of blood, so I concentrated on shrugging my pack off. Once off, I tried again and again to get myself sitting up in my harness but failed miserably. I was too weak and strangely uncoordinated. I gazed despondently down from an obtuse angle at the orange stain spreading in the salt water. I had a moment to reflect on what seemed to be my last view: a narrow corridor of pale gray cloud flanked by two black walls, with the white foam of the sea, which was turning quickly red, right there by my head as a ceiling to my fear. I could feel the life's blood draining out of me, literally, and there was nothing I could do about it.

Suddenly Celia was there, by me, telling me sweet lies about how it was all going to be OK.

"I heard a splash," she said in her Buckinghamshire-cum-Yorkshire accent. "You've taken a little rock on your head but you've had worse."

It's funny but those untruths are extremely comforting in moments like these. It's like you want to believe them, so you do. I was still hanging below the high water mark and had an irrational fear about my blood attracting sharks, never mind drowning when the tide turned. Imagine being engulfed by the tide and, ever so slowly, being overcome as the water rises inch by creeping inch. I was now in a fluffy dream world with cotton wool inside my head. Muffled voices were all about me and yet I was sure that only Celia was present. She fought to get me upright in slings and put her helmet on my head when she saw what a mess I'd made of it (several months later, in the back of an ambulance, I happened across the surgeon's report which stated that there was "much brain oozing out").

She prussiked the 100 feet back up to the ledge and rigged up a simple two-way pulley system through a carabiner. When I say simple, what I really mean is anything but simple, especially with only one bolt to use. It is just the simplest pulley system you can have. Now I weigh ten and a half stone (147 pounds) and she weighs nine stone (126 pounds), so you may ask how is this humanly possible? You must have heard about the child who lifted a car off her father who was being crushed when a jack failed. There are numerous such stories of superhuman strength fueled by adrenaline. I can only put this in the same category. She says it was hard, but it had to be done, she had no choice in the matter. She either did it or I died. So there was no decision to make.

Celia struggled in desperation for three hours to get me up to the ledge but faltered at the last hurdle. There was a right-angled edge to be surmounted to get me onto the ledge and the harder she pulled the tighter the rope became without moving me.

"You've got to help me here if we're to get you out of this," she barked. It was the first time I'd heard her lose her composure over this whole episode. I tried to placate her by telling her not to worry but a tired moan was all that came out of my mouth. Then was the first time I noticed something amiss with the limbs on my right side—well, I couldn't so much tell which side it was. I only knew that they had no feeling in them at all and however much I tried I couldn't move them. My arm was being thrashed around like a rag doll's and my leg was sustaining deep wounds as shinbone scraped sharp rock. I looked down at my leg and couldn't work out why it wasn't able to move. It was like a piece of wood, a cricket bat, for instance, being knocked on the edge of a stone tabletop. I remember thinking that it was just a temporary lapse in control of my body and I would soon be back to normal. With my left arm and leg I fought my way onto the ledge, first my chest, then my belly, then my legs. I lay exhausted on my front and all I could think about was going to sleep.

Celia put me in the recovery position (essentially lying on your front with your head turned to one side, a position that keeps your airway open and is sure to eject vomit). She gave me a hug, then told me she was going to have to leave me and get help. I was terrified that it was the last time I was going to see her but I didn't show my feelings. She was probably thinking the same thoughts. Celia then jumared back up the final 100 feet of the stack and crossed the Tyrolean traverse where I heard her shouting encouraging words. I answered with a groan, which she certainly could not hear.

⁊　　⁊　　⁊

The first time I met Celia was on a remote Scottish island. We went crazy. It was midsummer and light virtually all night long. It feels, in my vague memory, like we never slept, just partied round the clock. We soon got a reputation as the party crew, locals would turn up on tractors, their trailers loaded with ale at six o'clock in the morning. We joined the football team, playing on a cow field by the beach, with a dark silhouette of the Cuillin of Rhum just across the water. Eigg vs Muck. Taking part in the village ceilaidh, we spun each other drunkenly around until we stopped spinning, and only the room was left revolving.

Ed Stone and I had a plan to free climb the "last great aid route" in these islands, the Sgurr of Eigg. The Sgurr is a huge prow of columnar basalt, looking not so dissimilar to Venezuela's Mount Roraima, the fabled Lost World of Conan Doyle. Our ascent ended spectacularly when I fell off, clutching a colossal block. We decided to admit defeat and enjoy the midsummer madness for the rest of the week.

I fell hopelessly in love with Celia as soon as I set my eyes on her. It was her moodiness that intrigued me and I made notes about her in my little green book. She has high cheekbones, steel blue eyes, full lips, and a wonky nose. Back then she had permed blond hair. We gazed at each other across the campfire and went skinny-dipping on our private beach. She would often climb up into a tree and sulk about I didn't know what and didn't like to ask. It would be a further two years before we got together.

⸙   ⸙   ⸙

The seven hours that followed on the Tote were a fight to stay awake when all I wanted to do was drift into unconsciousness. But I was convinced that if I went to sleep I would surely die. Blood was pooling on the ledge from under Celia's helmet and I was blinded in my left eye. I foolishly put my hand under the hard hat to feel the damage for myself, and when I removed it, amidst the blood, there appeared to be a clear liquid which only served to confuse my already addled brain. I began talking to myself: "Hmmm, what have we here then?" I answered myself: "It looks as if you have a mighty hole in your head there, Mr. Pritchard." I remember having the image of a soft-boiled egg and toast soldiers just before blacking out for the first time.

Meanwhile Celia was running the eight kilometers back to the campsite, not knowing whether I was alive or dead. She met a couple of New South Walean climbers on the path who were coming to have a look at the Totem Pole and she pleaded with them to come down to be with me. As they had all their equipment with them they were very willing to oblige. They shouted, to see if I was still alive from the cliff top, but I still couldn't answer. I suspect it was a corpse they were expecting to encounter when they finally rappelled in to me. Later I learnt their names from the Tasmania Police report: Tom Jamieson and Andrew Davidson. I don't remember their faces but I felt their presence and heard their kind concerned voices.

I could now hear the all too familiar sound of helicopter rotor blades on the wind. The wind had been steadily picking up speed since we arrived and was now blowing through the narrow canyon with some force. I don't know the exact sequence of events. They appeared completely irrelevant to me and yet directly concerned me at the same time. I had chosen probably the most difficult place to get rescued on the whole coast line of Southern Tasmania. A twelve by 200-foot sea stack in the middle of a 160-foot channel with 400-foot cliffs on either side. And I was stuck on a ledge exactly halfway up it. A helicopter rescue was out of the question; it was just too dangerous, the rotor blades coming perilously close to the sidewalls.

Neale Smith, the only climbing paramedic in the whole of Tasmania, happened to be on duty that day and this was to be my one and only lucky break. He set about traversing the Tyrolean rope bridge and rappelling down to the New South Walean climbers and me. Meanwhile a rescue boat was radioed and on its way from Nubeena, about twenty-five kilometers away, that was our only hope of a rescue before dark. He sat by me for a couple of hours, with reassuring words, until I heard, as if in a dream, the screeching sound of a motor boat in the channel below. The boat handler had to negotiate submerged rocks at a depth of just a few feet. He then had to steer the craft in to the very base of the stack so that Neale could abseil down with me clipped to him, all the while trying not to disturb by head.

I remember being in the vertical again, now knowing at the time that here was the only guy of the paramedic team who knew how to perform such a technical operation. A blurred black wall was passing me by for what appeared to be an eternity. I remember being handled into the aluminum tub by the crew. What felt like a hundred hands groped me and attempted to make me comfortable. "Cut his harness off him," I heard one of the rescue team say as the driver skillfully slalomed in and out of the sunken rocks. Ian Kingston, the pilot, has since been nominated for a medal by the Tasmania Police Force, as has Celia for her bravery and skill.

It wasn't as pleasant a ride as we had taken with the Boy Racer and that is saying something. We battered up and down on each wave with people trying to hold me still in an attempt at stopping me being flung from the boat. The deafening whine of the outboard as it tore through the water still haunts me. There are times, as I write this book, when a lawn mower passes by the Rehab Unit window that for apparently no reason a shiver will run down my spine and I begin shaking. At the beach in Fortescue Bay I knew I was going to see Celia and made an attempt to compose myself and straighten my hair, which consisted of smearing the blood all over my face. Obviously she still didn't know if I had made it and it was with a certain relief that she saw me still hanging in there.

A stretcher was carried out of the boat and in to a helicopter, apparently with me in it, and it flew to the Cambridge Airport, about 100 kilometers distant. We couldn't fly direct to the Hobart Great War Memorial before getting picked up by ambulance, as is normally the case, because it is illegal to fly around the city after dark. I was then rushed by "ambo" across the Tasman Bridge to the Royal Hobart Hospital. I had seen this place many times because it is right there on the street corner; you pass it every time you leave or enter the city. I just have this image of concentric rows of windows and a fountain outside the main door. The stretcher was then put on a trolley and wheeled into the hospital. I recall the ceilings of corridors and lots of distorted faces as they stared down at me from twelve inches; ever so bright pen torches being shone into my eyes.

The paramedics decided against a morphine injection as it depresses the nervous system. Apparently they never administer opiates with head injuries. I wasn't in pain as such anyway, just out of it from blood-loss; I'm told there are no pain receptors in the brain. The surgeon's report reads that: "On arrival the patient was still conscious but grossly dysphasic with right sided hemiplegia," or to put it more simply, unable to speak and paralyzed down one side. Celia arrived a couple of hours later, alone and by car. Again she expected to be told, "Sorry we've lost him. We did all we could." But I was in the operating theatre and still hanging on in there. When the nurses were preparing me for surgery they took Celia's helmet off me and found that my brains were literally hanging out of the ten by five-centimeter hole in my skull. I was still in wet clothes and the doctor rebuked Neale for not undressing me, I don't know what he could have dressed me in alternatively. My long hair had to be shorn and two liters of blood transfused. The surgeon worked for six hours, in the dead of night, picking shards of bone and rock from the inside of my head.

The accident occurred on a Friday, which also happened to be February 13. As a rule I'm not a superstitious person and I still am not. I will walk under ladders or do dangerous things on the 13th just to tempt fate. Nothing has changed, only that I feel a slight uneasiness on subsequent Friday the 13ths. This new day was Saint Valentine's day. While lovers were exchanging pink gifts I was on the operating table having an "intracerebral hemorrhagic contusion" removed from my brain with a little vacuum cleaner in an operation known as an osteoclastic craniotomy. There were scans taken before and after the operation. The post-operative scan showed the "removal of bony fragments over the vertex after the evacuation (Hoovering) of a left fronto-parietal lobe hematoma (clot)."

Celia began the grim business of telephoning our friends and family to warn them that I might not make it. It was morning back home. She was careful to get the news to my parents first so they wouldn't hear it second hand. My friends' attempts to rationalize their sorrow manifested itself in a number of ways. Possibly the most bizarre attempt was Adam Wainwright's going climbing that very day on Craig Doris, perhaps the loosest sea cliff in Wales and not wearing a helmet! I climbed Trango Tower in the Karakoram with Adam, which makes him a particularly good friend. One can't go through something like a major climb without some special bond developing. My father, mother, sister, and brother all cried when they heard the bad news. Tracey, my sister who lives in Lebanon, offered to fly out to Tasmania with my mother. They all knew there was a chance I could die and they prepared for it in a number of ways.

Later my mother described how it felt like the bottom was falling out of her world, and how she lay on the bed shaking and sobbing at the prospect of losing a son. Afterward this was my deepest regret, more than never being able to climb again or run or even walk. Putting her through such a traumatic event was unforgivable. She telephoned my dad who did weep but he's much too much of a man to admit it. He went about his allotment with a hollow feeling in his stomach and lost weight through worry. Tracey prayed for me, and her husband, Kim, contacted Greg, a parson friend of his in Hobart who would shortly come and visit me. In fact there were people praying for me in Malaysia, where Kim's parents live, in Lebanon, where my sister and her husband work as missionaries, in Bolton, my home town, and in Hobart itself where Greg the parson's Taroona church congregation would pray for me whenever they met.

Obviously I wasn't aware of any of these goings on, as I was unconscious and hallucinating wildly for the best part of four days. When I awoke on the intensive care unit I had no idea where I was or that the course of my life had been drastically altered in one second. That's all it takes for a rock to impact.

⚐   ⚐   ⚐

As if by some cruel joke my bed was placed dead opposite the window, which looked straight over the roof tops, with a full view of the Organ Pipes. There was a skateboarder on a billboard, pulling a one-handed handstand on the lip of a half pipe, whilst advertising Coca-Cola with the other. He was grinning at me from his upside-down stance. I was in the Neurological High Dependency Unit of the Royal Hobart Hospital . . .

It had been five days since the Accident and I was starting to get a clearer picture of what I'd done to myself. I'd had two other hideous accidents but neither of these could remotely compare to what I was going through now. Neither could be said to be a capital letter Accident. But I believe that without that previous experience of trauma I would probably have died. I would have expired alone on that ledge were it not for the fighting to stay awake while the life's blood drained out of me. I relaxed and didn't panic, conserving my energy, that was the fight . . .

I still couldn't speak or move my right side. My face felt numb, like the right-hand side wasn't moving. I rang for a nurse and embarked on an almighty game of charades, but she didn't understand all my pointings at a plate, at my reflection in the stainless steel cot side and back at my face. All I wanted to ask for was a mirror. I was left exhausted. She thought I wanted food and then something to do with the cot sides. I think she was just as frustrated as I was at not being able to guess what I was on about.

I was desperate to see my face. It felt numb and swollen, my eye was almost closed and I still had blurred vision. I was dribbling saliva out of the right side of my mouth and I could just make out the looks on the faces of my few visitors, which registered pity and compassion or shock and horror. I felt like a real life Quasimodo.

Tubes still came out of my neck and nose and cock. As pain killers and liquid sustenance fed into my head, the waste would come in a steady trickle down the tube emanating from my bladder and down my pajama trouser leg. I still hallucinated every night and day, but that was getting less severe.

In the dead of night I felt a grinding pain in my abdomen. It seemed as though I was dying. I thrashed about in the clutches of my agony. With not an inkling of what it could be I rang the bell and the nurse came hurrying in. He put hot wet towels on my stomach to stave off the cramps, all to no avail, and told me not to worry, that it was just trapped wind. After an hour, where I was seeing all manner of colored patterns on the big screen of the inside of my eyelids, the pain dissipated.

The night staff had to turn me over whenever I rang the bell, which was about ten times a night. I became agitated and impatient if they didn't come straight away. It was only possible to lie on my left side or my back. I had to have a pillow between my knees, two pillows behind my back and one pillow to cushion my right arm, which lay out in front of me like a pauper I once saw on the pavement in Delhi begging for alms. An electric fan kept me cool, even though only a thin sheet covered me. A big Australian in the next bed asked the nurse to ask me if I could turn it off because he was chilled. Why he didn't ask me directly I don't know. I then proceeded to swelter and sweat my way through the long night. Just another long night of many.

I had some idea of what had happened to me now and I just kept breaking down in tears. Why me? Hadn't I been through enough these last five years? Two major accidents from which to convalesce, taking a year apiece, four illnesses, hepatitis, pericarditis, amoebic dysentery, and fatigue syndrome. I was weary and if I could I would have screamed out, "amputate the damned legs, they're fucking useless to me now. I'm better off without them."

If there'd been someone around with a saw I wouldn't have hesitated to have them lopped off. After all I couldn't feel a thing in them. In fact it was the opposite of the phantom limb phenomenon, where the leg or arm is amputated and for months, even years, after there is a ghostly feeling of the limb still in its place. The amputee will jump out of bed convinced that he has two legs and promptly fall over. My situation was the exact opposite. I could see I had the leg and the arm when I was looking at them, but when I averted my eyes they completely ceased to exist.

The last two accidents were my fault but this . . . I didn't even see it coming. I was aware of nothing. One minute I was jumaring, the next I was upside down on the end of the rope, trying to shrug my rucksack off my shoulders. One moment I was penduluming in a sweeping arc and fifteen minutes later coming round and wondering what all this blood was doing gushing from my head and staining the water crimson.

Lying there however I could now see how all three major accidents might be seen as subconsciously, subliminally self-inflicted. I had become bored with a pretty extreme lifestyle. What hope for me was there if I was disenchanted with doing just what I wanted, going right there to the edge of life and screaming, "You can't touch me, you bastards!" I never had anyone telling me what to do, never had a career apart from climbing, never worked nine to five. Most people have a climbing career that spans perhaps ten years and the rest is steadily downhill. There are some notable exceptions to this but even they would agree that there was a decade when they achieved most. For the last three years I was doing what I thought I should be doing and not what I really wanted to do. By continuing to climb I wasn't learning anything new, wasn't breaking into higher levels of consciousness or knowledge. So I knew something had to snap. I could feel it in my bones.

The first falling and drowning incident in Wen Zawn at Gogarth in '93 was because I was screwed up over a girl and thought she might notice me if I hurt myself. Let's put it this way, she was on my mind when I fell off, ripped all my gear and wiped out. It wasn't a conscious thought, but I'm sure it flashed across my mind.

The second, on Creagh Meaghaidh, in the Highlands of Scotland, was because I was desperate to change my life. I fell 200 feet off an ice climb. I was tired of it all and I recall breathing a sigh of relief when I awoke in hospital. There was a huge release of pressure. No more climbing, no more routes, no more egos, no more grades, no more sponsors trying to tell me what to do, no more weight crushing down on me and saying, "Excel!" Even if that pressure came from within. I didn't know what else to do at the time to find a replacement. That was the problem. So I drifted back onto the climbing treadmill. And so it all began over again.

I put myself in that situation purposefully but without knowing it at the time. I didn't willfully throw myself off the ice but I wouldn't have got myself into that situation—soft eggshell ice, miles out from an ice screw—if I was thinking rationally.

And this latest and final accident was because I felt trapped. I had it all, or that's what the majority of my friends figured—big house with a beautiful garden, nice car, as many holidays as I would care to take. Happy at home with Celia. Basically, I was very comfortable. I was taking too many risks and I didn't know why. Why was I not wearing a helmet? If there's a rock climbing situation which warrants wearing a helmet it was surely then. Why didn't I glance up and see the rock coming? I normally would have been much more aware of my surroundings. The only conclusion I can come to is that I was stressed out by my relationship and by climbing also, but on a subconscious level, without really mentally coming to terms with what I was challenging in my lifestyle . . .

⋆　　⋆　　⋆

Nicola MacKinnon and Dawn Lewis were my physiotherapists and they were a light-hearted pair. The trick is to get you moving from day one or as near as damn it. First lesson would be sitting on the side of the bed, which may sound easy, but with hemiplegia it isn't. I toppled over to the right again and again until I learnt how to balance on my left buttock. Though I would often get caught unawares and occasionally overbalance for weeks to come.

Once I'd vaguely mastered how to sit upright, I was whisked off to the physio gym where there were all manner of torture implements. Parallel bars, blocks, rubber balls from three inches to three feet in diameter, tilt boards, cupboards full of every terrible thing, splints, casts and slings, items that were going to become as familiar as the hairs in the ditch in my head over the coming months.

There they had me rolling a big ball whilst sitting down, my good hand holding my bad hand down. I would move it side to side and backward and forwards. Next I would be taught how to turn over, completely rotating, while lying down. Simple movements have a habit of becoming fights in desperation with a "dense hemi," as the doctors call my condition.

It was then that I saw that guy in the mirror at the end of the parallel bars.

I didn't recognize the man in front of me. Half his face was black and blue and he had a hemorrhaged eyeball. I knew this term because I'd had one before when my ice axe hit me in the orbit around my eye during the 200-foot fall on Creagh Meaghaidh. His whole eyeball was a deep cherry red, as if he'd been using cochineal eye drops. He was thin beyond belief. With the shaved head he resembled a Jew in the black and white Pathe News film footage of the liberation of the concentration camps. I couldn't take my eyes off the man in the mirror as I couldn't take my eyes off that black and white film. His head was poorly shaved with long bits on the sides and he still had matted blood in it and falling off sticky tape on top. He also had a "golden purse" with him, a catheter bag full of deep orange piss, which he hung on the parallel bars. That had to be emptied before every session but it soon filled up with the exercise.

Presently Marge Conroy the speech therapist tested me for swallowing ability. A kind, interested woman who had me sipping orange juice and eating ice cream by the teaspoon. I was then controlled for a number of days, eating little bits of easy to swallow food and tasting protein drink. Pretty soon I was being force fed, "to get my weight up," three massive meals a day, plus five protein shakes. My dietician would come round and make sure I was eating and drinking all I should. Celia told them that I had always been this weight but they seemed not to believe her. How could anyone look this emaciated? They obviously had not seen other climbers I could mention.

I was complaining to the nurse, by pointing at my throat, about my nasogastric tube and how it was choking me. Burnt chiles, that's what it was like. It was getting to the point where I couldn't even breathe any more without breaking into a coughing fit. Jane Boucher, a kind nurse, pulled it out because she felt sorry for me, but then faced stiff reprimands from the dietician who thought he was the one who should say whether it stayed or went. It was a momentous occasion. With the sliding out of that tube I suddenly felt free, the whole world was mine.

I preferred the chocolate to the banana milkshakes, but after a couple of days I got sick of the sight of either. I couldn't feed myself so well with my non-dominant hand. It would take more than an hour, lying down, and I would get most of the food down my front and onto the blue napkin. But it was bliss to be eating on my own rather than with the tube. My favorites were kidney bean casserole, followed by green jelly or ice cream. Celia brought me boxes of mixed bean salad in to ease my constipation but I still hadn't been for a week. I was on my third or fourth enema when I finally shat with great relief. They had been shoveling food into me all week and up till then nothing had come out the other end.

Marge's full title was speech and language therapist and she had me doing exercises with my mouth, making different shapes with it and saying "aaaaah" or "oooooh." She also made me look at picture cards and asked me to say what they depicted. I stared long and hard at a picture of a pen and raised my hands in disbelief. Then a picture of a house brick. "Don't know," I struggled to utter. An elephant, a horse, a shovel, a book, all manner of items and animals. I recognized them but just could not think of their names.

"We've all forgotten someone's name now and again and it's just a profound version of that," said Marge. "Anomic asphasia it's called."

My left from my right I persistently got confused and I had lost the actual concept of time. I couldn't say what clocks did. As the days passed, I found that I slowly came to understand, but there was still no way I could tell the time. So it was back to junior school for me with pictures of clocks and "The big hand is pointing to the nine and the small hand is pointing toward the three. No, Paul, it's not five to six!"

Then she would test my mental processing power and speed.

"Name all the animals you can think of in the farmyard in a minute?" she asked in her soft Tassie lilt.

"Er, pig . . . " There was then a long pause until the minute was up.

"OK, this time I want you to think of as many words as you can beginning with the letter 'C'."

I looked around the ward, hoping to cheat and there it was, as if in neon lights, "Australia's no. 1 Catheter provider.' She knew what I was up to straight away. I recognized the C and then the rest of the word as I stuttered out, "C-ath-et-er." And my minute was up . . .

⟩   ⟩   ⟩

I was slowly coming to terms with the fact that I may never go climbing again. This realization was aided by Dr. Khan's insistence that I would never be able to walk again, never mind climb. He looked a bit like a hare and had a little paunch squeezed into his expensive silk suit. "Just think yourself lucky that you still have one arm and one leg. Some persons have only their mouth that is usable." His remark made my heart sink and I began weeping. He came from Peshawar, near the Afghanistan border, and I wondered if he had grown up in a crueller environment than I had—a rocket launcher can be bought over the counter in Peshawar.

Once a day all the doctors and surgeons would come on a ward round. It could be any time. There was Mr. Van Gelder, my personal surgeon, Dr. Khan, Dr. Liddell, and the ward sister whose name I forget. They would all hover round the foot of the bed and make notes on their clipboards: "suprapubic catheter," or "naso-gastric feed out." I would stammer out my hello before any of them had a chance to beat me to it and they would, without fail, read my new faxes that I had received overnight. Some of them were very funny indeed. George Smith, a close friend from Wales, sent me numerous cartoons he had drawn with expertise and there were all manner of paintings and cards arriving all the time. And so they would all troop out in a line just as quickly as they had entered, muttering to each other under their breath.

Van Gelder wore round spectacles, had a square jaw, and the air of a Thunderbird about him. He was a climber himself, a damn fine one. He had climbed a couple of 8000-meter peaks, including Kangchenchunga in Sikkim, and Broad Peak in Pakistan. He was on K2 in 1986 when Julie Tullis and Al Rouse died in a ferocious storm. He knew his stuff, that is for sure, but he gave all that up to become a neuro-surgeon, finding he could get the same kicks without the risk to his own life. That out-of-body experience which you search for all your climbing life and only pick up about five times during your whole career, he now finds in surgery. He described looking down on himself at work just as a climber does when she or he is having one of those rare "special moments," usually in a very scary situation. He also thought that he could do more good saving people's lives than in the selfish act that is mountain climbing. Undeniably, I was indebted to him for having saved my life. He quietly voiced the opinion that, "There is too much senseless wasting of lives in climbing. I had to get out before it got me." I liked to think he took a little extra care because he knew we shared a love of the mountains, but I know that he uses the same expertise with all his patients.

He was interested in the use of helmets in climbing and discussed helmet design in great detail with Celia. He ruminated on the notion that I could have been in a worse state had I been wearing a helmet. Many motorcycle accidents result in quadriplegia because, when a smash happens, the motorcyclist breaks his cervical spine, whereas if he wasn't wearing a helmet he would have a head injury—the same as me. Obviously neither option is particularly appealing but at least I was "just" a hemiplegic. At least I had one good arm and one good leg. Had I been wearing a helmet maybe I would have been quadrapleged also . . .

>   >   >

It wasn't just the physical act of climbing a rock but the whole event: the crack with your mates before you tie into the rope, before you put on your serious cap; in the pub afterwards (where a good day's climbing invariably ends) discussing this move or that move; wild nights that you felt entitled to because you had burnt up so much energy during the day. And then there was the traveling which meant so much to me. I felt that I would rather die than not be able to go on expeditions ever again. Fifteen years of my life I had spent going on expeditions or "trips" as we called them, more or less back to back. I had witnessed flying saucer clouds from halfway up a wall in Patagonia, a plume of dust rising for thousands of feet during a gigantic rockfall, seen from the top of a mountain in Kirghizstan. And all of them watched, in awe, with special friends. I buried such memories and told Celia to drive on.

When we arrived at the summit of the mountain I transferred into my chair and took deep draughts of the rarefied air at 4000 feet. We wheeled down a plank-walk to the viewing gantry from where we could survey the whole of the Derwent estuary, its harbor and the city of Hobart. I could see the hospital from up here, model-like, and the Tasman Bridge, so clear was the atmosphere. It was a moving experience to be looking down upon the land and sea again instead of staring up at the ceiling from my hospital bed. To the west the Atlantic Ocean disappeared over the horizon, unchecked, as at 40° South, it peaked and troughed its way a clear half around the globe. In my over-emotional state I shed a tear at the vastness of the world . . .

FROM

STORM AND SORROW IN THE HIGH PAMIRS

BY ROBERT CRAIG

HOW COULD AN EVENT THAT BEGAN WITH SUCH GOODWILL and optimism end in such disaster, suffering and death?

One hundred sixty mountaineers from twelve nations came together in the summer of 1974 for an international climbing encampment in the central Pamirs Range, on the Soviet/Chinese border. Nineteen of America's best climbers, sponsored by the American Alpine Club, formed four teams for the encampment as the "American Pamirs/USSR Expedition." No Americans and few Europeans had climbed in these mountains before, and hopes were high for both record ascents and international cooperation.

Certainly, peaks were climbed, records were achieved, and friendships were built that continue today. But, just as the gathering of these mountaineers was unprecedented, so, unfortunately was the sequence of natural disasters that befell them—earthquakes, avalanches, horrendous storms that killed many and tested the endurance and courage of the others. One of the most tragic happenings during the expedition—indeed, in the history of mountaineering—was the death of an entire team of Soviet women on Peak Lenin as their pride held them to the storm-lashed mountain, high up beyond any hope of timely rescue.

Craig, deputy leader of the American contingent, recounts the growing horror and frustration of the listeners as radio transmissions from the Soviet women's leader, Elvira Shatayeva, convey the exhaustion, gradual weakening and eventually the deaths of her comrades, one by one. Unbearable sadness comes over everyone as Elvira finally clicks off with "Please forgive us. We love you. Good bye."

This selection is a slightly abridged version of Chapters 10 and 11 of *Storm and Sorrow in the High Pamirs*, pages 144-166.

I n Base on August 4 we were almost ankle deep in mud after another night of snow and rain. Climbers came down off Peak Lenin in a steady stream. Roskelley and Lowe had returned from Nineteen; Schoening, Higgins, Kopczynski, and Sarnquist from Lenin, and the American sector of Base came back to life again. Austrians, Swiss, English, Russians, and Bavarians all came in as afternoon clouds again enveloped the range.

Jeff [Lowe] and John [Roskelley] rapidly crossed the meadow into Base and while they were not jubilant at having completed the best route of the season, there was the quiet sense of satisfaction at having accomplished a worthwhile task. Peak Nineteen had been a challenge, a drama, a tragedy, and now what had begun with such high spirits and sunlight was completed quietly and in storm. There was no triumph, only a grave on the mountain and two friends safely returned.

With Pete Schoening back, we tried to take stock of the various Americans. Everyone seemed okay at Camp II and ought to be back in Base on August 5. We had not heard a thing from Jock Glidden, Al Steck, and Chris Wren since they left Base Camp. Then there was the report of the Siberians having sighted the Americans on the Lipkin on the 2nd, but the latest long-range weather report had come in forecasting an extremely dangerous new storm. If they were not transmitting we wondered if they could be receiving. There was some reassurance for their safety in the many years of big mountain experience of Steck and Glidden, but the big Pamirs storm, with hard snowfall already hitting Base, was the beginning of real anxiety for all of us.

It snowed moderately the night of the 4th; still the storm did not materialize and we awoke with hopes that conditions would hold until everyone was in a safe position. The morning report of the Soviet coaches; at Camp III on the 5th indicated relatively calm conditions with little wind and partly cloudy skies. It had not snowed any appreciable amount the night before.

What was disturbing about their transmission, especially to Abalakov and the other Soviet officials, was the report that climbers were still setting off for the summit in spite of the warnings from Base. Abalakov decided to send up several of the Soviet coaches to be in position to render assistance for those climbers on the Lipkin and Razdelny routes, should they need it on their way down the mountain. Boris and Valodya were already in Camp I and he would immediately dispatch Kostya and Oleg. They would go as high as they could, perhaps to the ice cave camp on the Lipkin.

Abalakov, Gippenreiter, and Monastyrski were in a corner of the mess tent in mid-afternoon when Pete [Lev], John Evans, and I approached them. We said we would like to help if support was needed. Abalakov noted it was too soon, that not enough was known about what was happening on the upper mountain. Monastyrski conveyed a sense of deep concern. By nature he was cheerful, and often humorous, even while functioning in a low-key, business-like manner. He was obviously worried and tense, and appeared to be smoking one cigarette after the other. Gippenreiter, normally outgoing and urbane, looked thoroughly exhausted and was distinctly concerned. He had been high on the Lipkin with the Siberians and the Scots. He had had a meal with the Soviet women. Having climbed Lenin four times, he had decided to descend alone after reaching the point where the Lipkin joined the northeast ridge at about 22,000 feet. He said the conditions were as bad as he had ever seen on Peak Lenin. Abalakov was more impassive than ever.

Late in the afternoon of the 5th the storm, which we observed lashing the upper levels of Peak Lenin and the other peaks of the Pamirs within our view, moved down into the Achik Tash Valley. It began again to snow heavily, the wind rose, and we knew the major storm forecast by Osh had arrived. To make things even more ominous, the Soviet Meteorological Service was forecasting "winds of hurricane force." At about 5:00 P.M., Allen North came down off the Lipkin and reported the three Americans were camped solid at about 21,000 feet and planning to go for the summit with the first good weather.

At about 7:00 P.M. we were called to the communications tent, and informed by Abalakov and Monastyrski that the Soviet women had indeed reported from the summit of Lenin that they were going to camp on top and that they were having trouble getting their tents up in the storm. It was never clear how many they were able to pitch, though it seemed they had started with three. Abalakov again had ordered them to descend immediately in the morning, returning down the Lipkin as that was the route they knew. It was almost a 4,000-foot descent to Camp III at Razdelny Pass with virtually no protection in between. By contrast, to the Lipkin ridge from the summit and some sort of lee shelter it was a 1,000–1,500-foot descent. In the back of his mind he hoped, too, that the women might encounter the Japanese or Americans holding out in the storm on the Lipkin. Abalakov suggested further that, as the storm was out of the southwest, they would gain some benefit from the lee of the northeasterly trending Lipkin ridge.

Equally ominous was Monastyrski's report that Viktor and Georg had called in a few minutes earlier with the news that it appeared the International Women were in trouble and that a rescue group was being formed at Razdelny to give assistance in the morning. They reported violent winds, heavy snow, and rapidly falling temperatures. Michael [Monastyrski] also noted that a large group of Siberian and Polish climbers was descending the Lipkin and northeast ridges but was too far below to be of possible assistance to the Soviet women.

The atmosphere in the mess tent that evening was extremely subdued. Over forty people were at 20,000 feet or above, eight of them at 23,400 feet in a great storm that had not even reached its peak. Still, there was no certain indication that anything had gone wrong. The movies went on as scheduled, but attendance was light, and as we returned to our tents it was snowing hard.

There were 5 inches of snow on the ground when we got up early the morning of August 6. The sun came out and took some of the chill from the air and we had the impression that things might be improving. But a look toward Peak Lenin was not reassuring: clouds enveloped the whole mountain down to the base, and where a rent occurred to reveal layer upon layer of clouds well above 30,000 feet, one could estimate that the winds aloft had to be enormous. This was soon confirmed.

At 8:00 A.M., Viktor and Georg reported from Camp III that the night had been desperate: two tents had been blown apart and the occupants forced to double up with others nearby. The three International Women, Heidi [Ludi], Eva [Eisenschmidt], and Anya [last name unknown], were still 1,500 feet or so above Camp III in God knows what shape. There had been over a foot of snow and the wind was blowing 70 to 80 miles per hour. A rescue team of Peter Lev, François Valla, Michel Vincent, Sepp Schwankener, Hans Bruntjes, and another Netherlander named Louie had left to render assistance in getting them back to the relative safety of Camp III. Three Japanese and a Swiss man were also unaccounted for, and the two Soviet coaches could only hope they managed to bivouac safely.

The Soviet women reported in rather matter-of-factly with a strong signal from their position on the summit of Lenin. They had had a bad night. The wind had destroyed two of their tents in the night. They were now four in each of the two remaining military tents. One of the girls who had been in a collapsed tent was feeling poorly.

The tents had no zipper closures, but rather a double flap system of folds which were secured along the seams by wooden toggles passed through string eyelets attached to the flaps. This closure system hardly kept out the storm in the same kind of tents which were provided for us at Base, and a number of us were dumbfounded when we learned that this equipment was what the Soviet women were depending on. Even more depressing was the knowledge that the four poles providing the A-frame suspension at either end of the two-man tents were made of wood, and at least three or four of these poles had broken in various instances in Base Camp, most not involving heavy winds, but snow loads of a mere few inches. We made no mention of our feeling about the tent to the Soviet officials, but fervently hoped the women could somehow dig snow caves.

[Elvira] Shataeyeva did not specify how or to what degree her teammate was sick. She was apparently one of the two youngest. Michael Monastyrski and Eugene Gippenreiter translated for us alternately as Abalakov, speaking directly to Elvira, the leader, and to each of the women as teammates, ordered an immediate descent to the shelter of the Lipkin. As they verified their understanding, the roaring wind periodically obliterated their voices. Abalakov, speaking slowly, told the women they had to get down the mountain far enough to find snow suitable for snow caves. He repeated that snow caves and some lee shelter out of the wind were absolutely essential. Again, they must go down the Lipkin immediately. He did not say it directly, but it was implied that if the sick girl could not move and they could not achieve adequate shelter, they must leave her for the good of the group as a whole. He said this softly but he was adamant that they descend. He exacted a promise from Shataeyeva that they would do so.

As we walked back to the American tents, Pete said, "We've got to do something! We've got to persuade them to bring helicopters. There must be some way. They're all going to die up there! Jock, Allen, Chris—they're up there too. At least let's put a rescue or support team together." We agreed to talk to the Russians, the English, and the French and see what could be arranged.

At about 3:00 P.M. on August 6, Viktor called Base from Camp III saying

Eva Eissenschmidt had died while being evacuated to Camp III. The other two women had been returned safely, but frostbitten. He noted there was other frostbite amongst the climbers in the camp and that supplies of fuel and food in the camp were dangerously low. The three Japanese and the Swiss had survived their bivouac and returned to Camp III as the rescue of Eva proceeded. When Abalakov asked Viktor whether they could descend in the storm, he said Peter Lev, the American avalanche specialist, had stated emphatically that snow conditions were just too dangerous for a descent at that time. He noted that he, Georg, and Franqois Valla, another avalanche expert, tended to agree, but he felt they would be in equally grave danger if they remained too long at III.

At 5:00 P.M. the Soviet women called Base from just below the summit of Lenin on the short, steep snow and ice slope leading northeasterly down to the Lipkin. One of the women had died, apparently while assisting the others down. It sounded as if she had frozen to death while belaying the others down to a bivouac position. The girl who had been reported sick was worse and another ill. Under the circumstances of storm and extreme cold and 23,000 feet, being "ill" could only mean that two more were, in fact, dying.

Shataeyeva said they were trying to pitch tents on the steep ridge. Abalakov tried to be stern as he questioned why they had not dug snow caves, but he visibly sagged and seemed more desolate than ever as Elvira replied they had tried but the snow was too hard and that they were very cold and rapidly weakening.

Abalakov then said they must continue to climb down, there was nothing they could do for the sick—they would all die if they tried to remain in that spot. Shataeyeva replied with some detachment that she understood, that they would continue to try, and that they hoped to get further down the next morning. The Russian woman translating in English next to us said tearfully, "It is like a dream; she doesn't seem to realize what is happening to them."

As Elvira ended her transmission on a note of what seemed deep sadness and resignation, if not of a dangerous kind of vagueness, the steady moan of the raging storm could be clearly heard above her voice, and, as it was snowing again at Base, one could only guess at the temperature at 23,000 feet, some 12,000 feet above us. At the adiabatic cooling rate of 5 or 6 degrees per 1,000 feet, it was probably somewhere between 60 and 70 degrees below freezing—30 to 40 degrees below 0°F. If one added the velocity of the wind, probably well over 70 miles per hour, the prospect of the women's surviving the night seemed very slight.

A crowd of climbers from every national group in Base Camp milled around the communications tent area in the falling snow and gloom. The final realization that a disaster of overwhelming proportions was in the making—a disaster that very conceivably might involve everyone on the upper slopes of Lenin—was painfully evident.

Pete and I talked with the British and French about mounting some kind of rescue or assistance effort. The response from Doug Scott and Benoit Renard had been immediate and affirmative. If the Soviets would agree, we would add four English, four French, and four Americans to their coaches at the bottom of the Lipkin and Razdelny routes. We would recommend bringing up helicopters at the earliest moment—tomorrow, the 7th (but requesting them immediately), if possible to attempt an airdrop to the women. An airdrop or any use of helicopters assumed a lessening of the storm, but experience had indicated that it took at least a day to move machines into position in the Achik Tash Valley. We would also recommend that the Soviets strongly urge the evacuation of Camp III, despite the known avalanche hazard, in light of the strong possibility that its inhabitants, like the Soviet women, might soon experience the beginnings of hypothermia and reduced function.

We approached our three Russian friends after dinner. We outlined the situation as we saw it and told them of the willingness, indeed the eagerness and necessity, of a group of top climbers' trying to assist the others. At first there was reluctance, even slight annoyance, and Michael said, "We feel this is our problem. We appreciate your spirit but we will do everything that can be done.

I replied, "Michael, we understand you are doing everything you can, but it is not enough. You have a rescue operation underway on the Saukdhara Glacier, your coaches are thinly scattered on Peak Lenin, and now there is a real question about the safety of over forty people distributed all over the mountain, a good many of them in places we're not even sure of. We have twelve or so international class climbers, including a doctor, who are willing to go up to help. They may not succeed, but we must at least try. You must know we are your friends—we will do nothing to embarrass you."

Monastyrski looked at us, eyes slightly brimming, and said, "I know, we have already become better friends. I will discuss this with Evgeny and Vitaly." The three were in session for over an hour. They called us back to the command post at about 7:30 P.M.

Abalakov was, as we had expected, uneasy about the thought of any further exposure of foreign climbers to the hazards of the full storm that was now enveloping the Pamirs, yet he recognized the soundness of our logic. There was no denying that Soviet personnel were stretched too thin. Too many things had happened, even the safety-conscious Soviets could not have predicted so many misfortunes.

Abalakov affirmed that he knew the British, French, and Americans would do nothing to embarrass or distort the situation. Still, what really could be done?—the "girls" were 12,000 feet above Base Camp.

Gippenreiter and Monastyrski, knowing as did Abalakov that the chances were very slim for the Russian women, felt there was a chance to render real assistance to those at Camp III and perhaps the Americans, Japanese, and Siberians on the Lipkin. They quietly urged the joint effort. Abalakov, for whom we had by now developed real affection in addition to respect, looked at us sternly and sympathetically and finally said in German, "Yes, we must, in the last analysis, try to do something."

Vitaly Abalakov staked his reputation and prestige on the enterprise of an all-women's traverse of Peak Lenin. There had been considerable resistance to Abalakov's progressiveness in certain circles of the Soviet Federation of Mountaineering. Although the general lot of women in the Soviet Union is touted by the authorities as a kind of co-equal existence in all walks of life, and clearly Soviet women in athletics have been a formidable force in international competition, there had been a reluctance in the area of mountaineering to allow female teams to operate on their own in the highest mountains.

We outlined our thoughts regarding the form we thought the rescue group ought to take: the English would be Tut Braithwaite, Guy Lee, Paul Nunn, and Doug Scott; the French would send Bernard Germain, Yves Morin, Benoit Renard, and Michel Revard; and the Americans would include John Evans, Jeff Lowe, John Roskelley, and Frank Sarnquist.

The three Soviet leaders agreed they should go up in the morning and join forces with Kostya, Boris, Oleg, and Valodya. They had already requested heli-copter assistance from Dushanbe and from Osh. There was no way to estimate when they could reach the Achik Tash. So far as the evacuation of Camp III was concerned, they agreed the Soviet coaches should be urged to descend, but that Peter Lev's concerns about avalanche hazard should be taken most seriously. In any event, the rescue group should divide to provide assistance to both the people on the Lipkin and those descending from Razdelny Pass.

The Soviets agreed to our assessments and recommendations, by now too overwhelmed by the staggering sequence of events to dispute, and apparently trusting our objectivity in a situation that involved a good many of our own teammates.

At 8:30 P.M. on the 6th, Shataeyeva came on the air again and the roar of the storm at various moments simply obliterated her transmission; the wind seemed to snatch her voice away from time to time, but the message was all too clear. Two more of the women, the youngest two, had died in the last 3 hours. One more of their tents had been shattered by the wind and five of them were in the tent without poles on a ledge they had scooped out of the steep ridge.

They were taking turns going outside of the collapsed tent and trying to dig into the hard, wind-blown snow of the ridge. The snow under the surface was granular and very loose and did not submit to the forming of a cave. It was like digging in a tub of dry, loose sand.

Elvira was clearly beside herself with grief, yet she somehow maintained an almost eerie composure, talking calmly about problems with the tents, no stoves, no water, etc., faltering only when she referred to her dead compan-ions. We remembered the lady interpreter's comment of just that morning—Elvira had seemed to have entered a dream.

It snowed another 6 inches at Base through the night of the 6th. By early morning of August 7 the temperature had dropped to around 22°F. The Achik Tash appeared as if in winter. Elvira came on the radio at about 8:00 A.M. She sounded very weak, very tired, and distinctly disoriented. She repeated herself as she tried to describe the night just passed. They were all very cold, they had eaten nothing for a day and a half, and they had little strength left.

Abalakov pressed her to determine whether they were still trying to descend to the Lipkin ridge. She hesitated, did not answer the question directly, but said almost fiercely, "Three more are sick; now there are only two of us who are functioning and we are getting weaker. We cannot, we would not leave our comrades after all they have done for us. We are Soviet women. We must stick together, whatever happens!"

Abalakov knew well what was taking place and that whoever remained of his "girls" had little time left before their strength to go down would be totally exhausted. He again tried alternate haranguing and gentle persuasion to get them to abandon their hopeless position on the ridge, but by that time the pattern of their agony seemed irreversible. In the spirit of group solidarity they were committed to stand by each "sick" teammate and, as they did so, one by one they began to die themselves.

As Abalakov kept the main transceiver open for instant communication with the women, we reached Jed Williamson and Peter Lev at Camp III with a Sony transmitter the Dutch team had brought. We apprised them of the overall situation involving the Soviet women and the lack of any communication from Jock Glidden's group. We stated that the weather forecast was for even worse weather for the next 2 days. We noted that Georg and Viktor had earlier reported that tents had been destroyed and that food and fuel supplies were crucially low. In the face of all this, we asked them how they felt about things. Through Jed, we gathered that Peter's position was that any party descending from Camp III under the current conditions was "in the most dire danger of becoming caught in an avalanche and if not buried, getting lost in the blizzard during the descent."

Jed seemed to lean toward descending and reported that several others felt the same way, and thus it was left that when they decided what they were going to do and if they decided to go down, they should call Base. In the meantime, on the chance that they might decide to descend immediately, a support party would leave Camp II that day to help guide them down. John Evans and the support group from Base should arrive at Camp I that evening. They would join Bruce Carson at I. Early in the morning, John and Bruce and anyone else who was available would leave for Camp II to back up Valodya. All the other rescuers would proceed toward the Lipkin ridge. In the meantime, Valodya would leave Camp II immediately and begin placing wand markers in the snow from Camp II upward toward III. The Russians instructed Valodya to proceed with whomever he could persuade to go in the direction of Razdelny Pass. It was urged that he try to communicate by radio with Georg and Viktor every hour and, failing that, by voice signals.

Elvira came back on the air at 10:00 A.M. The roar of the wind was almost constant as she transmitted, but several standing nearest the receiver thought they could hear one of the women weeping.

"We are holding on. We cannot dig in; we are too weak. We have had almost nothing to eat or drink for 2 days. The three girls are going rapidly. It is very sad here where it was once so beautiful."

Her voice broke and she sobbed for the briefest moment, then regained her composure and said in a tremendously weary but steady voice, "We will carry on and talk again soon. Over."

We all asked: How could they have survived so long? Thirty to 40 degrees below zero, consuming wind, no tents, no food. What keeps them going? Why do those smiling, happy, cheerful women have to die?

It snowed intermittently but hard through the morning at Base. The mess tent was crammed to overflowing with people from the many nationalities who made up the International Camp. We continued to wonder what could be happening to Steck, Glidden, and Wren. The real (perhaps the only) hope of the day lay in Evans and Valodya giving assistance to the large group retreating from Camp III.

Shataeyeva came on again at noon. One more had died. Four were dead. Two were dying. The condition of the last two we could only guess. The transmission was brief. Elvira almost seemed delirious, but she said, "We will go down, there is nothing left for us here. They are all gone now. The last asked, 'When will we see the flowers again?' The others earlier asked about the children. Now it is no use. We will go down."

The mountain was totally closed in by clouds and the great wind roared across the ridges high and low. At Base we could just see across the valley, nothing above. The wind was gusting to 40 miles an hour across the meadow and the temperature remained around 28 degrees. In zero visibility, with the possibility of descending to the right and over the huge east face or to the left and onto the not so precipitous, but avalanching north face, the dying Soviet women had run out of alternatives. It was only a matter of hours and, though no word was spoken, virtually every person in camp hoped they would be mercifully few.

There was no transmission at 2:00 P.M. from Elvira and we wondered if they were moving down or if the end had come. The receiver had been on continuously since 6:00 A.M., so the batteries were changed to ensure that there was no failure either in transmission or receiving.

The rescue group called in from Camp I and reported that Jeff Lowe, the Englishmen, and the French were going to try to go up with Kostya and Boris to the ice cave camp on the Lipkin. We briefed them on the status of the women and reminded them we were still concerned for the Siberians, Japanese, and Americans.

Roskelley had contracted diarrhea and would remain at Camp I with Frank Sarnquist. Frank would treat the sick as they came down off the mountain.

Evans was on his way to Camp II with Bruce Carson, who had joined the rescue group at Camp I. One of the Swiss named Hans had joined up as well. They were to support Valodya and assist the large group descending from Camp III.

The Japanese on the Lipkin had been in touch with their people at Base, but not with anyone else. They must have been transmitting on a different frequency than any of the other groups since their voices were not heard on the communications tent receiver. Nor did the Japanese at Base make known until somewhat later that their four men on the Lipkin had heard the transmission from the Russian women and, though they spoke no Russian, sensed something was wrong. When this was confirmed by the Japanese at Base, two of the four set out to try to rescue the women. The storm was so violent and visibility so limited, the wind chill factor so great and loss of location of their own camp so likely, that they were forced to turn back after getting only a short distance. Several times in the attempt they were blown off their feet. They were probably less than 1,500 yards from the women when they started.

The barriers of language and cultural differences in judgments of value and importance within those barriers added the final sense of confusion to the International Camp. The Russians may never have known about these transmissions, but they never revealed it if they did; nor did they suggest at any point a tie-in with the rescue effort being mounted from Base. Most likely in the great confusion of large numbers of people in apparent trouble, they didn't know. In the face of the frightful conditions, it is significant that the Japanese on the Lipkin even tried to reach the Soviet women.

Elvira came on the air at 3:30 P.M. She spoke incoherently and then seemed to have lost track of time and referred to the illness of two of the women who had already died. The sound of the storm had momentarily eased and someone beside her (Valentina?) was audibly weeping. Then Elvira began to sob, "They are all dead; what will happen to us? What will happen to the children? [The two women who had youngsters had already died.] It is not fair, we did everything right."

Abalakov sat at the transmitter cutting in, trying to console Shataeyeva, "Viretska, my dear, beautiful girl, you have been very brave, all of you. Please hold on, we are trying to reach you."

Elvira came back on calmer, but distinctly weaker than she was 3 hours earlier. "We are sorry, we have failed you. We tried so hard. Now we are so cold."

"Elvira, don't give up. Stay awake; try to move your limbs. Kostya and Boris and others are trying to reach you. Keep calling us on the radio. We will not leave the receiver." The sad, thin-faced lady interpreter did a brave job of keeping us informed of the conversation as, frequently on the edge of tears, she helped us understand that Abalakov was not cynically trying to raise the hopes of his doomed friends, but simply trying to make their deaths seem less forlorn. He felt that anything he could do to ease the anguish of their slow and certain dying was a merciful thing.

The transmission at 5:00 P.M. was garbled, but we sensed one more had died, leaving three still alive. The storm seemed to be continuing to build in intensity and for a brief moment we caught a glimpse of the clouds racing across Krylenko Pass. We estimated the wind velocity at 80 to 100 miles per hour.

Further below, Kostya and Oleg called in to report they could make no progress in the storm. They were worried about the large group of Siberians which was descending, but thought they were safely below the upper ridge line and thus somewhat protected from the most punishing winds. They said they would go up with the rescue team, whom they could now see below in breaks in the storm, in the morning.

At 6:00 P.M. we got the tremendously cheering report that the entire group from Camp III had made it down to Camp II and that some were continuing down to Camp I. It was thought that Heidi Ludi, Anya, and Sepp Schwankener had fairly serious frostbite and would need medical assistance if not helicopter evacuation from Camp I. Everyone else was apparently okay.

At 6:30 we heard several clicks of the transmitter key and then above the roar of the wind the very faint voice of Elvira, "Another has died. We cannot go through another night. I do not have the strength to hold down the transmitter button."

At this, the Russian lady interpreter burst into tears. People looked at one another in embarrassed silence. We saw Zina, the Russian camp dietician who had been so kind to all the Americans, across the meadow with tears streaming down her face.

At 8:30 the receiver registered a few of the clicks we heard earlier and then Elvira came on in a voice almost drained of passion. "Now we are two. And now we will all die. We are very sorry. We tried but we could not . . . Please forgive us. We love you. Goodbye."

The radio clicked off and everyone in that storm-lashed meadow knew the cheerful Soviet "girls" were gone forever. Everyone in the meadow wept unashamedly as the fact of finality was driven home by the utter silence of the radio and the unforgiving wind. The Soviet men and women wept the hardest and caused the rest of us to weep even more as they, several Russian generations removed from the Church, made the sign of the cross and with that almost forbidden gesture signified the end had come. And then there was only the wind.

⸱   ⸱   ⸱

As the crowd at Base gathered around the radio hearing the last transmission of Elvira, the rescue team of Doug Scott, Tut Braithwaite, Jeff Lowe, the two Soviet coaches, Boris and Kostya, and the four French climbers, Bernard, Yves, Benoit, and Michel, had arrived at Camp I below the Lipkin ridge.

The death of the Soviet women numbed everyone's awareness of the storm which continued to build until it reached its peak about 10:00 P.M. It was difficult to focus on the plight of Chris, Al, and Jock whom we knew were camped somewhere up there above 21,000 feet. I damned and double damned the Soviet Customs for having confiscated our radios. It was not inconceivable, in light of the fate of the Soviet women, that they, too, had perished in the storm. The recurring and reassuring thought was of the collective experience of the three climbers.

I went by Monastyrski's tent and we looked at each other for some time. He pulled out a bottle of brandy and we drank from mess cups in silence. He finally said, "We did everything possible, Robert—now this."

I returned at midnight to my tent, thinking we must inform Evans and the others on the first radio call in the morning that all the Soviet women had died and that we did not know anything about Jock's group. We wanted them to remain on the mountain until we knew something more. It was now quite cold in Base—perhaps 15°F. At the top of Lenin? It could easily have been –40°F. to –50°F.

I awakened around 2:00 A.M. The Soviet Army two-man mountain tent was stiff with ice. It was bitterly cold. I forced the frozen toggled flaps apart and I remembered the "girls," their tents, and their deaths. Up the valley it was sparklingly clear, the sky daylight bright with stars, the landscape totally plastered with the new snow, looking like winter, while the winds aloft continued to roar. The upper levels of the peaks were cloaked in blowing snow.

It was hard to think in positive terms of our friends' night on Lenin, for the storm had been so staggering in its force that our convictions about their well being were extremely shaky. I was afraid of what daylight might reveal and I took a Seconal to numb any further thought about anything.

The tent was showering down droplets of water on my sleeping bag as I woke at 8:15 A.M. A blinding sun now beat down. In the soggy mess of the Base Camp quadrangle, it was quickly apparent that though the sun was melting the snow on every surface it touched, it was still very cold. As I looked up at Lenin, the whole mountain was clear and the northeast ridge was characterized by snow plumes blowing high into the sky. Great billowing gusts of snow raced across the ridge from the northwest. I clocked the blowing clouds over a series of estimated distance segments and they checked out at 70, 80, and 85 miles per hour. It continued to be dangerous up there.

We reached John Evans at Camp I. He had gone to Camp II from Base and back down to I the night before. Everyone was safe from Camp III and many would reach Base before the day was over. Heidi Ludi had fairly serious frostbite of the hands and some in her feet, but her spirit was good considering what she had been through. Anya was okay, but with a small amount of frostbite, and Sepp Schwankener, who had been a great help to Peter Lev in the rescue effort, had some frostbite in his hands. Frank Sarnquist recommended sending a helicopter up to Camp I for the more seriously afflicted. He said they would stamp out a landing pad.

Evans reported that the Siberians were now coming down off the Lipkin and that they had seen the Americans in the afternoon of August 5. They seemed fine. Somehow there was a bit of hope in that, but the last 3 days of giant storm had to change the odds somewhat. The Siberians also seemed to be indicating something that did not square with Ronnie Richards's account of August 5; namely, that they felt the women were leaving for the summit on the 6th. They claimed to have seen them on the 5th. Perhaps in all the storm and confusion on the mountain the Siberians got their dates confused. Perhaps, too, the women left for the summit from their high camp later than anyone imagined.

By mid-morning the wind along the summit ridge of Lenin had begun to let up. We borrowed the powerful 850 x 15 glasses the Englishmen had brought along and began to grid the upper Lipkin and summit ridges in search of Jock and the Japanese. There was a strong possibility we wouldn't find anything. Working down the summit ridge there were a couple of dark spots in the snow that could have been rocks, or—the thought that they might have been bodies had an eerie unreality about it. Further down the ridge no sign. No tents visible on the Lipkin. Much further down and on a different ridge five climbers were descending, but they were too low and too far from the line of ascent to be our friends. They had to be the last of the Siberians.

At about 10:30 A.M., emerging from the shadow of the north face and diagonally left up a snow slope leading to the summit ridge, three figures moving together appeared. "There they are! They're okay!" There was a scramble for the glasses, first John Marts, then Molly [Higgins], and finally Pete who passed the glasses back, beaming with relief. In a few more minutes, four more climbers were to appear to the right of the three—also heading up for the summit ridge. They had to be the Japanese.

Shortly after we had spotted the two teams climbing toward the summit of Lenin, Abalakov came to our sector of the camp, smiled faintly as we told him the good news, and took the glasses for a personal look.

"Perhaps they will find the 'girls,' but it really doesn't matter—after all, they are finished, aren't they!" The rock-like old man wandered across the meadow to the memorial we had been building (with his considerable assistance) for Gary Ullin [who died earlier in an avalanche]. In a very short time the unique, solitary rock with its large cruciform cross of heavy stones originally erected in Gary's memory had become a tribute to fifteen dead climbers, nine of them women.

The two ropes proceeded in unison toward the summit pyramid and we wondered how much longer it would be before they stopped. It was not long. As we observed the seven climbers milling around in the saddle below the final summit ridge, there was great commotion at the communications tent. We arrived as Al's voice came through saying, "Bahza, this is Sasha Four. This is Allen Steck. We are transmitting on the Japanese radio. Something very strange, something very sad has happened here." They had arrived. Al's voice came slowly; they were above 23,000 feet and literally in the midst of a summit attempt and they had stumbled on a tragedy of which they had no forewarning. The Japanese did not speak enough English to give them any notion of what had befallen the Soviet women. "We have found one of the Russian women frozen. I suppose the rest are above, there are signs farther up the slope. We will communicate in a few minutes as we get higher up. Please stand by. Over."

We acknowledged Al's transmission with great relief and asked them to determine what they could about the death of the women, but above all to get down off the mountain safely. They had come upon Elvira's body stretched out as if sleeping, face up, in the small saddle below the summit on the north side. She appeared to be asleep. Her face was composed and peaceful. Chris Wren commented later that he recognized the striking face of Elvira and realized an unbelievable tragedy had occurred.

Steck was back on the transmitter in about a half hour; it was 12:30 P.M.

and he said in a now distinctly shocked voice, "We found two more, half buried in drifting snow and above them what appears to be three more ladies. Above us is another, apparently in a belay position with a rope leading down the slope. It is pretty grim. We will go on up to the top and see if we can locate the eighth."

Al asked us to put Eugene Gippenreiter on the radio. "Eugene, we are stunned by the magnitude of this tragedy . . . we share in your grief over the loss of the girls. Over and out." Al recalls that as they probed amongst the wreckage and the bodies, he wept and then climbed higher.

Glidden noted in his diary: "As we climbed higher we came across more stations of horror—one group of three huddled together—tent obviously swept away. Then the seventh and highest leaning over sleeping or tent material as if belaying the others below—we stepped over their belay rope."

They went on to the summit where they found no trace of the eighth woman. It was not until Elvira's husband, Vladimir, went up with a support team 7 days later that the eighth was found buried in the ruins of a tent under the four bodies previously discovered.

The two teams descended off Peak Lenin past the bodies of the women at about 2:30 P.M. to conclude one of the strangest and most tragic episodes in mountaineering history. They had too little energy in reserve to do anything about the bodies save place dowel wand markers around them. We at Base had strongly admonished them to get off the mountain as quickly and safely as possible.

Even as the dramatic events had been unfolding high on Lenin, members of the American team not involved in the rescue attempt were putting in many hours chiseling an inscription in the great rock commemorating Gary's loss, but which had become, as well, a memorial to all the fallen climbers of the summer of 1974.

The inscription said simply, "In memory of Jon Gary Ullin, who died in avalanche, on 19th Party Congress Peak, July 25, 1974. A graceful man." The cross, erected on top of the great rock by Abalakov and made with 75- to 100-pound flat rocks hauled up on the rock by several of us, had transformed the remote and beautiful meadow from a scenic sheep pasture into an international memorial.

Helicopters began arriving on Thursday afternoon, August 8. One was a sleek turboprop carrying the Assistant to the Minister of Sports. It never seems to take very long for inquests to get underway. Word quickly spread that an investigation was about to begin into the deaths of Gary Ullin, Eva Eissenschmidt, the Estonians, and (most important to the stunned Russians and Kirghiz) the Soviet women. Others would arrive the next day for the inquiry and there was rampant speculation amongst the international teams as to what the proceedings would yield.

Some thought Abalakov would be blamed for letting the women attempt the traverse of Lenin, especially in light of the opposition amongst the conservatives of the Mountaineering Federation. One sensed the Soviets might be caught on the horns of their own dilemma—either they were for equality of women in the eyes of the international climbing delegations or they were not. Others thought it was a *pro forma* procedure, necessary to establish a sense of Soviet solidarity in the face of the tragic series of events that had befallen the Pamirs camp.

The tribunal went on for a number of hours. As it turned out, Abalakov was vindicated because he had ordered the women to turn back at least a day before their ordeal began. The official gathering concluded that the Soviet women had been unavoidably overwhelmed by an unprecedented storm and that all the others died in circumstances over which they had no control.

The Soviet women died because of a combination of faulty judgment, inadequate equipment, and obvious bad luck. If they had not been warned of an impending storm of major proportions and had not been admonished to retreat or remain in a secure position, their decision to continue their traverse of Lenin (which in turn determined their decision to camp on the summit) would have been at least understandable.

They never revealed their reasons for moving up to the summit in the face of the storm. They could have been running low on rations and decided to make a run for it, rather than risk laying siege by waiting out a large storm with insufficient supplies. They may have reasoned that they would never get a second chance once the storm of the predicted magnitude struck.

Their decision to camp on the summit of Lenin, taken with the failure of the tents and the unprecedented storm, removed virtually any chance of escape.

The tents the Soviet women were using simply failed. We knew from our experience with tents of the same design at Base that they were not adequate for more than moderate winds, that the tent poles collapsed under modest snow loads, and that the closure system would not prevent blowing snow from seeping in and filling the interiors.

Once the tents failed the first night and some of the women began to die of hypothermia, they lost whatever chance they might have had to effect a successful retreat, for they would not leave any of their teammates behind so long as they were alive. Thus, struggling to survive in the storm, but losing strength hour by hour, they died one by one in the unrelenting wind and snow.

Psychological and physiological deterioration at high altitude is still imperfectly understood. It seems judgment is one of the most acutely affected cognitive processes, especially when combined with the stress to survive. Climbers have done strange things in such situations: gloves have been forgotten at the price of frostbite; oxygen valves have been left closed during periods of crucial need; climbing and logistical strategies have been ignored. Some of these forces may also have worked against the Soviet women in subtle ways.

Equally, the psychological force of their commitment to demonstrate that Soviet women were a strong and perhaps special breed (which no one ever doubted) had its ultimate effect on the situation. It robbed them of the flexibility that is so vital in making prudent decisions on high mountains. In a sense, once they had announced to the Scots on the summit, "We are strong. We are Soviet women. We will camp here and go down in the morning," they never really had a chance.

The Soviet women died climbing alpine-style on an extremely cold, very high peak under what had become siege conditions, insufficiently understood by them. They had all of the above factors working against them plus a storm of the greatest ferocity in the memory of the oldest Kirghiz.

When Elvira said, "We are sorry we have failed you," she and the others had really only failed in the understanding that humans are at best only privileged trespassers on high mountains. There is no real conquest beyond a kind of convergence of self and the mountain, and a realization that even on the most brilliantly planned and executed ascents luck is always a major factor. . . .

"LUCKY JOE"

FROM
The Price of Adventure:
Mountain Rescue Stories from Four Continents
BY HAMMISH MACINNES

SOME MIGHT THINK BRITISH CLIMBER JOE SIMPSON IS A DISASTER waiting to happen . . . he has been part of an unprecedented number of accidents in the mountains, yet survives to climb again. Is it luck, or some subtle application of skill that the observer, aghast at the circumstances, fails to see and properly credit?

In this selection, Scottish mountain rescue expert Hamish MacInnes recaps two hair-raising events in the life of "Lucky Joe" that took place in just two years. In the first, his life literally hangs by a thread on the Bonatti Pillar in the Alps. In the second, on Siula Grande in the Andes, he is once again hanging by a rope, but this time he's severely injured, and his partner is in trouble and has to cut the rope that joins them. The story of Joe's subsequent fall, near death and incredible, agonizing self-rescue electrified the world in his best-selling book *Touching the Void*.

MacInnes quotes both Simpson and his climbing partner in presenting this version of a story that leaves the reader amazed at the strength of human endurance. From *The Price of Adventure* by Hamish MacInnes, pages 17-33.

Joe Simpson fell the best part of 2000 feet in the Alps in an avalanche on the North-East Face of Les Courtes. "I didn't have any helmet on. Only my legs were buried when I finally came to rest, and apart from a cut head and bruising, I was otherwise unhurt. I was bloody stupid and I deserved to die."

Joe Simpson had already had one dramatic demonstration that someone somewhere was keeping half an eye on him when climbing the Bonatti Pillar in 1984, and in 1985 he was to survive an even more spectacular climbing accident on the other side of the world on the West Face of Siula Grande in the Peruvian Andes.

But first the Bonatti Pillar.

Joe and his climbing partner, Ian Whittaker, had virtually finished the climb and managed to get to a bivouac ledge in gathering darkness and swirling cloud. Probing the corners of their lair for the night with the aid of their headlamps, they saw that it was in fact a huge pedestal which formed the right wall of a high-angled corner they had just ascended. Above the pedestal there was no continuing corner, only a vertical smooth wall. There was no way up there, so they counted themselves lucky that they had come across this providential ledge when they did.

Joe found an old piton above the ledge, which he decided to use for a belay, but this wasn't much good for protecting Ian, who was farther along. Ian tied a belay rope to a rock flake which was close to him and passed the end to Joe who secured it to the peg. The rope now acted as a sort of handrail between the two of them. Joe also found an additional spike behind him and put a couple of slings over this to which he tied himself for added security, then he clipped on to the handrail and settled in for the night, the great void beneath them masked in the darkness. Joe had zizzed off when he heard Ian's voice.

"Do you think we're safe from rocks here? I was going to sleep without my helmet on."

"Safe as houses," Joe returned, for above them were great overhangs and any rocks falling would be well out from the face and their ledge. "But," he continued, hedging his bets, "I'll keep mine on just the same." In the light of his headlight Joe watched Ian take off his helmet and place it beside him, then clip himself on to the handrail in case he literally dozed off during the night.

As if on cue there was a frightening noise, a sort of groaning followed by a violent tug on both their safety ropes. They were falling, cocooned in their bivy bags. Then they jerked to a halt on their handrail rope, both hanging like socks on a clothesline. The old peg and the rock spike had fortuitously held. The ledge, now disintegrated, crashed 2000 vertical feet down the face to the couloir, then bounced another thousand feet to the glacier.

Presently in the anonymous darkness all was quiet. Joe wondered about his companion, he seemed to recall a cry. Had Ian plunged to his death? But Ian's reassuring Lancastrian accent floated out of the night. He was all right and needed a drink! He had a head injury and, hanging there, Joe examined his scalp by the light of his headlamp. It wasn't too serious. They were grateful to be alive. Had the ledge collapsed only five minutes before, when they weren't belayed, they would now be mutilated messes on the Dru Glacier.

Gradually they took stock of their position and found that they had lost all their gear, even their boots. Joe in fact still had one and he now disgust-edly tossed this useless item in the wake of the rock fall. Ian had even lost one of his socks and had to utilize a woollen climbing mitt in lieu.

With the beam of Joe's headlamp they saw that their climbing rope, their lifeline, was shredded by the fallen rocks and hung uselessly down the cor-ner below them. The two young men then examined their belays with some trepidation. They saw to their consternation that the spike which Joe had put the slings over as an added safety precaution had disappeared, though the carabiners were still clipped to his harness. The slings must have parted when the ledge went. Joe next examined the old ring peg to which they were attached at his end of the now V'd handrail. He observed that it had bent and then, pulling sideways on it to get a better look, he saw to his horror that it moved. On Ian's side the case was no better. The other handrail belay, the spike, had sheared off at the bottom with the ledge but somehow still held, even though they saw splinters of rock still falling out of the gap sur-rounding it.

The climbers were now in an unenviable position, unable to move, with a loose peg at one end of the rope and a shaky spike on the other. They had no gear left to help safeguard themselves and any violent movement could send them both crashing down the face. Even to climb up the rope would involve too much disturbance and anyhow they were still trapped in their bivy bags.

Joe and Ian hung on their line for twelve hours, frightening themselves when they had to move to overcome cramps. They were both forced together at the bottom of the V in the rope. It was like Russian roulette where any movement could trigger off the vibration which would dislodge the peg or loosen the flake further.

They shouted throughout the night and signaled with their headlamp to the Charpoua hut, for it was in line of sight from where they were. In the cold light of dawn the frightening drop they could now see below worked overtime on the imagination. Salvation came in the form of an Alouette III helicopter. Their distress signals had been seen. It eased its way toward the face until it hovered like a giant hummingbird not fifty feet away. The two climbers pointed at their stockinged feet, then held their arms up in a V to indicate that they required help. Possibly the understatement of the year. The pilot took all this in and after giving a thumbs up he swung down toward Chamonix.

Members of the Chamonix rescue team were dropped by helicopter on a ledge above the pair and set up a hand winch. Some time later a guide came down on the steel winch wire to evacuate them. After they were both taken up to the ledge, the Alouette came in and they were picked up on a helicopter winch and lifted up into the cabin.

Joe has since speculated on his rashness in throwing away his remaining boot, for he heard a few days later that a French climber had found a climbing boot in the couloir at the bottom of the Dru and it worried him to think that this may have been the other one of the pair.

⸕   ⸕   ⸕

The scene changes to the Peruvian Andes in 1985. Joe's companion is twenty-two-year-old Leicestershire-bred Simon Yates, now living in Sheffield. Their objective was one of the highest unclimbed mountain walls in Peru, the 6360-meter (17,447-foot) West Face of Siula Grande. They set up their Base Camp at 4500 meters at the top of the high Quelrada Sarapoquoucha, a superbly isolated place.

After one abortive attempt on the wall, driven back by bad weather, they set off again on Tuesday, June 4. They were now on their own, in a remote spot and on a serious climb, their only contact with the outside world being non-climbing Richard Hawkins, down at Base Camp.

They climbed to the high point of their first attempt and found the equipment they had cached in a snow hole. The snow hole itself had been destroyed in an avalanche and Simon and Joe were lucky to recover their gear. In view of the avalanche danger at this spot, they dug out a safer snow cave to the south, which was also closer to the face.

The route began up an avalanche cone which was fortunately consolidated. The climbing proper then started with a bang. It was unrelentingly steep and an icefield which they ascended was a constant 80°. They slanted to the right as they climbed and the angle eased to about 65–70°, then got through a rock band via a steep twenty-meter cascade pitch of ice.

Difficulty after difficulty presented itself, often with avalanche risk. To the right a 300-meter yellow rock wall dropped to the base of the icefield. Their problem was to get across this wall by a ramp, access to which was blocked by séracs. It was dark by the time they got to a very steep fall of ice at the foot of a secondary ramp line.

But there were no bivy sites, so Joe carried on up this. It started as overhanging honeycombed ice for about eight meters, and thereafter was hard ice leading up through a galaxy of large icicles. This pitch was vertical in places and exited in a frightening funnel pitch on to a snow gully. Simon came up then and led through. They were amazed to see on the left of the gully a twenty-meter-diameter "golf ball" of snow just stuck on to the face, apparently defying the force of gravity. Fate smiled on them now, for they found a huge natural cave inside.

In the morning the difficulties continued unrelenting. From the cave they traversed right and fought their way up another cascade of ice at a high angle. After a farther pitch, they at last managed to get on to the main ramp, their key to the higher part of the route.

The ramp was in fact an enormous hanging gully with fortifications at each end in the form of séracs and cornices. Getting there had been desperate and by the looks of things getting out at the other end would be equally exacting. Now they did a rope length to the right, followed by 250 meters up the left side of the gully. This wasn't so steep, between 50° and 60°, by far the easiest climbing so far.

They stopped to take stock of this next problem: the exit from the gully ramp. There was a broken rock wall on the left with a nasty icefall running down parallel with the gully. This looked just possible if they avoided some large icicles on its left, but the snow and ice looked like unstable nougat.

It was Simon who started up this pitch, thrutching up the rotten snow which was plastered at a high angle, but he had to give up after fifteen meters and abseiled from an icicle—not the most reassuring anchor. He next moved left on to the rock face in the hope that this would get him high enough to make a traverse into the gully beyond the ice. He managed to insert a Friend (a cam-type device which he used as a running belay) and was about three or four meters above it when both of his handholds came away and he peeled off the rock. It was his good Friend which possibly saved his life.

The two young men were now faced with the last option in this dicey trinity. They would have to climb the icicles direct. With care, Joe took the lead up the overhanging ice, and soon it eased to vertical, when he paused for an instant, hanging by the wrist loop of his ice axe. With his other hand he put in an ice peg called a Snarg. It was then a matter of smashing a mass of icicles to enable him to get over this crux. While engaged in this risky occupation he cut his chin. He made a rush to climb the remainder of the steep section which was strenuous and hard. Beyond lay an eighty-meter ice funnel which led to a ridge, a ridge both sharp and airy.

Simon came up and Joe then led on, traversing once more to the right, looking for a way through to the top. It was hair-raising stuff, the basic material for future nightmares. He was back on rock now, it was loose as well as being covered with crappy snow. Tantalizingly, he could see the summit cornices less than 300 meters from him, but en route were ghastly steep powder snow-flutings, like a plowed field, huge furrows tilted at a ridiculous angle. They found that once in a chosen channel it was almost impossible to change lanes. Just a hundred meters of this took all of five hours!

They felt like high-altitude navvies, forcing a trench up the trough in the flutings. Darkness overtook them and it was two tired, worried climbers who excavated a snow hole on the side of their chosen "flute." It had been a frustrating and dangerous section, possibly worse for the second man who could do nothing but sit on his insecure bucket seat excavated from the loose snow and be covered in a cascade of spindrift sent down by his partner, who struggled up to his armpits forging the deep trench.

They were forced to spend the night in their unstable snow hole, hoping that it wouldn't collapse beneath them: to go any higher that night would have been suicidal.

The next morning was June 7. They were poised for the push to the summit which was only 150 meters away, but despite starting just after first light they didn't top the summit cornice until 2:00 P.M., relieved to be off those horrible flutings.

They stayed on the top for half an hour, taking photographs. Then gathering clouds to the east told them that it was time to move. They studied their way down, by the North Ridge. As this route had been first climbed by a German party in 1936, Joe and Simon had assumed it would not present them with too many difficulties but, seeing it now, they knew better. It looked horrendous, sweeping away to bristling cornices overhanging the West Face.

They set off down but were soon enveloped in thick cloud.

Simon takes up the story:

> Shortly after starting the descent we were engulfed in cloud and snow, and lost contact with the ridge. At this point I became completely disoriented and was trying to lead Joe in totally the wrong direction. Fortunately Joe's argument to go the other way prevailed and after a lot of nasty traversing through flutings at the top of Siula Grande's East Face, we saw the ridge again through a break in the cloud. I led up toward it and when I was about thirty feet from the crest an ominous cracking sound filled my ears. This was instantly followed by a falling sensation and the thought that we were both going to die. After what seemed to be a very long time the falling stopped and I was left hanging upside down with an unnerving view of the West Face beneath me. It didn't take long to realize that I'd stepped through a huge cornice. I climbed back up and informed Joe that I'd found the ridge! The event only served to emphasize the dangerous and unstable nature of our chosen descent route.
>
> The ridge continued to be an assortment of snow mushrooms, steep flutings, and occasional crevasses. The stress involved in descending it was immense. The fear was suppressed slightly by the concentration required for this technical "down climbing" and it left me with an uneasy feeling. The day came to an end with about a third of the ridge behind us. The wildest bivouac on the route, a snow hole in a near vertical fluting, did little to relieve my uneasiness.

Joe was in the front now, leading down the ridge, and he describes what happened:

I had thought that the worst of the ridge had been completed but soon found that this was not the case. It became very tortuous with large powder cornices and steep knife-edged ridges. It was not possible to keep below the line of cornices owing to the fluted and unstable powder slopes on the east side.

We descended roped together fifty meters apart. The climbing was never technically hard but always extremely precarious and very tense. Toward eleven o'clock the worst was past and the ridge now formed large solid broad whalebacked cornices. Simon was out of sight as I contoured round the first large cornice and approached the second one. Beyond the ridge dropped to our West Face descent point.

I was surprised to find an ice cliff on the other side of the cornice. This was about fifteen feet high at the crest of the ridge and nearly forty feet high farther down the East Face. It wasn't possible to abseil, as the snow on top was unstable and the ridge too dangerous to attempt. I therefore began traversing the cliff edge looking for a weakness, an ice ramp or a crevasse, by which I hoped to get down the cliff.

Suddenly a large section of the edge broke away beneath me and I fell twenty feet on to the slope of the East Face, and then somersaulted down. I knew I had broken my leg in the severe impact as my crampons hit hard ice.

Simon knew that Joe had fallen by the tug on the rope and he was worried:

The reality of the predicament did not come home to me until I had done the precarious abseil to where Joe was. I got out some painkillers from my rucksack and gave them to him. His right leg was quite obviously broken. My immediate thoughts were that the situation was quite hopeless and that Joe was as good as dead. But eventually I realized that I would have to make some kind of effort to try and get him off the mountain.

I traversed back toward the ridge and saw that reasonably

*angled snow slopes led down to the Col Santa Rosa. Fortunately
Joe's accident had occurred on the last technical part of the ridge.
After returning to him, I then climbed up to free the abseil ropes
which had stuck. While I was doing this Joe managed to traverse
toward the ridge on his own.*

*Getting back up to the abseil point was for me the most fright-
ening part of the epic. It involved climbing the ice cliff at its
lowest point. This place, unfortunately, also happened to be on
the corniced edge of the ridge. Climbing the ice solo took a very
long time with terrifying views of Siula Grande's West Face
viewed through fracture lines in the cornice. When I reached
the anchor point I made sure the doubled rope would now run
freely and abseiled again. There was no trouble this time and
the rope pulled down easily. I then caught up with Joe who was
making slow and painful progress.*

*I'm not exactly sure whose idea it was, but a system for low-
ering Joe was devised. The two fifty-meter ropes were tied together. I sat in a seat-shaped platform dug out of the snow and
started lowering Joe through a Sticht plate, a friction device.
After fifty meters the knot which joined the two ropes together
reached the plate. Now Joe took his weight off the rope so that I
could swap the knot to the other side of the plate and lower
him a further fifty meters. I then down-climbed to him and as I
was doing his he cut a platform for me to belay from for the
next lower. While I was lowering, Joe would lie on his left side
to stop his broken right leg from being jarred. Even so it was
obviously very painful but I only stopped lowering him when
the pain was intense, because of the urgency of getting him off
the mountain.*

Joe recalls:

*Simon was very much in control and all I had to do was cope
with the pain and execute any maneuvers as safely as possible.*

We both began to feel optimistic about getting to the glacier and the sanctuary of a snow hole that night. We worked well as a team and made steady progress down the 650-meter face. Already Simon had lowered me 200 meters to the col.

By nightfall we reckoned we were only two and a half rope lengths from the glacier. On what should have been the second-last lower, disaster hit when I was lowered accidentally over an ice cliff. The situation suddenly changed from possible to hopeless. When the lowering ropes reached halfway point at the belay plate I was hanging free fifty feet above a huge crevasse!

Simon, who could not now see Joe, was also in a desperate situation:

After about fifty feet the rope came tight, and I knew Joe had gone over a steeper section. I carried on lowering until the knot in the rope came up and gave tugs on the rope to tell Joe to take his weight off the rope.

Joe did not respond. I carried on tugging at the rope and screaming for Joe to do something. As time went by my screaming became more desperate. I was getting very cold. My already frostbitten hands were getting worse, my legs were going numb and the snow seat was gradually collapsing.

Back to Joe:

This, I thought was the end. I was exhausted and very cold, and felt cheated, as if something was determined to finish me off, irrespective of what we tried to do to prevent it. I was giving up the ghost.

In darkness, with avalanches pouring off the cliff edge above, a strong biting wind and a temperature of −20°C, I felt too numbed to attempt anything. My efforts at prusiking failed as one of my frozen hands dropped a loop and I felt too shattered afterwards to do any more.

I distinctly remember thinking of Toni Kurtz who was left hanging on a rope from an overhang on the North Wall of the Eiger. He froze to death. I thought that at last I knew what he must have felt like. Approaching death wasn't as bad as the books led me to think. I tried and failed—tough shit! I was spinning from my waist harness, too weak to hold myself upright, and I could see in my mind's eye that horrific old black and white photograph of Kurtz's corpse on the rope with long icicles hanging from the points of his crampons. My legs were numb and I was grateful because I could feel no pain now. I wondered if Simon would die with me and if anyone would ever find us.

The longer I hung there, the more relaxed I felt about everything, even feeling quite calm about knowing I was going to die fairly soon. In a lazy sort of way it didn't really bother me, seemed to have nothing to do with Joe Simpson. It was just a fact of life—of death.

Simon must have had a terrible time on the slope above struggling to hold on to me and realizing his belay seat was collapsing beneath him and all the time being in the full force of the avalanches.

Simon's predicament was indeed desperate. He realized that if he didn't do something soon they would both perish.

I remembered Joe had given me his Swiss Army knife for cutting abseil slings. After getting the knife out of my rucksack I cut Joe's rope. It seemed a very rational thing to do and I did it very calmly.

On the end of the rope Joe must have known that what was about to occur was the only logical solution:

When I felt myself slip several inches I realized what was about to happen. I wondered whether he would be able to cut himself free in time. I looked down and knew I wouldn't survive a free fall into the crevasse.

I was looking up the rope when I suddenly felt myself hurtling down. I wasn't scared, more confused. I hit the snow roof of the crevasse very hard and twisted sideways as I broke through it, then accelerated down again. I couldn't see but felt all the snow roof cascading past. Farther down I hit a snow bridge in the crevasse on my side—very hard—and banged my knee, which made me cry out.

It took me a long time to recover and sit up. I think my left hip had been dislocated because when I moved it popped back in. I could only feel my knee at the time.

Simon had now to act quickly or he could freeze to death on the exposed face:

I immediately set about digging a snow hole as it was necessary to get into my sleeping bag as quickly as possible. Excavating the hole took a very long time. My mind was full of quite bizarre thoughts. At first they were speculative: what had happened to Joe? I knew we were nearly on the glacier and hoped Joe had not fallen on to the avalanche chute leading to this. I wondered if the fall had injured him further and if he could survive the night. Eventually I became convinced that my action was bound to have resulted in Joe's death. I got into my sleeping bag and felt terrible. My mind was working at an incredible rate, jumping from one subject to another. Occasionally I would smell the water in the surrounding snow and wish for a drink. Eventually I had a little sleep.

Joe, after his fall:

That Sunday night in the crevasse was the worst thing I've ever experienced in my life, for I suffer slightly from claustrophobia. The first thing I did was put an ice peg into the side wall of the crevasse and tie myself to it. Then I looked around with my torch. There seemed no way out but up. The roof I came through was about fifty feet above. It was impossible to climb up there but in desperation I tried four times before giving up.

I'm sure I went mad from about 11:00 P.M. to 3:00 A.M. and I was convinced that Simon thought me dead. I had no reason to presume this, I just felt it in my bones. It was a living nightmare, a turmoil of thoughts ricocheting within my head. I reckoned it could take me days to die in that crevasse. I've never felt so isolated and abandoned in my life. I seriously thought of untying and jumping down the hole to my left into the bowels of the ice, but I knew I wouldn't be able to do it. I just huddled up against the ice wall like a frightened child and cried, shouted, moaned, and generally felt very sorry for myself. I then tried to rationalize, thinking that we all have to die some time and that this was just my time, this was my way. I wondered how many others had died in a similar way and what they had done and how they had coped. It felt strange to think I was now just another one of those reports you see in Mountain Accident statistics. I had now an awful realization of what all those tales of climbers' deaths in the mountains really meant. I felt sad for all of them.

This went on and on, recurring thoughts, getting nowhere. I had deliberately not got into my pit—my sleeping bag or my bivy sack. At about 3:00 A.M. a wave of anger and resentment swept over me and I made a resolute effort to control myself. I decided, fuck it, I've got this far, why give up now? Maybe in the morning I'll see a way out. I never once believed that Simon would find me or get me out. It was as if I had banished him from my mind. When I did struggle into my sleeping bag it was with the greatest difficulty. The pain was intense but eventually I did get some disjointed sleep.

I awoke about 6:00 A.M. and at once started screaming, "Simon. . . . Simon." I felt dehydrated and it was difficult to *shout. But no sign of Simon, perhaps he too had fallen? He wouldn't be able to see me where I was and maybe my voice was too weak.*

Dawn for Simon wasn't a bed of roses either:

When I awoke it was still dark and I began to think about getting down to Base Camp. This made me very afraid. I was quite convinced that I would be killed as a form of retribution. When it got light I packed my rucksack and geared up, very slowly and meticulously as though it was a sort of peculiar last ceremony.

After getting out of the snow hole I saw the slope beneath ended in a cliff edge and below that the avalanche chute led down on to the glacier. I traversed rightward above the cliff toward a couloir that I could see would bring me down on to the glacier. Once in the couloir I had to abseil and as I went down the doubled rope I could see across to the ice cliff that I had lowered Joe over. At the bottom of it was a huge crevasse. Joe had obviously fallen into it. I shouted, "Joe, Joe," while abseiling, but I was totally convinced that he was dead, and didn't bother going over to the crevasse.

Walking back across the glacier was tiring due to the deep snow and my general condition. Only when I reached the moraine was I convinced of my own survival. I began thinking then of how to break the news to Richard at Base Camp. I realized that I could fabricate a less controversial story to tell him and later other people, but I dismissed this idea immediately, knowing that I was simply not capable of it.

Coming over the final moraine before Base Camp I met Richard on his way up to look for us. I told him Joe was dead and explained how it came about. In a very subdued mood we went back to base.

Joe in the bowels of the ice decided to get to grips with his situation:

Look around, I told myself, see what it's like. Is there a way out? Not up, impossible, not left, not right. Hang on. I can see a ledge. Is it a false bottom to the crevasse eighty feet down? There's light on it. Maybe there is an exit from down there, I rambled on. No. Can't go down deeper, don't want to go down. But what if that snow floor is just a thin cover? I'll never get back up to this ledge again.

I pulled the rope down from the blocks of snow in the roof above and saw the frayed end of nylon fibers. Seeing it sort of made my mind up for me, as if it confirmed the situation that I was in and forced me to face facts. If there was no escape down there then it would make no difference to me now. I was going to die if I stayed here so what difference would it make if I did so eighty feet lower? It was Hobson's choice but I still cringed from going down. It might mean a quick death if I fell and I wasn't as prepared for that as I had thought.

In the end I weighted the frayed end of the rope with carabiners and abseiled down. Once on this lower snow bridge or platform; I was delighted to find that the floor was reasonably solid though I didn't detach myself from the rope.

I could see holes going deep down on the outer side of the crevasse, so obviously it continued beneath what I was lying on. The floor must have been made by avalanches pouring in from above and they had formed a powder cone rising right up to the roof which began about twenty or thirty feet in front of me. At the top I could see a small circular hole, head width, with a column of gold sunlight angling in on to the back wall of the slot. Seeing this gave me the most incredible lift. All the time I was in the crevasse and especially then at its deepest point I had the most overwhelming sense of isolation and of being completely cut off and abandoned. It was the eeriest feeling, all light blue and shadowed, everything totally lifeless, like being in a crypt, where nothing living had ever been or would ever come again.

That shaft of sun however dispelled all this and gave me a link with the outside world, even though I had great doubts if I would be able to climb the slope, knowing how hard the climbing had been for me up above.

The angle was about 50° at the bottom, gradually steepening to 60° near the roof and in the region of twenty-five feet wide at the base and six feet broad at the top. I crawled over to it, still tied to the abseil rope fixed to the ice peg eighty feet above. It was very soft powder and after much faffing around I sorted out a system by which I could tackle it. I cut out then stamped down a small platform-step with another step just below it to the right, then I hefted my bad leg into this and with axes and armpits buried deeply above, executed a big hop to get my good leg on to the platform, then I lifted my injured leg up to it as well and started all over again.

The pitch was about 130 feet and when I got higher the abseil rope hung almost horizontal behind me. The steeper it got the more precarious and strenuous it became to step up. Several times near the top I very nearly fell off.

After six hours of this hell I popped my head out through the roof exit and saw before me all the world. My world. The feeling of exultation was quite indescribable. I couldn't believe that I had done it. I could see the glacier about 150 feet below me and the route back to camp. I was yelling and shouting like a mad thing, just shouting for no reason except perhaps relief. I wanted to cry but couldn't.

It was about 12:30 P.M. on a bright sunny day. When I reached the glacier, I knew that Simon had returned presuming me dead. I saw his tracks and started to crawl after them. The rest was just crawling. For another three days I clawed my way down, getting weaker each day. Despite being out of it a lot of the time, hallucinating on the glacier, talking to myself, shouting then shouting some more, I just kept going mechanically, detached, like an automaton. I was very methodical about it. I am surprised in retrospect how controlled I was, fixing stages to reach, not thinking beyond them, snow holing and bivouacking when I wanted to keep going on yet knew the weather would kill me if I did. I know that if I had been in that situation at eighteen, I would not have survived. There was a lot of experience in me that made me do the right thing at the right time.

By far the hardest thing was being alone, having no one to talk to or to encourage me. The great temptation was to just lie still and say sod it, I'm going to sleep for a while. It was so hard to fight on my own. This was especially so the two days on the boulder field when I fell a lot; I always seemed to be lying still, waiting for pain to subside.

I had continuous conversations with myself as if I were talking with another person. On the last day, June 11, I saw Simon's and Richard's footprints in the mud and was convinced that they were with me. There was an uncanny sense of someone else following along quietly. It felt very comforting. I was absolutely sure for about three hours that Richard was in front and Simon behind, out of sight because they didn't want me to be embarrassed by my condition, but encouraging me along. When I fell over and it hurt badly they didn't come to help. I thought it was because they wanted me to do this thing by myself and that seemed all right, really. I was just glad that they were there and someone knew I wasn't dead.

Suddenly the bubble burst and I knew they had never been there and that I was alone and dead as far as they were concerned. That came as quite a blow to me mentally.

Until halfway through the third day dehydration was very bad. I had had no water or food since Sunday night. It now was Tuesday and I felt terrible. I couldn't raise saliva and my tongue was swollen and dry. I had trouble breathing evenly, always being excessively out of breath. When I got to water I drank liters and liters. It tasted like nectar and at once I be-

gan to feel stronger and had less trouble breathing.

I knew having no food was bad but didn't miss it and I was very much aware that I was getting progressively weaker and slower. That last, usually ten-minute, walk to camp took me six and a half hours! I could just shuffle a bit and then lie back shattered. I've never felt so fucked in my life.

Simon and Richard were meanwhile packing up camp:

The night before we had arranged to leave, just as it was getting dark, I heard a distant cry that sounded like "Simon." I thought little of it as there had been a few locals about tending to their cattle. But Richard and I were awakened shortly after midnight by a clear call of "Simon, help me."

We shot out of our sleeping bags and dashed outside the tent. It was an eerie sight that greeted us. The night was misty with gently falling snow. Joe was slumped on a rock about fifty yards from the tent. He was in an appalling physical state. His face was incredibly thin, his eyes sunken, he was covered in mud, stank of fleas and urine, with a smell of acetone on his breath from starvation.

Joe said later:

I believe that was as far as I would have got. When Simon's and Richard's torches came bobbing across the snow everything seemed to drain out of me; all the fight which had kept me going evaporated. There was no longer a need to boost myself, now others would help. I felt myself just give up and pain came rushing in, the exhaustion, everything. I sometimes wonder if that wasn't the point at which I was most at risk, whether I could suddenly just have keeled over and died. I felt like death, and no doubt smelt like it as well.

At this point a helicopter would have been an answer to prayer, but this was not the Alps or Glencoe. It was one of the remoter corners of the High Andes, and evacuating Joe Simpson involved a tortuous haggling first with muleteers, then with police in the nearest town, followed by a truck ride to Lima with an obliviously drunken driver, before Joe was deposited in hospital three days later. He was not yet rid of the trauma of his ghastly experience and in hospital during pre-sedation had one more of those weird dreams he had suffered during the long nights and agonizing days after the accident.

Joe:

> *I was back in the crevasse again and a passage from Shakespeare's* Measure for Measure *came to mind where a condemned man contemplates execution. I had had to learn it about fifteen years before and hadn't seen or even thought about it since. It was a dream with words. When I woke up I wrote it on my plaster cast:*

Death is a fearful thing . . .
>> To die, and go we know not where;
> To lie in cold obstruction, and to rot;
>> This sensible warm motion to become
> A kneaded clod; and the delighted spirit
>> To bathe in fiery floods or to reside
> In thrilling region of thick-ribbed ice . . .

"THE FATAL ACCIDENT ON THE MATTERHORN"

BY EDWARD WHYMPER

FROM
Peaks, Passes and Glaciers: Selections from the Alpine Journal
EDITED BY WALT UNSWORTH

ONE OF THE MOST FAMOUS OF ALL MOUNTAIN ASCENTS WAS ALSO the scene of one of the worst of all mountaineering tragedies. The elegant, classic Matterhorn, at 14,688 feet crowning the Alps in an isolated position between Italy and Switzerland, is probably the best known mountain in the world next to Everest. Attractive in form, with four distinct faces and ridges meeting at a knife-edge summit ridge, the Matterhorn is everything a grand mountain should be. The first ascent of any such mountain, then, becomes a milestone in mountaineering history. The first ascent of this peak, however, was marked as well by an appalling disaster.

London-born Edward Whymper first visited the Alps with a commission to create wood engravings of Alpine scenes, and he returned again and again to make his mark on a number of the unclimbed peaks. Whymper made the first English ascent of Mont Pelvoux in 1861, and by 1865 had completed more than a dozen first or early ascents on other challenging peaks in the Alps. At this point he set his sights on the Matterhorn.

The ascent on July 14, 1865, via the Hornli Ridge, went quite well, and the party that included a number of well-known local guides reached the summit early in the afternoon. On the way down, however, catastrophe struck as there was a slip, a fall, a broken rope, and four men plunged to their deaths.

The press of the time was full of commentary and speculation on the disaster, and, finally, on August 7, Whymper responded to pressure and prepared a letter to the editor of *The Times* of London giving his version of the events. This selection comprises that letter as published in the newspaper, and republished in Walt Unsworth's book *Peaks, Passes and Glaciers*, pages 46-52.

S ir,—After the direct appeals which I have received from the President of the Alpine Club and from yourself to write an account of the accident on the Matterhorn, I feel it is impossible to remain silent any longer, and I therefore forward to you for publication a plain statement of the accident itself, and of the events that preceded and followed it.

"On Wednesday morning, the 12th of July, Lord Francis Douglas and myself crossed the Col Théodule to seek guides at Zermatt. After quitting the snow on the northern side we rounded the foot of the glacier, crossed the Furgge Glacier, and left my tent, ropes, and other matters in the little chapel at the Lac Noir. We then descended to Zermatt, engaged Peter Taugwalder, and gave him permission to choose another guide. In the course of the evening the Rev. Charles Hudson came into our hotel with a friend, Mr. Hadow, and they, in answer to some inquiries, announced their intention of starting to attack the Matterhorn on the following morning. Lord Francis Douglas agreed with me it was undesirable that two independent parties should be on the mountain at the same time, with the same object. Mr. Hudson was therefore invited to join us, and he accepted our proposal. Before admitting Mr. Hadow I took the precaution to inquire what he had done in the Alps, and, as well as I remember, Mr. Hudson's reply was, 'Mr. Hadow has done Mont Blanc in less time than most men.' He then mentioned several other excursions that were unknown to me, and added, in answer to a further question, 'I consider he is a sufficiently good man to go with us.' This was an excellent certificate, given us as it was by a first-rate mountaineer, and Mr. Hadow was admitted without any further question. We then went into the matter of guides. Michel Croz was with Messrs. Hadow and Hudson, and the latter thought if Peter Taugwalder went as well that there would not be occasion for anyone else. The question was referred to the men themselves, and they made no objection.

"We left Zermatt at 5:35 on Thursday morning, taking the two young Taugwalders as porters, by the desire of their father. They carried provisions amply sufficient for the whole party for three days, in case the ascent should prove more difficult than we anticipated. No rope was taken from Zermatt, because there was already more than enough in the chapel at Lac Noir. It has been repeatedly asked, 'Why was not the wire-rope taken which Mr. Hudson brought to Zermatt?' I do not know; it was not mentioned by Mr. Hudson, and at that time I had not even seen it. My rope alone was used during the expedition, and there was—first, about 200 ft. of Alpine Club rope; second, about 150 ft. of a kind I believe to be stronger than the first; third, more than 200 ft. of a lighter and weaker rope than the first, of a kind used by myself until the Club rope was produced.

"It was our intention on leaving Zermatt to attack the mountain seriously—

not, as it has been frequently stated, to explore or examine it—and we were provided with everything that long experience has shown to be necessary for the most difficult mountains. On the first day, however, we did not intend to ascend to any great height, but to stop when we found a good position for placing the tent. We mounted accordingly very leisurely, left the Lac Noir at 8:20, and passed along the ridge connecting the Hörnli with the actual peak, at the foot of which we arrived at 11:20, having frequently halted on the way. We then quitted the ridge, went to the left, and ascended by the north-eastern face of the mountain. Before 12 o'clock we had found a good position for the tent, at a height of 11,000 ft.; but Croz and the elder of Taugwalder's sons went on to look what was above, in order to save time on the following morning. The remainder constructed the platform on which the tent was to be placed, and by the time this was finished the two men returned, reported joyfully that as far as they had gone they had seen nothing but that which was good, and asserted positively that had we gone on with them on that day we could have ascended the mountain, and have returned to the tent with facility. We passed the remaining hours of daylight—some basking in the sunshine, some sketching or collecting, and when the sun went down (giving, as it departed, a glorious promise for the morrow) we returned to the tent to arrange for the night. Hudson made tea, myself coffee, and we then retired each one to his blanket bag; the Taugwalders, Lord Francis Douglas, and myself occupying the tent, the others remaining, by preference, outside. But long after dusk the cliffs above echoed with our laughter and with the songs of the guides, for we were happy that night in camp, and did not dream of calamity.

"We were astir long before daybreak on the morning of the 14th, and started directly it was possible to move, leaving the youngest of Taugwalder's sons behind. At 6:20 we had attained a height of 12,800 ft., and halted for half an hour, then continued the ascent without a break until 9:55, when we stopped for fifty minutes, at a height probably of about 14,000 ft. Thus far we had ascended by the north-eastern face of the mountain, and had *not* met with a single difficulty. For the greater part of the way there was, indeed, no occasion for the rope; and sometimes Hudson led, sometimes myself. We had now arrived at the foot of that part which from Zermatt seems perpendicular or overhanging, and we could no longer continue on the same side. By common consent, therefore, we ascended for some distance by the arête—that is by the ridge descending toward Zermatt—and then turned over to the right, or to the northwestern face. Before doing so we made a change in the order of ascent; Croz now went first, I followed, Hudson came third, Hadow and old Taugwalder were last. The change was made because the work became difficult for a time, and required caution. In some places there was but little to hold, and it was therefore desirable those should be in front who were least likely to slip. The general slope of the mountain at this part was less than forty degrees, and snow had consequently accumulated and filled up the irregularities of the rock face, leaving only occasional fragments projecting here and there. These were at times coated with a thin glaze of ice, from the snow above having melted and frozen again during the night. Still it was a place over which any fair mountaineer might pass in safety. We found, however, that Mr. Hadow was not accustomed to this kind of work, and required continual assistance; but no one suggested that he should stop, and he was taken to the top. It is only fair to say that the difficulty experienced by Mr. Hadow at this part arose, not from fatigue or lack of courage, but simply and entirely from want of experience. Mr. Hudson, who followed me, passed over this part, and, as far as I know, ascended the entire mountain without having the slightest assistance rendered to him on any occasion. Sometimes, after I had taken a hand from Croz or received a pull, I turned to give the same to Hudson; but he invariably declined, saying it was not necessary. This solitary difficult part was of no great extent, certainly not more than 300 ft. high, and after it was passed the angles became less and less as we approached the summit; at last the slope was so moderate that Croz and myself detached ourselves from the others and ran on to the top. We arrived at 1:40 P.M., the others about 10 minutes after us.

"I have been requested to describe particularly the state of the party on the summit. No one showed any signs of fatigue, neither did I hear anything to lead me to suppose that anyone was at all tired. I remember Croz laughing at me when I asked him the question. Indeed, less than ten hours had elapsed since our starting, and during that time we had halted for nearly two. The only remark which I heard suggestive of danger was made by Croz, but it was quite casual, and probably meant nothing. He said, after I had remarked that we had come up very slowly, "Yes; I would rather go down with you and another guide alone than with those who are going." As to ourselves, we were arranging what we should do that night on our return to Zermatt.

"We remained on the summit for one hour, and during the time Hudson and I consulted, as we had done all the day, as to the best and safest arrangement of the party. We agreed that it would be best for Croz to go first, as he was the most powerful, and Hadow second; Hudson, who was equal to a guide in sureness of foot, wished to be third; Lord F. Douglas was placed next, and old Taugwalder, the strongest of the remainder, behind him. I suggested to Hudson that we should attach a rope to the rocks on our arrival at the difficult bit, and hold it as we descended, as an additional protection. He approved the idea, but it was not definitely settled that it should be done. The party was being arranged in the above order while I was making a sketch of the summit, and they were waiting for me to be tied in my place, when some one remembered that we had not left our names in a bottle; they requested me to write them, and moved off while it was being done. A few minutes afterwards I tied myself to young Taugwalder and followed, catching them just as they were commencing the descent of the difficult part described above. The greatest care was being taken. Only one man was moving at a time; when he was firmly planted the next advanced, and so on. The average distance between each was probably 20 ft. They had not, however, attached the additional rope to rocks, and nothing was said about it. The suggestion was made entirely on account of Mr. Hadow, and I am not sure it even occurred to me again.

"I was, as I have explained, detached from the others, and following them; but after about a quarter of an hour Lord F. Douglas asked me to tie on to old Taugwalder, as he feared, he said, that if there was a slip Taugwalder would not be able to hold him. This was done hardly ten minutes before the accident, and undoubtedly saved Taugwalder's life.

"As far as I know, at the moment of the accident no one was actually moving. I cannot speak with certainty, neither can the Taugwalders, because the two leading men were partially hidden from our sight by an intervening mass of rock. Poor Croz had laid aside his axe, and in order to give Mr. Hadow greater security was absolutely taking hold of his legs and putting his feet, one by one, into their proper positions. From the movements of their shoulders it is my belief that Croz, having done as I have said, was in the act of turning round to go down a step or two himself; at this moment Mr. Hadow slipped, fell on him, and knocked him over. I heard one startled exclamation from Croz, then saw him and Mr. Hadow flying downward; in another moment Hudson was dragged from his steps, and Lord F. Douglas immediately after him. All this was the work of a moment; but immediately we heard Croz's exclamation Taugwalder and myself planted ourselves as firmly as the rocks would permit; *the rope was tight between us, and the shock came on us both as on one man.* We held; but the rope broke midway between Taugwalder and Lord F. Douglas. For two or three seconds we saw our unfortunate companions sliding downwards on their backs, and spreading out their hands endeavoring to save themselves; they then disappeared one by one, and fell from precipice to precipice on to the Matterhorn Glacier below, a distance of nearly 4,000 feet in height. From the moment the rope broke it was impossible to help them.

"For the space of half an hour we remained on the spot without moving a single step. The two men, paralyzed by terror, cried like infants, and trembled in such a manner as to threaten us with the fate of the others. Immediately we had descended to a safe place I asked for the rope that had broken, and to my surprise—indeed, to my horror—found that it was the weakest of the three ropes. As the first five men had been tied while I was sketching, I had not noticed the rope they employed, and now I could only conclude that they had seen fit to use this in preference to the others. It has been stated that the rope broke in consequence of its fraying over a rock: this is not the case; it broke in mid-air, and the end does not show any trace of previous injury.

"For more than two hours afterward I thought every moment that the next would be my last; for the Taugwalders, utterly unnerved, were not only incapable of giving assistance, but were in such a state that a slip might have been expected from one or the other at any moment. I do the younger man, moreover, no injustice when I say that immediately we got to the easy part of the descent he was able to laugh, smoke, and eat as if nothing had happened. There is no occasion to say more of the descent. I looked frequently, but in vain, for traces of my unfortunate companions, and we were in consequence surprised by the night when still at a height of about 13,000 feet. We arrived at Zermatt at 10:30 on Saturday morning.

"Immediately on my arrival I sent to the President of the Commune, and requested him to send as many men as possible to ascend heights whence the spot could be commanded where I knew the four must have fallen. A number went and returned after six hours, reporting they had seen them, but that they could not reach them that day. They proposed starting on Sunday evening, so as to reach the bodies at daybreak on Monday; but, unwilling to lose the slightest chance, the Rev. J. McCormick and myself resolved to start on Sunday morning. The guides of Zermatt, being threatened with excommunication if they did not attend the early mass, were unable to accompany us. To several, at least, I am sure this was a severe trial; for they assured me with tears that nothing but that which I have stated would have prevented them from going. The Rev. J. Robertson and Mr. J. Philpotts, of Rugby, however, not only lent us their guide, Franz Andermatten, but also accompanied us themselves. Mr. Puller lent us the brothers Lochmatter: F. Payot and J. Tairraz, of Chamonix, also volunteered. We started with these at 2 A.M. on Sunday, and followed the route we had taken on Thursday morning until we had passed the Hörnli, when we went down to the right of the ridge and mounted through the séracs of the Matterhorn Glacier. By 8:30 we had got on to the plateau at the top, and within sight of the corner in which we knew my companions must be. As we saw one weather-beaten man after another raise the telescope, turn deadly pale, and pass it on without a word to the next, we knew that all hope was gone. We approached; they had fallen below as they had fallen above—Croz a little in advance, Hadow near him, and Hudson some distance behind; but of Lord F. Douglas we could see nothing. To my astonishment, I saw that all of the three had been tied with the Club, or with the second and equally strong, rope, and consequently there was only one link—that between Taugwalder and Lord F. Douglas—in which the weaker rope had been used.

"The letters of the Rev. J. McCormick have already informed you respecting the subsequent proceedings. The orders from the Government of the Valais to bring the bodies down were so positive that four days after the events I have just related twenty-one guides accomplished that sad task. The thanks of all Englishmen are due to these brave men, for it was a work of no little difficulty and of great danger. Of the body of Lord F. Douglas they, too, saw nothing: it is probably arrested in the rocks above. No one can mourn his loss more deeply or more sincerely than myself. Although young, he was a most accomplished mountaineer, hardly ever required the slightest assistance, and did not make a single slip throughout the day. He had only a few days before we met made the ascent of the Gabelhorn—a summit considerably more difficult, I believe, to reach than the Matterhorn itself.

"I was detained in Zermatt until the 22nd of July, to await the inquiry instituted by the Government. I was examined first, and at the close I handed in to the Court a number of questions which I desired should be put to the elder Taugwalder; doing so because that which I had found out respecting the ropes was by no means satisfactory to me. The questions, I was told, were put and answered before I left Zermatt; but I was not allowed to be present at the inquiry, and the answers, although promised, have not yet reached me.

"This, Sir, is the end of this sad story. A single slip, or a single false step, has been the sole cause of this frightful calamity, and has brought about misery never to be forgotten. I have only one observation to offer upon it. If the rope had not broken you would not have received this letter, for we could not possibly have held the four men, falling as they did, all at the same time, and with a severe jerk. But, at the same time, it is my belief no accident would have happened had the rope between those who fell been as tight, or nearly as tight, as it was between Taugwalder and myself. The rope, when used properly, is a great safeguard; but whether on rocks, or whether on snow or glacier, if two men approach each other so that the rope falls in a loop, the whole party is involved in danger, for should one slip or fall he may acquire, before he is stopped, a momentum that may drag down one man after another and bring destruction on all; but if the rope is tight this is all but impossible.

"I am, Sir, your obedient servant,

"Edward Whymper

"Haslemere, Aug. 7"

"SOLO WINTER ASCENT: FADDEN, 1936"

FROM
The Challenge of Rainier
BY DEE MOLENAAR

THE LINE BETWEEN DETERMINATION AND OBSESSION IS A FINE ONE, and those who review mountain history can choose for themselves the appropriate term to apply to Delmar Fadden. A young man of considerable artistic and poetic talents, this Puget Sound resident had, from his childhood, shown a marked interest in mountaineering. Weekends with the Boy Scouts soon led to extended backpack excursions and finally to a month-long solo trek across the Olympic Mountains.

Friends were hardly surprised, then, when Fadden turned his sights on Mount Rainier, highest of the Cascade peaks. He was 22 and had already ventured high up on the peak, even summiting it solo, when he set off alone in late January 1936 for a winter climb of Rainier. Over the next two weeks, the nation waited anxiously as the news covered the extended search for Fadden, who had gone missing. What was hoped to be a rescue became instead the recovery of a body when Fadden was found, frozen, high up on the Emmons Glacier.

Noted climber, cartographer, and Rainier historian Dee Molenaar profiles Fadden and describes the search and recovery efforts in this selection, taken from his book *The Challenge of Rainier*, pages 247-253.

As a note of interest, a present-day relative of Fadden's, also named Delmar, himself became a mountain climber and even served as president of The Mountaineers, Seattle.

F ew mountain tragedies in the Pacific Northwest held the public attention so long as that which befell 22-year-old Delmar Fadden during his solitary winter climb in late January of 1936. The story took 2 weeks to unfold to its climax as nation-wide news coverage kept the public informed of events high on the icy slopes.

At 5 P.M. on January 20, 1936, Chief Ranger John M. Davis received a radio message from a winter seasonal employee, Larry Jensen, at the White River Entrance Station. Jensen reported a young man, Donald Fadden, had visited the station, saying his twin brother Delmar had not returned from a week of solitary skiing at Glacier Basin. Upon this word of a possible missing person, Davis directed District Ranger Oscar A. Sedergren and Ranger

Bill Butler to collect their gear for a trip to the basin. Also notified was White River District Ranger Charlie Browne, who was in Seattle on leave at the time.

Davis, Sedergren, and Butler left Longmire for White River early on January 21. There they met Donald Fadden, who said his brother had gone to Glacier Basin to ski, snowshoe, paint, and sketch, and that he might hike up to Steamboat Prow. He said Delmar had gone by the ranger station at 11 P.M. the week before in his solitary trek into the Park. With this information, and after a brief stop at the ranger station, Browne, Davis, Sedergren, and Butler continued on snowshoes to the White River Campground, which was reached at dark. From there they were able to maintain radio communication with Larry Jensen at the ranger station. They noted Fadden's tracks went past the patrol cabin without approaching it.

The next day, January 22, they continued on Fadden's tracks to Glacier Basin, noting where he had spent a night or two at an old mine cabin at Storbo Camp. Evidence of food and cooking suggested Fadden had left the cabin not later than January 19. The search party continued as far as the lower end of Inter Glacier, then returned to White River Campground. It was there they learned by radio from Jensen that Donald Fadden said his brother was carrying a supply of wands to mark the route up the mountain and might have gone for the summit.

Early on the morning of January 23 the group ascended to Steamboat Prow, finding two wands in the snow a little way above. It was bitter cold and they retreated, searching down the north edge of the Emmons Glacier to about 4800 feet before crossing over the ridge to Glacier Basin and returning to the White River Campground long after dark. Radio contact with Longmire advised them another search party was enroute from Seattle, all men experienced on Rainier.

On January 24 Jack Hossack and Bob Buschman, a close climbing friend of Fadden, headed for Summerland to check the shelter for signs of the missing man; Ome Daiber and Joe Halwax set out for the White River Campground; Sedergren, Butler, and Browne climbed to Yakima Park. Browne remained at Yakima Park to observe the summit area with the powerful telescope mounted there, while the next day Butler and Sedergren hiked to Mystic Lake to check the shelter cabin. Hossack and Buschman found no signs of Fadden at Summerland, so proceeded up the mountain to Steamboat Prow by way of the lower Emmons Glacier. The journey was a long one and they spent a night on the glacier before meeting Daiber and Halwax at the Prow next morning.

On January 26 Butler and Sedergren returned from Mystic Lake, while Daiber, Buschman, Hossack, and Halwax climbed above Steamboat Prow. They found two more wands, then two snowshoes, separated. At 11,000 feet they began searching crevasses but an approaching storm drove them back to Glacier Basin. Next day all returned to Seattle except Butler, Davis, Browne, and Sedergren, who remained at the entrance station to await further word following a proposed flight over the mountain by Daiber.

On January 29, from a small plane piloted by Elliott Merrill, Ome Daiber and photographer Charles Laidlow spotted the body of Delmar Fadden lying on the upper slope of the Emmons Glacier at about 3,000 feet. The long search was over—now a difficult evacuation remained.

A large party including packers and climbers gathered the next day, and with long delays enroute, arrived at Glacier Basin about midnight. After a short rest the group headed up the mountain at 5:30 A.M. Skis took them a couple of miles, then hard snow necessitated the donning of crampons for the ascent to Steamboat Prow. At the Prow a recovery party was roped as follows: Daiber-Davis-Gilbreath; Butler-Buschman. The glacier surface was windpacked and easy traveling, but when the sun went behind the mountain the temperature dropped rapidly to 0°F and below. The body was reached by Daiber, Buschman, and Gilbreath (Davis had tired and re-roped with Butler) at 3:10 P.M.; Butler and Davis arrived a few minutes later.

Fadden was found face down, head downslope, solidly frozen. The crampon on his left foot was missing; his other crampon was partly off the toe of his soft-soled muckluck boot (an Eskimo boot coming above the knee). His hands were bare, he had no axe, his mouth and nostrils were filled with snow. It was apparent he had suffered a fall, been knocked out, then froze to death without regaining consciousness.

The body was lashed into a canvas tarp and lowered by the five weary, cold men down the steep glacier. Great difficulty was encountered owing to the awkward weight, roughness of the surface, and very cold temperatures. The body was continually anchored during the descent to prevent it from slipping loose. A little moonlight helped after dark and the Prow was reached at 7:15 P.M. The body was left there for the night as the tired party returned to Glacier Basin, all badly frostbitten, Gilbreath so much so he continued hiking out even though near exhaustion. Wendell Trosper, who had come up to the Prow with Harland Eastwood to assist the evacuation, was also severely frost-bitten and accompanied Gilbreath back to Seattle for treatment. Several well-known Northwest climbers and skiers played significant roles in the perilous midwinter evacuation of Fadden's remains from high on the mountain. Among those bringing the body down from Steamboat Prow to the White River Ranger Station were Harland Eastwood, a powerful, one-armed mountaineer who served as patrol ranger at the White River Campground during the early 1930s, and Ken Syverson, who ran the ski school at Paradise in those days. Along with The Mountaineers' Amos Hand, from Tacoma, and the Park Service's Art Collins, Charles Drysdale, Don Loehrke, and Dan Pryde, they worked in temperatures reported by Wendell Trosper as "pushing the mercury to the bottom" of a thermometer that recorded to minus 25°F. (57 degrees below freezing).

On February 1 a support party returned to the Prow for the body, which was carried down on a toboggan. The following day marked the end of the long ordeal as Fadden's still solidly frozen remains were placed in a hearse waiting at the White River Ranger Station.

As an aftermath to the tragic affair, a roll of film found in Fadden's pocket was developed. It showed views across the summit crater and verified the belief he had made the top and met his death on the descent. The cloud and lighting conditions in the photos were compared with weather records of the previous 2 weeks and indicated he probably had reached the summit January 17. The summer after Fadden's death, Arnie Campbell and Jim Borrow followed the youth's trail markers to the summit and located his camp in the crater. According to Campbell (written communication, January 1969), the number of empty cans lying about gave evidence Fadden had spent several days on the summit.

Ranger Butler's part in the heroic search and evacuation operations was recognized by his being given permanent appointment as Park ranger by President Roosevelt. Several efforts were made by public-spirited citizens to reward those taking part in the lengthy search operation, but when one prominent businessman attempted to capitalize on the project the climbers withdrew from further participation.

In retrospect we might ask: what manner of man was Delmar Fadden? What sort of person would venture alone to the summit of Rainier in the middle of winter? With these queries in mind after perusing Park records of the climb decades later, in 1969 I had the pleasure of a visit with Fadden's sister, Mrs. George Gilbert, and his older brother Gene; Delmar's twin brother Don was in Alaska at the time. I was provided full access to Delmar's photo albums and scrapbooks of the 1930s and gained an insight into the young man's character and aspirations.

From his early childhood in the Seahurst area of southwestern King County, Delmar displayed an unusually energetic interest in outdoor activities of all kinds, but particularly in mountaineering. He was a talented artist and writer and very popular at Highline High School. As a Boy Scout he had worked his way to Eagle rank. In 1930 and 1931, in company with two companions on each occasion, he made his first extended climbing trips into the Olympic Mountains. The notations in his photo album give itemized lists of food, equipment, and clothing used on each trip. The following summer, from July 31 to August 29, Fadden made a highly publicized solo trek across the Olympic Mountains.

Stating that he was going unarmed—"to see things, not shoot things"— Fadden started his hike from Lake Quinault under a 56-pound pack which held all he considered necessary, including a few fishhooks, and a camera "to get close-ups of a cougar and Mount Olympus in the moonlight." To spice the adventure, after his parents had driven to the lake and departed, Fadden deliberately destroyed his compass and a few days later burned his map ("I'm free! Whoopee!") He then crossed several passes and climbed a few peaks, including Mounts Tom and Olympus, the latter ascent timed for a night on the summit during full moon. At the end of the 30-day trip the youth arrived at the mouth of Big Quilcene River on Hood Canal, barely recognizable to his parents after losing 30 of his normal 160 pounds. To augment his food supply Fadden had stoned several grouse and during the final days he had survived on plant bulbs, frogs, and polliwogs. The journey had its rough moments of near-starvation and of rain and lightning storms, but Fadden's poetic bent was undismayed:

> It isn't raining rain to me,
>> No pretty daffodils.
> It's just raining misery
>> With pains and aches and chills.

Fadden first responded to the challenge of Rainier in 1931 when he hiked to Steamboat Prow from Sunrise via Burroughs Mountain. The following year on October 7–8 Fadden and a friend, Bert Kattron, repeated the climb to the Prow, where Kattron remained while Fadden continued alone to about 12,000 feet on the heavily crevassed glacier of early autumn. He turned back owing to lateness of the hour, but his photo album clearly shows the icy conditions; he made several explorations into shallow crevasses. A week later, following the first heavy snowfall of the season, Fadden returned to the route with Bob Buschman. Wintry conditions, and the fresh snow covering the crevasses that had been so widely exposed the previous week, stopped the two at the Prow. Near there they spent the night huddled in one sleeping bag at the bottom of a crevasse. Fadden's album notations read: "Slept at the bottom of this crevice—cold! Shoes froze (not oiled), took ½ hr. to get them on—had to warm them in bed; gloves like bent wire or steel clamped on ice pick just where I left them last night. 2 slept in one sleeping bag—broke side—wet, freezing, snow—What a night; can of half frozen beans for supper." Fadden's desire for exploration was not dampened, however. He added: "Bob tied rope to me and lowered me further down in to another ice cave where I snapped this picture. Only little light. Notice snow mound which sifted in from hole above."

Fadden came back to the mountain with Buschman December 26–27, 1932, this time via the south side. They climbed to Anvil Rock but were again rebuffed by bad weather. The following year, on September 1–2, 1933, Fadden finally realized his goal—a solo ascent to the summit via the Emmons Glacier. Because his film of the climb turned out blank, he returned the next weekend. Leaving Sunrise at midnight, he climbed to the Prow in 4 hours by way of Burroughs Mountain and Inter Glacier and reached Columbia Crest at 10 A.M., exactly 10 hours from the parking lot. After 2 hours on the summit, during which he took a photo of himself by means of a cord attached to the camera, he started down. He reached Sunrise at 6 P.M., completing an impressive, though unpublicized, 18-hour round trip of this very long route.

Though the weather was good on the summit, Fadden included notations in his album that describe the descent of the Emmons Glacier in fog:

> *Clouds obscure crevasses such as this one until immediately upon it. Fortunately I was following my footsteps—But to come upon such a scene further up the mt. is most confusing. You don't know which way to follow it. And as I found I chose the wrong direction back on the mt. and came near coming down the Emmons Glac. (too far to south). Bad business—traveling in fog. I got lost on Burroughs Mtn. and wandered around for 2½ hours.*

In 1934 Fadden began his efforts to attain Rainier's summit in winter:

> *It has long been my determination to scale the mount & when I could get no one to try with me, I willingly went alone. Although unsuccessful because of weather, I am all the more confident of Future success . . . Dec. 27, hiked to Prow alone, deep snow, wearying trip, broke snowshoes, 60 lb. pack, slept in snow, very cold. Began hike 10 PM, planned to reach Starbo at dawn, but deep snow prevented this . . . it seemed hopeless to continue; yet to turn back before I had actually begun was ugly to me . . . Reached Starbo on 3rd day after dark. Cleared up, continued to Prow for night there. Returned next day.*

Delmar Fadden's life was cut short at its prime, but his soul doubtless would have had it no other way. Many lines in his scrapbook reveal his deep passion for the quiet beauty of dark forests, starry skies, winter storms, and icy heights. Perhaps he anticipated his manner of passing:

> *If a dream*
>> *Meant anything to me*
> *Would it seem*
>> *A bold reality?*

> *If I knew*
>> *My hand of fate,*
> *Would I do—Or hesitate?*

FROM

MINUS 148°: THE WINTER ASCENT OF MT. McKINLEY

BY ART DAVIDSON

AT 20,320 FEET, ALASKA'S MOUNT MCKINLEY, OR DENALI, HAS A greater vertical rise than any other peak on the planet. Its icy slopes and ridges are swept regularly by some of the foulest weather anywhere. It was to this inhospitable place that a group of young climbers tried to make the first winter ascent in January 1967. Tragedy struck them on the second day out when one of their strongest members, Jacques "Farine" Batkin, died in a crevasse fall.

Shaken and grieving, the remaining seven climbers considered abandoning the expedition but struggled through more falls and bad weather. The party did put three men on the summit on their second attempt while their four companions—leader Gregg Blomberg, Shiro Nishimae, John Edwards, and George Von Wichman—waited in a snow cave 3,000 feet below. Descending in the dark and sorely needing rest, the three who had summited—Dave Johnston, Ray "Pirate" Genet, and Art Davidson—decided to bivouac at 18,200-foot Denali Pass. They woke to 100-mph winds that sent the windchill plummeting to 148 below. What was intended to be a short respite turned into an epic six-day battle with death that came within a hairsbreadth of disaster. The expedition was split between Denali Pass and the 17,000-foot snow cave where the others were waiting. With no means of communication, each group had no way of know what was happening to the other.

Davidson keeps the reader enthralled as he writes of the unrelenting cold, frostbite injuries, and rapidly diminishing food, as the three summiters lie crammed into a tiny ice cave, listening to the unrelenting wind and, day by day, growing weaker. Diary entries by Greg, John, and George record their feelings about the ordeal as they come to accept that Art, Dave, and Pirate have perished. That they finally escape what so easily could have been their tomb still seems nearly impossible.

This selection is abridged from pages 143-200 of Davidson's book *Minus 148°: The Winter Ascent of Mt. McKinley.*

DENALI PASS: ART, DAVE, PIRATE

The wind woke us. The wildly whipping parachute billowed and snapped with reports like those of a bullwhip or rifle. The wind blasted against the rocks we were nestled among with a deafening eruption of noise; crosscurrents in the storm fluctuated its pitch to a groan or a prolonged whine. A dull, aching pressure along my backside was the cold, pressed into me by the wind.

I twisted in my sleeping bag to grope for the loose section of parachute thrashing me from behind. The moment I caught it my hands were pierced with cold; groggy with sleep, I'd forgotten that the nylon, like everything else outside our sleeping bags, was about –40°. The cold sank into my fingers while the parachute, jerking and cracking erratically, resisted my attempts to anchor it. As soon as I managed to gather the slack material under me, the weight of my body holding it down, I shot one hand under an armpit and the other into my crotch for warmth. I was out of breath from the effort.

Drawn tighter, the parachute made less noise, and I was able to relax for a few moments. My fingers, aching inside from being deeply chilled, began to gradually rewarm with strong tingling sensations. I pressed the length of my body against Dave to be warmer on that side, and I felt Dave shift inside his bag, trying to press against me. I snuggled close to him and lay quietly for a long time, hoping I'd fall asleep again, as if not thinking about the wind and cold would make them disappear.

I couldn't sleep, and the wind only grew more vicious. I tried to ignore the cold along my backside, away from Dave, but when the first shiver ran through my body I turned to check the sleeping bag where it touched my back. To my horror it was no thicker than its shell, two pieces of nylon. The wind had pushed the down away. I could hardly believe it possible that the parachute, designed to resist wind, was letting the wind eat through it and into my sleeping bag.

The parachute began cracking again. "Oh, hell," I mumbled. The cracking meant a portion of the parachute had broken loose again. Feeling I didn't have the strength for another attempt at anchoring it, I curled up in my bag, shivering occasionally, waiting for something to happen; I didn't know what.

After what seemed like several minutes but was probably only a matter of seconds, I heard Pirate trying to tie down the parachute.

"Art." Pirate's voice sounded far off and unfamiliar. "Help me hold it."

Hearing his voice made me realize that the three of us had been awake for more than an hour before anyone had spoken. Burrowed into my sleeping bag, I didn't want to budge from its security, false as it was, for even a moment. While I was deciding whether to help Pirate or prolong my rest, I felt Dave get to his hands and knees and begin wrestling with the parachute, which was now pounding his head and back as it billowed and cracked back in rapid succession. Yanking and cursing, Dave managed to pull part of it around him again, only to have it whip off as soon as he settled down into his bag.

"Look, we gotta get outta here!" Dave yelled.

"Where? We'd never make it down!" I said, grabbing onto the piece of parachute that Pirate was clinging to. "Maybe it's a morning wind that'll die down."

"Morning wind?'" Dave looked at me with disbelief. "It's a bloody hurricane, you fool! I'm checking the other side of the rocks."

"Awwghaaaaa. . . ." Pirate growled, staring up into the wind.

Instead of getting completely out of his bag, Dave tied the drawstring at the top tight around his middle. With his legs still in the sleeping bag and his arms free, he lurched toward the crest ten feet away. I was horribly apprehensive. If he lost his grip on the rocks he could easily be blown off the mountain. On the other side we'd never hear him again if he called for help. How far was he going? Maybe he'd be hidden behind a rock where we wouldn't be able to find him if we needed his strength. Besides the logic of my fear, I recoiled emotionally against Dave's leaving because it seemed to break our trust; it violated a fundamental law of survival—stay together.

"Dave," I cried. "Wait! I think it's safer here."

"Stay if you want!" he hollered back. "This wind's bad, and I'm gettin' out of it!"

"Where are you going?" Dave didn't hear me. "It's exposed over there!" He had disappeared over the crest.

Since my mittens were too bulky to grip the parachute, I pulled thick wool socks onto my hands; my fingers were nearly numb already. I was astonished as I looked up to see Pirate holding the parachute with his bare hands. Just as I yelled at him to get something over them, one of my socks started to slip off. Pulling it back on, I shifted position, and the wind seized the wind parka I had been sitting on. Inside its main pocket was the tape recorder I had been using for the physiological testing, but at that moment I was much more concerned about the loss of the half dozen cookies I'd stashed in the pocket. One moment the parka had been next to me, then I saw it whirling through the air, fifty, a hundred feet up, sailing in the direction of McKinley's summit.

With Dave gone, his loose end of the parachute caught the wind, and this threatened to rip the entire piece of nylon from our grip. We gave up trying to wrap the parachute around us; the pull on our arms wrenched our whole bodies as we clung to it to keep it from escaping. The parachute was our only shelter.

"My hands are bad!" Pirate's voice was weak, almost a whimper. His face was drawn up into a hideous, painful grin. Ice caked his beard.

"Bring them in!" I yelled, though his head was only inches from mine. His fingers felt like chunks of ice against my stomach.

"They're stiff!"

"Move them!" I reached for a better grip on the parachute. It slipped. I lunged. Pirate caught it as it whipped past him. He winced in pain.

"Aw, the hell with it!" Pirate sighed. As he let loose, the parachute twisted through the air. It snagged on a rock. I saw it starting to rip, then it was gone.

For the first time I noticed the sky. It was a blue wall, smashing into the mountain. Thin pieces of cloud shredding—everything grew blurred. My eyes were watering and stinging from squinting into the wind. Compared to anything I had ever experienced, this wind was like another element. It was as if gravity had shifted and, instead of holding us down, was pulling us across the landscape.

Pirate began digging his hands in under my parka. The top of my bag had fallen open to the wind. As I pulled it shut, I fell against Pirate. We grabbed each other.

"Hold onto me!"

"Art, let's get into one bag."

"How? There's no room. . . . Give me your hands." I felt his icy fingers grabbing the skin around my middle. My bag had opened again, and to keep the wind from getting to me Pirate pushed himself over the opening. I just leaned against him, trying to catch my breath. Shivering, teeth chattering, my whole body was shaking with cold.

"Pirate, it's no good!" Wind was coming into my bag. We were both losing our warmth. "Each in his own bag . . . it's better."

"I can't feel my fingers!"

"Put 'em between your legs!"

"I don't want to lose my hands!"

I remembered Dave. If it was less windy on the other side of the rocks, he would have come back to tell us. If it was just as windy, I thought he would have returned to be with us. Something must have happened to him. But maybe he had found a sheltered corner. How could he abandon us?

"Pirate, let's try the other side!"

"Naw . . . the wind's everywhere!"

We huddled together, hunched upright in our sleeping bags, wedged tightly between two rocks. Whenever we relaxed the wind caught us, started us sliding along the ice which gradually sloped away, and forced us to push and fight our way back up into the rocks. Leaning against Pirate didn't make me any warmer, but it was comforting—I wasn't alone. We didn't talk. I could breath more easily with my head inside my bag. I wondered what the others [Shiro Nishimae, Gregg Blomberg, John Edwards, and George Wichman] were doing down in the cave. Shiro's cough, Gregg's foot, John's swollen ear—it was too frightening to think about.

Beneath me I felt the ice sliding. Slipping onto my side, I brought an arm out in time to grab Pirate's knee. I pulled myself back against the rocks. My arms trembled from exhaustion. Pirate stared blankly out of his bag. His head turned slowly toward me with a groggy nodding motion. Was he slipping into a stupor? I wondered whether I looked as awful.

"It's no use here," I sighed.

I could barely keep myself up against the rocks. There was nothing I could do for Pirate. Maybe Dave had found a safe spot. I had to check the other side of the rocks, but that would be deserting Pirate. Yet there was no way I could help. How could I just leave him? I had to do something for myself!

"I'm going over." He didn't move. "Pirate," I yelled, "I'm going after Dave!"

His head shook from side to side as he half mumbled, half shouted, something I couldn't understand. I grabbed at the rock above me and pulled myself up the slope. Another rock; its sharp cold cut through the wool socks. Another pull. I reached the crest. To my tremendous relief I saw Dave crouched on the ice only about fifteen feet away. His back was toward me.

"Dave!" He couldn't hear me. I worked a little closer to him. The wind threatened to throw me off the crest. Beyond lay bare glacier where I'd never catch anything to hold onto if I was blown from the rocks.

"Dave!" This time he turned and saw me. I was out of breath and must have been gasping as much as yelling. "Is it better where you are?"

"What? . . . It's the same. Go back!"

I didn't want to go back, and waiting here on the crest was impossible because it was completely exposed to the wind. Before I'd decided which way to go, a crosscurrent gust caught me. I grabbed for rocks. One came loose. I caught another one nearer Dave. Somehow the sock on my left hand had blown off. I shoved the bare hand into my sleeping bag. The other hand held onto a rock. The wind flung and tossed my body as though it were weightless.

My right hand ached with cold front gripping the rock, and my forearm began cramping from the strain. I couldn't go back into the wind, but neither could my right hand cling to the rock much longer. The only other rock I could reach was three feet to my left, near Dave. My numb right hand had become so dead that I couldn't feel the rock it held onto. My shivering body seemed on the verge of going into convulsions.

I tried to think. If I lost my grip, I'd be blown across the ice. My mind was racing. I had to grab for the rock near Dave with my left hand: it was bare, no mitten or sock. It would be frozen. I had to. Suddenly, my bare hand shot out to grab the rock. Slicing cold.

I saw Dave's face, the end of his nose raw, frostbitten. His mouth, distorted into an agonized mixture of compassion and anger, swore at me to get a glove on. I looked at my hand. It was white, frozen absolutely white.

I pulled my body onto the rock. Dave was only five or six feet away on the ledge; he had chopped in the slightly sloping ice.

"Christ, Art." His voice cracked. "You froze your hands!"

I pushed off from the rock, letting the wind throw me against Dave. He flung his arms around me. All I could do was lie across him, wheezing and shaking, trying to catch my breath.

"Man," he said, "we gotta dig in!"

　　　　　➤　　　➤　　　➤

Dave cradled Pirate's feet against his belly and massaged them gently until they began to rewarm.

"Dave," I said, "you know you saved us out there." My words sort of hung in the air. They sounded hollow, and Dave bit at his lip self-consciously. I didn't say more, but my eyes followed Dave with admiration and a kind of love as he tucked Pirate into his bag and then reached for the stove.

For more than an hour I had clung to the ledge on the ice, feeling the frostbite blisters swell on my hands and watching helplessly while Dave dug a cave in the ice. Just before he had completed it, Dave had collapsed from exhaustion; by then Pirate had pulled himself together, and despite his hands and feet, which were beginning to swell with frostbite blisters, he had somehow made it over the crest to finish hollowing out the cave. Dave had recovered enough strength to help me through the small hole in the ice which was the entrance to our new home.

Now inside our cave, Dave leaned on his elbows, and steadying the stove with one hand, he prepared some food with his free hand. In this cramped chamber under the ice cooking was more miserable than it had ever been in the last four weeks; Dave had quietly accepted the job because his were the only hands capable of working the stove. At least he had found some good food to fix—four pound-and-a-half cans of ham, bacon, and peas which had been cached by a previous expedition among the rocks we had bivouacked against. Since our pot had blown away, he heated the ham in its own can, then used the can to melt water in.

Flattened against the wall while Dave cooked in the middle, I realized how small our cave was. At the wide end there was barely enough room for our shoulders, and at the narrow end our feet in our sleeping bags were heaped on top of each other. Because of the rocks behind us, Dave and Pirate had been unable to make the cave long enough for us to stretch out completely. Over our feet the ceiling was about a foot and a half above the floor; toward the larger end there was just enough height to turn or lie on our sides with one shoulder touching the ice on the floor and the other touching the ice on the ceiling. We were quickly learning that our every movement bumped the next person. This cave certainly wasn't pleasant or comfortable by ordinary standards, but it kept us safe from the wind, and that was all that mattered, for the moment.

Dave looked for his journal and found it missing. We had lost too much to the wind—the use of four hands and two feet, an incalculable amount of body warmth, two packs with half our food in them, the parachute, my wind parka, and— perhaps our greatest loss—the foam pads which would have insulated us from the ice and helped to keep our bags dry. Yet we felt secure thanks to Gregg's foresight. We were supplied with enough gas to make water for another day, maybe two more days if we stretched it. With four lunches left, and three remaining cans of food, we needn't worry about starving.

That night ham and hot water were a feast, not filling, but delicious nonetheless; it was our first warm food since leaving the cave down at 17,200 feet more than thirty hours before. My hands had become so inflexible that Dave had to place each bite of ham—there were five of them—in my mouth, then tip the can to my lips to let me drink. Eating made us giddy with pleasure and almost got us feeling warm.

We were actually exultant, not from any sense of conquering the wind, but rather from the simple companionship of huddling together in our little cave while outside in the darkness the storm raged through Denali Pass and on across the Alaska Range.

We agreed that the wind coming out of the northwest was funneling through the pass at least 130 miles per hour. We remembered that a wind of such velocity, combined with the –30° to –45° air temperature outside our cave, created an equivalent wind-chill temperature somewhere off the end of the chart; the last figure on the chart was minus 148°.

"One hundred and forty-eight degrees below zero."

It was frightening to say, but the worst was over, we thought. In the morning the wind should slack off; we would descend, greeting the others at 7,200 feet with the news that we had made the summit; we would get off the mountain and go home. We wanted to believe the climb was over, that in a couple of days everything would, be warm and easy again. Yet the wind, howling and pounding the slope overhead, reminded us that we couldn't move until it died down. We talked of the cave as our refuge, but the suspicion that we were being held captive in the ice must have entered each of our minds as we fell asleep listening to the wind.

17,300 FEET: GREGG, JOHN, SHIRO, GEORGE

Gregg's diary: The nightmare goes on. I can't believe this is happening . . . It is windy and white out this morning, very bad conditions. The waiting is hell. The wind stops and you listen for footsteps. I can't remember a more prolonged terror in my life.

DENALI PASS: ART, DAVE, PIRATE

Through the night I had slept restlessly, waking every time Dave's knees and shoulders pushed into me. Each time my mind started to clear, the thought that the wind might be down rushed up, but before I'd be fully awake the damnable roar would be running through my head. A shift of legs, or a roll to the other side—in any position the ice was too hard to be comfortable. Sleep made time pass, but the altitude caused a nervous wakefulness.

Staring at the ice, supposing the others were asleep, I looked forward to discussing a plan of action when they woke. Eventually their shifting to find a more comfortable position convinced me that they must already be awake. I asked, and they both said they had been lying silently for an hour or more. I realized there was nothing to say. It was horribly simple. We would have to wait here until the wind stopped, at least until it died down. One sleepless hour after another we listened for the first lull.

During the morning the wind remained constant. The fluctuations in its monotonous tone were so slight that it reminded me of the perpetual roar inside a conch shell—only much, much louder. Later in the day, extraordinary blasts of wind hit the surface of the ice overhead with enough force to actually shake the roof of our cave, causing loose ice crystals to fall from the ceiling.

There was no joking, no idle conversation, hardly any talk at all. We retreated into ourselves, silent, waiting, staring at the ice on the ceiling, staring at the ice on the sides of the cave, staring into the darkness inside our sleeping bags. I tried to think constructively, develop a plan or project for the next summer, but it was useless. The altitude was heckling my mind—the same restless lightheadedness that was keeping me awake also prevented me from concentrating. Wandering thoughts always returned to the sound of the wind and to the dreary question repeated continually—"When will it stop?"

The only event during the day which aroused any interest at all was our one meal, stretching from late afternoon till after dark. Dave, manning the stove again, thawed and melted more than he actually cooked. Patiently, he dropped chunks of snow and ice into the can, watched them melt, added more snow and ice, and finally—with what Pirate and I agreed was a stroke of genius—he dumped in a package of gorp. When the grog became hot the chocolate bits melted into a fascinating brew, filled with cashews and raisins. Flavored partly with my considerable thirst, it was undoubtedly the best drink I had ever tasted. However, when I had gotten my portion down, a curious, mildly unpleasant aftertaste remained.

About an hour after the hot drink, Dave served the rest of the ham. He heated it over the stove only long enough for it to thaw. Warming it would have meant wasting fuel, which we would need in case the wind held us here another day. Dave placed two pieces of ham, each about the size of an apricot, in my mouth, followed them with several slices of cheese and salami, and finished with three pieces of hard candy.

After another hour Dave melted enough snow and ice to fill the can with water. When it was warm he emptied a tiny can of chopped pork into the water to make a thin soup. Before I drank my portion I felt the need to relieve myself. Going outside was unthinkable.

"Dave," I asked, "isn't there a spare can or a plastic bag we can use for a pee bottle?"

"Nope, Art," he answered. "All we've got is the cooking can."

"Then what did you use?"

"Well," Dave started uncertainly, "I thought you wouldn't eat or drink if I told you, but I used the cooking can."

Now I recognized the scent or flavor that had remained as an aftertaste—urine. It didn't matter. I thought it should, but it just didn't.

After Dave poured the last of the soup into me, I prepared to use the can myself—inside my sleeping bag. This would be the first thing I had attempted to accomplish with my swollen fingers; it was a task that even under more normal conditions required considerable technique. An accident would not only be wretchedly unpleasant but disastrous as well, because the extra liquid in my bag would consolidate the down, thus ruining its insulation.

I listened anxiously as the can began to fill. The liquid level rapidly approached the rim, but in the nick of time I managed to maneuver out of what would have otherwise been a shameful and uncomfortable predicament and looked about for a place to empty the can. Not finding a suitable spot to my left and realizing Dave was guarding against my dumping it to my right, I raised the can precariously over my head and sloshed its contents against the ice behind me. Most of it melted in, but a little stream trickled under my bag. No matter, it would be frozen in seconds.

Dave calmly observed that my performance of holding the can was so skillful that I could damn well feed myself from now on.

I had heard Pirate's voice only two or three times throughout the day. Even though he lay along the opposite side of the cave, only four feet from me, I could barely hear his voice above the wind the few times he did speak. The altitude had cut off his exuberance and made him a slowed-down version of his old self. When I asked Dave whether Pirate was all right, he simply said that Pirate was worried about his feet, which had become worse than his hands. The swelling had leveled off, Dave told me, but most of his toes were insensitive to touch.

One particularly excruciating aspect of waiting was knowing that the longer we were held down the worse our frostbite would be. As our bodies began to dry up as a result of an inadequate liquid intake, they became more difficult to warm. Dave's toes were cold, but he didn't complain because he thought that was a good sign; better that they feel cold than numb. Only Dave and I had down booties, yet we had to frequently wiggle our toes to keep the circulation flowing through them. I considered lending my booties to Pirate, but the thought of my feet freezing while I slept discouraged me.

My main concern was my hands, which were swollen to nearly twice their normal size. To flex the tips of my fingers I had to painfully clench the muscles in my hand and forearm. I recalled the last time I had played my flute before leaving for McKinley. I had carefully watched my fingers run over the keys; I had wanted to appreciate them in case I lost them, and at the same time I had promised myself that I wouldn't lose them. I had begun to fear that was exactly what was happening every hour I lay in the cave. I caught myself wondering if I would still be able to play my flute with the first and second joints of my fingers missing.

Our stomachs hadn't really been full since we had left for the summit. An empty sort of craving had settled into my belly; I hoped it wouldn't develop into the cramps which I had heard afflict people suffering from malnutrition. The others down below would be running short of food soon. Maybe they would have to retreat down the mountain. I asked Dave whether he thought the others had given up on us. He didn't answer; maybe he was asleep. Surely they'd come looking for us when the wind died down.

That night, long after it was dark, I found myself repeating the words of a Dylan Thomas poem: "Light breaks where no sun shines." Before I'd come on McKinley I had known the verses by heart; now I couldn't remember the first one past "Where no sea runs the waters of the heart push in their tides." Further on there was something about the things of light filing through the flesh. I couldn't remember. Just the first line—"Light breaks where no sun shines"—ran over and over in my mind.

I lay a long time in the dark, unable to sleep. The wind, a persistent, audible ache in our heads, had been with us for so long that its incessant sounds were like a silence that had settled over our lives. That silent, paralytic quality in the wind recalled images of unalterable bleakness; I remembered seeing the wind run through the broken windows of an abandoned cabin, the wind in the dried grass of a beach in November after the birds had migrated, the wind over the delta of a frozen river.

I couldn't remember what it was like not to hear the wind, but the three of us knew that if we heard it in the morning, our situation would become critical. There appeared to be only enough gas to melt one more can of water.

Through more than thirty-six hours the wind had not even for a moment relinquished its hold on the mountain and on our lives. Surely, we reassured ourselves, the wind's force would be diminished by morning.

The infernal noise filled our heads.

The wind's vicious, I told myself. It's diabolical. Silently cursing it became a pastime. I tried to think of all the words that described its evil nature—fiendish, wicked, malicious. I called it a vampire sucking the life out of us.

But the wind didn't hear me, and I knew my words were irrelevant anyway. The wind wasn't malevolent; it wasn't out to get us; it had no evil intentions, nor any intentions at all. It was simply a chunk of sky moving about. It was a weather pattern, one pressure area moving into another. Still, it was more satisfying, somehow more comforting, to personify the wind, make it something I could hate or respect, something I could shout at. I wished I were an old Eskimo shaman, seeing devils and demons in the storm and understanding the evil spirits that lived in the mountain. I thought that a good shaman would blow a chant that would chase away the wind. But I didn't know any magic, and I knew all my cursing was only an attempt to escape the simple facts; we had to descend, we couldn't descend in the wind, and the wind showed no sign of letting up.

We needed water most desperately. There was very little gas left in the stove; I wanted Dave to melt ice with it. I tried to think of the most pleasant ways of reminding him that we needed to drink, but whatever I said he growled at. I knew he felt the strain of having to do all the chores for Pirate and me. I felt too thankful, too dependent, almost too much at the mercy of Dave to pester him about the water. He told me that "later" he would melt some ice and thaw the bacon or peas, but gradually the day slipped by without our eating or drinking. Yet, if my hands had been all right, I would have put off the cooking the way Dave did because the altitude had cut away our motivation; it was so much easier to say "later" because, though we didn't really believe it, we always thought the wind might suddenly stop, letting us run down to the cave at 17,200 feet.

It was toward the middle of the afternoon when I heard Dave beginning to coax the stove back to life. He fiddled with it for several minutes without any luck, then decided to let it sit while he opened one of the large cans of bacon, ham, or peas.

It was the moment I had waited for all day.

"Which one do we want first?" he asked.

"Mix 'em all together," Pirate suggested.

Dave scraped the ice off the can of bacon with his knife, clearing the top so he could open it. I could already taste the bacon.

"Damn!" Dave swore in disgust. "Holes in the can! We can't eat the bacon! It's rotten!"

He reached for a can of peas.

It could certainly not happen again. Those holes had been an accident. Nevertheless, Pirate and I listened intently as Dave cleared the ice from the can of peas.

When only about half the ice was off, he swore again. More holes! Then he tried the ham, our last can. It was the same!

We sank back into a numb depression. For two days we had anticipated the flavor of the bacon. We had let ourselves dream of the juice of the peas in our mouths. Suddenly the food we had counted on was gone. The gnawing cramps in our stomachs weren't going to be quieted.

Immediately we were angry for being so cruelly cheated, but only after several minutes did we realize how the spoiled food had transformed our trial with hunger into a confrontation with starvation. We had almost nothing left to eat—three bags of gorp, a dozen slices of cheese, some hard candies, a little coffee, a three-ounce can of chopped pork, and maybe a dozen cookies. The combined calorie count of our remaining food was probably adequate for one person for one day. Solemnly, Dave divided a little less than half of the remaining food into three equal portions.

Although Dave battled with the stove long after his fingers were insensitive from handling the cold metal, he failed to get it going. There was so little gas left that he couldn't build up enough pressure to vaporize it. At thirty below the gas was sluggish—he had to give up. Just like the punctured cans of food, our last drops of gas mocked us with their uselessness.

Our one hope was a gallon of gas Dave had cached on the far side of Denali Pass when he had climbed McKinley in the summer three years earlier. It might still be there; Dave had spotted the bottle of gas the first day we had tried for the summit. He thought we should take a look, but no one volunteered to go out. He said he had originally cached the gas only about two hundred feet from where we lay. No one moved. Dave was the most fit to go out, and the most certain of the place it was cached, but the horror of entering the wind overcame the slightest inclination Dave might have had to go after it.

We tried to imagine what the others at 17,200 were doing. They had shelter, but only a limited supply of food. I remembered how a week or two before we had been concerned for the strength of John and George, about Shiro's cough and hemorrhoids, and about Gregg's unpredictable emotions in a crisis. Now they were entirely dependent on their own resources; and the three of us who had once been the strongest might soon come to depend on their judgment and strength to be rescued.

We hoped the others would not attempt anything rash for our sake—that the strain of their fear for us wouldn't break them. We thought of the gallon of gas. We imagined how delicious a cup of water would taste. We shifted our hips and shoulders to relieve the hard cold beneath us.

We talked very little. The grayness inside the cave faded into darkness.

17,200 FEET TO 14,400 FEET: GREGG, JOHN, SHIRO, GEORGE

> *John's diary: We decided today that Gregg and I should go down to call for a helicopter overflight . . . Set off about noon into heavy wind. Just near the gendarme above 16,000 feet Gregg wrenched his ankle. We encountered terrible winds here and had to cling to the ridge rocks to save from being blown off our feet. Sometimes the wind blew up, sometimes down, unpredictable. Very difficult to maintain balance. On hands and knees to the fixed ropes in a screeching wind . . . Pieces are coming off my bad ear.*

DENALI PASS: ART, DAVE, PIRATE

I woke elated. The wind had stopped. I heard a helicopter.

Just outside the cave I heard the steady whir. Gregg must have gotten a rescue started. It sounded as if the copter had already landed. People must be searching the pass for us. I was afraid they wouldn't find our cave; it was such a small hole in the ice. Maybe they'd give up and leave.

"Dave!" I rolled toward him. "Dave, do you hear the helicopter? We'd better get outside right away."

"Go to sleep . . . it's the wind."

"No! It can't be. It's too steady, too constant. It's a copter . . . Dave . . . "

He didn't answer.

"It's a copter," I repeated to myself. "It's the steady whir of a copter." I listened to be certain; but I wasn't certain. Maybe it was the wind; it couldn't be. I almost asked Dave to listen; but I knew he was right; yet I strained my ears for a voice, any sound that would let me believe there were rescuers outside.

There was only the wind.

After a long silence Dave admitted that he had been susceptible to my delusion; he had convinced himself for several minutes that the sound of the wind really was a rescue helicopter.

"But you know," Dave said, looking toward me, "it makes you feel kind of humble to know a helicopter couldn't possibly get to us."

Dave went on to explain how he felt good to know that no device of technology nor any effort on the part of our companions could conquer the storm, or even reach through it to help us. He said the three of us were alone in this sanctuary of the earth's wilderness, and that our only security lay in ourselves, in our individual abilities to endure, and in our combined capacities of willpower and judgment.

I said, "Dave, it may sound funny, but I feel closer to you than ever before."

Dave beamed and said, "Yea, I know what you mean. If we can't fight our way out of this storm, at least we can stick together, and try to live in harmony with it."

I thought to myself how the storm itself was helping to protect us from its own fury. Ever since the McKinley massif had been thrust upward out of a flat land, the wind had been packing the snow and ice of Denali Pass into contours of least resistance. We were sheltered inside ice that conformed to the pattern of the wind. We had suffered and nearly succumbed to the storm that first morning when we had fought it head-on in the open, but now all the force of the wind only pounded more stability into the roof of our cave as it swept across the slope above us.

The altitude riddled our attention span into fragments of thoughts. Discomfort was the only thing on which my mind seemed able to concentrate. My lips were deeply cracked in several places. Moving my tongue along the roof of my mouth I felt clumps of dried-up mucus; other experiences with dehydration had taught me that if I didn't get water soon, the rawest areas in my mouth would begin bleeding. The ligaments in my legs ached as they dried up. It was especially painful to stretch or change positions; unfortunately, the hardness of the ice made my hips and back sore whenever I remained still for more than a few minutes. I complained very little, not because I was naturally stoic, but because there was no one to complain to—each of us experienced the same discomforts; pain had become a natural condition of our life under the ice.

I was probably warmer than either Dave or Pirate because their sleeping bags were icing up faster than mine. Every time Dave had cooked, steam from the warm liquid had been absorbed into his bag, where it soon froze. As the down had matted together, its resilience had disappeared. It was particularly unsettling when Dave pointed out a number of lumps of ice mixed with the down. I didn't see how his bag could retain any warmth. Pirate's bag was a little better, but his down was fast becoming clogged with moisture from his breath because, against Dave's advice and mine, he persisted in burying his head in his bag, where his exhaled moisture had no escape. All of us sorely missed the foam pads. Without them, we were only able to place a spare wind parka or pair of wind pants under our buttocks and shoulders, leaving the rest of our sleeping bags on bare ice.

Pirate's hands were swollen, but he said he was worried most about his feet. He asked about my down booties. Though he didn't say it outright, I could tell he wanted to wear them. I tried to ignore him, acting as if I hadn't heard. My feet were cold with the booties; without them I thought they would surely freeze while I slept, or even while I lay awake. I avoided thinking about it, but that was exactly what was happening to Pirate's feet. He knew I didn't want to give them up, and didn't ask again. As he kicked his feet inside his bag to relieve their numbness, I knew he must be thinking of the warmth of my booties. Pretending to be asleep, I tried to forget about Pirate's feet.

I couldn't remember how many days we had been in the cave. The day we had gone to the summit, then that first day of the wind, the day we ate ham, then a day without water—it must have been the fourth day, but I was uncertain.

Sometime during the middle of the day Dave rationed us each a fig bar and two hard candies. Sucking on the candies brought a few minutes of relief to the rawness in my mouth. I put the fig bar aside. I wanted to save it for later in the afternoon as a break in the monotony of hunger. After about an hour I couldn't wait any longer. I had looked forward to saliva coming back into my mouth as I chewed the fig bar, but the crumbs only stuck to the gums and roof of my mouth. With some effort I swallowed the sticky wad, feeling it tumble into my stomach, where it set off a series of cramps. The pain constructed a morbidly amusing picture of four or five hands in my stomach grabbing for the fig bar, fighting each other for it, tearing and ripping at it. After a few minutes the cramps died down and the usual steady ache returned.

Silently I cursed the punctured cans of food. Some careless climbers must have punched holes in them with their ice axes as they tried to chip away the ice that covered them. We all wished we had never seen the cans. Without them we might have been able to accept our hunger, but knowing that ham and peas, rotten as they were, lay within arm's reach while we were actually starving was almost unbearable. The cruelest twist to the irony was the uncertainty; the canned food might still be good. Perhaps the food had remained frozen ever since it had been brought to Denali Pass. It was doubtful that there were any bacteria living at 18,200 feet. At least a portion of the ham, peas, and bacon might not be rancid, but to find out would be risking food poisoning.

Early in the afternoon it became obvious that we were going to spend another night in the cave. Even if the wind let up toward evening, we wouldn't have the time, nor perhaps the strength, to descend. We knew our dehydration was critical. We hadn't drunk a cup of liquid for more than thirty-six hours. Because our circulation was down we were all chilly inside our bags with all our parkas and wind pants on. Occasionally, I could feel Dave's body tense and shake with shivers. We needed water, which meant we needed gas—which we didn't have.

The only possibility was the gas Dave had cached at Denali Pass three years before. If one of us went for the gallon of gas, he might not make it back through the wind to the cave. The gruesome reality of this possibility had kept us from retrieving the gas, but there was no longer any alternative. One of us had to go for the gas! Who? I couldn't go because of my hands, so I lay quietly in my bag, letting my silence ask someone else to go.

Dave resisted the thought of his going. He had dug the cave. He had cooked for us when there had been gas. He knew his efforts had kept Pirate and me alive. And we knew it.

It wasn't right that Dave go out into certain misery to possibly disappear in the wind. Yet, knowing Dave, I sensed he was struggling with his weariness and fear to find it in himself to go out. Since he was the only one of us who knew for certain where the gas should be, it was logical that he go. Neither Pirate nor I could ask him. Semiconscious from the altitude and the numbing hypnotism of the wind, we retained a sense of justice.

There was another reason we weren't anxious for Dave to go. He was our hands! We needed him to cook if we ever got some gas. We would need him to tie the rope around us and hold us on belay when we descended, whenever that might be.

Quietly—I don't remember hearing him say he would go—Pirate got out of his sleeping bag. When he started to pull on his boots, he found it difficult and painful to force his swollen feet into them. I offered him the use of my down booties. He took them and quickly had them tied on. Dave described the rocks among which the gas had been cached. Pirate pulled down his face mask.

The wind had become more erratic: there were gusts and then short—ten- to thirty-second—lulls of comparative calm. Pirate lay on his stomach, facing the entrance, listening for the lull that sounded right to him. A resigned determination seemed to be all that was left of his former fierceness. Suddenly, he gave a short and not too loud "Arahhaa!" and began squirming out the entrance, uphill, through loose snow. Dave and I cheered, not loudly, but with all our remaining enthusiasm. For a moment we heard Pirate placing the pack across the entrance again. Then the lull ended abruptly, and all we heard was the wind.

For the longest time Dave and I listened without saying a word. Ten, fifteen minutes passed. We knew Pirate should have returned, but we said nothing. He might call for help only ten feet from the cave and we'd never hear him. I couldn't help imagining what we'd have to do if he failed to return. Maybe Dave would make a try for the gas. Maybe the two of us would attempt to dash down from the pass. If Pirate didn't return within a few minutes there would be no reason to go looking for him. Maybe Dave and I would simply lie in the cave, waiting until Gregg, Shiro, George, and John could reach us, or until we passed into delirium.

We heard a movement at the entrance. Two immediate whoops of sheer joy expressed our relief. A flurry of snow, then a plastic jug shot into the cave, followed by an exhausted Pirate.

"Bad!" He was gasping. "I couldn't stand up, even in the lulls. Something's wrong with my balance." I had never before heard Pirate say anything was rough or dangerous. "I crawled all the way, clawing into the ice with two ice axes. I can't feel my feet now."

We had gas! We could drink water!

With a merriment we'd forgotten ever existed Dave melted chunks of ice and piles of snow. The first can of water, especially, smelled and tasted sweet; we did not remember that the sweetness was the scent of urine. Dave heated can after can of water till they became hot. We drank, and drank, and always waited for yet another canful. For the first time in five days we went to sleep with full stomachs. That we were only full of water mattered not at all—or so we thought.

My feet had become colder. I had to constantly wiggle my toes to keep them from becoming numb. Still, I was glad I had not asked Pirate to return my booties after his trip for the gas.

17,200 FEET: GEORGE, SHIRO

> George's journal: The wind is still making a sound like Niagara Falls. All kinds of things enter our minds, one of which is: what could we do even if we did find the three above and they need help? . . . it is a very helpless feeling and a helpless situation.

Time had become critical and we just don't have the slightest hope for the three above. This is a transition between life and death . . . Invariably the picture of Farine comes to mind because it happened the same way. The night we left him on the glacier he was still Farine, warm. And the next day he was just a frozen body, like a piece of ice.

I have a horrifying dull bone ache in my shoulder. Even with straps around my shoulder I don't have full use of my arm— not because something is dislocated, but because of the pain. It feels as if it will give out. Our packs are quite heavy and the wind is severe, but we head down.

14,400 TO 8,000 FEET: GREGG, JOHN

Gregg's diary: John had such a heavy load coming down that he fell twice. He slid more than anything. He was above me with the first fifty-foot fall. The second time I caught him with an arrest. We need a little good weather before we will be safe. I try hard to forget the situation that the three above are in, but it is a gnawing sickening feeling that won't go away.

DENALI PASS: ART, DAVE, PIRATE

The gusts and lulls of the wind sounded hopeful when we woke to another cold, gray morning under the ice. The ragged end of the storm seemed to be blowing itself out, and had we been strong we probably would have tried to dash down from the pass immediately. Unfortunately, we had become so weak that the wind would have to be completely gone before we could descend with any confidence. Yet, regardless of when the wind disappeared, this had to be our last day in the cave, because by the next morning there would be no food at all. For the three of us we had only a handful of gorp, four slices of cheese, and three little hard candies. When this food ran out the cold would take over our bodies unless we could make it down. We lay silent and brooding in our bags; cheerless as our situation was, I felt a curious sense of relief that it was so simple—without food, it was either descend or perish in this wretched cave.

Pirate refused to believe what the wind had done during the night. On going to sleep, he had fixed a rope to the pack which closed the cave's entrance, then tied that rope around his arm to keep the pack from being blown away if a gust dislodged it. He woke to find both the rope and the pack gone. As the wind had begun packing the entrance full of snow, some loose, fine-grained crystals had sifted into Pirate's sleeping bag; the bag had so little warmth that the snow lay in it without melting. Pirate stared at the snow for ten or fifteen seconds, then mumbled hoarsely that he'd leave the snow in his bag because it might help insulate him. His reasoning sounded absurd. I thought of telling him to get the snow out of his bag as fast as he could, but it was easier to lie silent than begin talking. Then I began wondering whether Pirate might be right about the snow helping to insulate him—his bag and Dave's were now little more than matted down and chunks of ice held together by the nylon shell.

Even after Pirate placed his boots and the gas bottle in the entrance to block the blowing snow from sealing us in, snow still blew through every time a gust of wind hit the slope above. Because the entrance wasn't tightly closed off from the storm, a steady draft circulated the –35° air through our cave. With the chill factor increased, I began shivering again. This wasn't particularly painful, but it was unnerving to watch my body shaking uncontrollably. What happens after you lose control of your body? I thought of asking Dave, but said nothing.

My thoughts wandered back to my childhood. I recalled my parents saying that when I was first learning to walk I enjoyed toddling around in the snow naked. I remembered the times when I was eight and nine and we'd run out into the spring windstorms that sweep across the plains of eastern Colorado; with bales of straw we built shelters from the driving wind and dust, and considered ourselves pioneers. In those days it had been great fun to run shouting from tree to tree in a thunderstorm or when the rain turned to hailstones the size of marbles and golf balls. How had those games in storms led to the desperate mess the three of us were trapped in? All I wanted now was to be free of the fear of freezing and being buried under the ice. I started imagining what we'd look like frozen solid. The feel of my mouth on Farine's cold lips came back. I saw his last expression frozen in his cheeks and eyelids. How much of a body could be frozen before the heart stopped? Was I acting cowardly to think this way? It wouldn't happen to us, not to me; yet, there was the cold in our hands and feet.

To get these thoughts out of my mind, I asked Dave if it seemed to him that the gusts were becoming less powerful and the periods of calm longer. He said, "Don't think about it." But I couldn't help being attentive to every fluctuation of the wind, even though I knew as well as Dave that it was only depressing to hear every lull end in a blast of wind.

Only food occupied our thoughts as much as the wind, especially the food in the punctured cans. Those cans haunted us. I felt the little holes staring at me whether the cans were in plain sight or hidden under a sleeping bag or out the entrance. After Dave had emptied the cans of their contents, he classified most of the food as definitely rotten, but there remained at least a pound of peas and a half pound of ham that he thought might be edible. He even thawed and heated some of the ham. It didn't smell or look bad; still, it had come from a partly spoiled can.

"Aw, I'm going to eat it," Pirate insisted.

But we wouldn't let him. There was no question in our minds that, weak as we were, food poisoning would do us in. As long as we could just resist the canned food we had a chance; if we gave in and ate the doubtful ham and peas we might eliminate that chance. Of course, the food might be good, and it could easily provide the extra strength we might need to get down.

As our stomachs lightened with cramps and the deafening repetition of gusts and lulls whittled away our patience, each of us changed our minds about eating the canned food. One moment Pirate would declare he was going to eat the ham, and the next he would be restraining Dave or me from trying it. So far we had been able to check ourselves, but every moment of hunger increased the temptation.

We dreamed about feasts, banquets, exotic dishes, all our favorite foods. For what seemed like hours Dave and I listed every type of food we could think of. Sometimes we would be silent for ten or fifteen minutes, as if the conversation had ended; then as soon as I'd mention something like "crab,"

Dave would say "Wow, oh honcho boncho! I'd forgotten crab!" Another ten minutes might pass before one of us would remember a forgotten delicacy.

Once Dave said, "Stuffed green peppers!"

"Yea . . . with lots of raisins in the stuffing!" I answered.

We tantalized each other with difficult choices between different foods. "Dave," I asked, "would you prefer a mushroom pizza or a pepperoni pizza?"

"Mushroom, and if you could have one fruit, what would it be?"

"Awaarraghaa. . . . I want some bloody meat!" Pirate interrupted. There was enough gas to make as much water as we could drink; however, Dave had only enough motivation to make a minimal amount. As our dehydration continued, our frostbite became more severe. The swelling in my fingers had started to go down; I didn't know whether this was a sign of improvement or an indication that my body simply didn't have enough liquid to keep the swelling up. Much as I worried over the blisters, I realized they were my body's way of trying to save the tissue that had been frozen.

Dave couldn't feel the large toe on his right foot, nor parts of several other toes. There was so little he could do for his feet—rub them, wiggle the toes. He said they were becoming steadily colder. The scabby, frostbitten skin on the end of his nose was sickening to look at, but not nearly as frightening as the freezing that was beginning in his feet. The frostbite on his nose was isolated and had come about because he happened to have a long nose which protruded from his face mask, while the frostbite taking hold in his feet was not isolated; it was a sign that the cold was steadily creeping into his body. It was happening to each of us.

At times I was surprised that I wanted Pirate to continue wearing my down booties, which I had previously guarded so selfishly. I knew I hadn't overcome my selfishness; Pirate was sort of included in it. Since his feet had suffered on his trip to get the gas, I had felt almost as protective toward his feet as toward my own. Later in the day Pirate passed one bootie back to me. Perhaps one bootie each would not be a practical way to halt the freezing in our feet, but, even if it was only a gesture, it was still the most touching thing I had ever seen Pirate do.

The one advantage of being dehydrated was that we rarely had to jeopardize ourselves by urinating into the can inside our sleeping bags. Likewise, our lack of food had saved us from the ordeal of a bowel movement in the wind. Nevertheless, our hour of reckoning came. We had postponed the moment until it appeared we wouldn't be safe another minute. To go outside would be risking the possibility of contracting a humiliating case of frostbite while our pants were down. By comparison, it was almost pleasant to contemplate attempting the feat inside our sleeping bags. Dave's ingenuity developed a technique which produced little packages, nicely wrapped in toilet paper. With some coaching from him I managed to get my bundles safely wrapped and out the cave's entrance. However, Pirate, who hadn't been very attentive, got himself into trouble. Soon after he had completely disappeared into his sleeping bag we heard him begin to mumble and swear. When the shape of his sleeping bag began shifting frantically, we offered him some advice.

"Oh, you had paper?" he moaned. "I didn't know you guys had used paper."

During the first days of the wind, sleep had been an effective way of waiting. Now it had become a continual twisting of hips and shoulders away from the hardness of the ice, a twisting away from the cold that seeped into our bags from the ice beneath. None of us had even a momentary respite from hunger cramps and the cramps and aches in our dried-up ligaments and muscles. Nevertheless, wakefulness continued to be a worse kind of half-consciousness; pain was felt more acutely by a more alert mind, and we realized that we weren't dreaming, that we were not going to wake up to find everything friendly and warm.

At times I was unable to tell for certain whether I was awake or asleep. Dreams of Farine lying on the ice, of John calling from the bottom of that crevasse, of Shiro coughing, of our hands and feet turning black, filled my sleep and drifted over into the different levels of wakefulness, that stretched through the day. Hours no longer existed. I once asked Dave how long we had been trapped under the ice; he said he didn't know.

In the afternoon, during one period of what I thought was clear-sightedness, it seemed as though the wind was finally dying. The lulls had become much longer, maybe as long as five or six minutes, and the gusts were less frequent and no longer hit with the force which had shaken our cave for so many days. I dozed fitfully, then woke in the dark to a strange sound. I was startled. To ears that had become unaccustomed to quietness, the silence sounded nearly as loud as the wind's roar had that first morning.

"Dave, the wind's gone! We can descend!"

"Yea man, I'm cooking us up a farewell dinner to this awful hole," Dave said. In a moment his headlamp flicked on and several minutes later I heard the cheery purr of the stove. It was all over, we thought; we had made it through. Our farewell dinner was a farewell to the very last of our food, to the cave, and, we hoped, to the wind. Dave passed the hot water and divided up the four slices of cheese.

14,400 FEET TO 10,200 FEET: GEORGE, SHIRO

> George's diary: "Gloomy, very, very gloomy—it was a condi-
> tion of despair under which we climbed down . . . the wind was
> very severe again. We almost didn't make it; the snow began
> blowing—it was deep. It was getting dark . . . There is a sliver
> of hope—as anyone would have hoped—but logically we reject
> the possibility that any of the three could come down alive . . . we
> try to avoid the sentiments of death."

7,500 FEET: GREGG, JOHN

> Gregg's diary: "What a fight! Woke up in partial white out and
> spent till noon finding our base camp igloo. . . . Settled into my
> wet bag now. Worked at my black (frostbitten) toe. Looks bad,
> but it will make it . . . Bad weather predicted. Thank God we
> are here. After a week, I can't imagine much hope for Art, Dave,
> and Pirate.

DENALI PASS: ART, DAVE, PIRATE

In the gray light and quietness we anxiously prepared to leave the cave, but it took us several hours to get ready. Dave melted ice. Pirate was a long time cramming his swollen feet into his boots. My feet and Dave's weren't swollen, but during the night we had both lost feeling in several toes. With my hands still mostly useless, I relied on Dave to stuff my feet into my boots, then lace them up.

Keyed-up by our departure, we felt more alert than we had at any time since the first day of the wind. When I decided to give the mental tests before we went down, Dave helped me with the stopwatch and the sheet of subtraction problems since my fingers were unable to hold them. Dave said he was thinking as clearly as he ever had; the test results did not agree. It took each of us twice as much time to answer a series of subtraction problems as we had needed to answer a similar series down on the Kahiltna. Although this was only a rough indication of one way in which our logical thought processes were impaired, I made a mental note to be damn careful if we had to make an important decision.

But we weren't really worried. There was no wind. After sticking out the storm we felt there was nothing we couldn't do. In a few hours we'd reach 17,300 feet; we might descend all the way to the 14,400-foot igloos before night, it was going to be great to walk in on the others; they had probably given up on us by now. A new excitement quickened our movements. We were going down, going home! Dave was the first outside. With one word he cut short all our excitement.

"Whiteout!"

"Whiteout." The word hung in the air. We had never considered the possibility of a whiteout after the wind. Dave could see only twenty to thirty feet. A mile of ice stretched between us and the 17,200-foot camp if we took a direct course; but on the slope below us there were four or five square miles of ice, in the basin below there were another four or five square miles of ice, and the basin fell away through forty or fifty square miles of heavily crevassed glacier. Blinded by the whiteout, we might wander about the ice forever, or rather, until we collapsed, or walked off an edge, or fell into a crevasse.

We hoped the whiteout was merely a small passing cloud that would sift away in an hour or two. We dreaded to think of what would become of us if the whiteout proved to be the beginning of a week-long snowstorm.

I followed Pirate out of the cave only to see his hunched form stumble into Dave, who was also unable to straighten his back. For a moment I just watched the two lean against each other like drunks trying to maintain their balance. A mist of ice crystals crept silently over the rocks behind them.

With short, painful jerks of his head, Pirate twisted his face up to look Dave in the eye: "Dave," he said in a hoarse whisper, "I think I'm too weak to go down."

For the first time since the night we had pulled Farine out of the crevasse, Dave's face went blank with shock. In an instant his confidence had been broken. It wasn't only Pirate's words that had shaken him. In the half-light of our cave we had been unable to see each other's features clearly, but now nothing was hidden. Pirate's appearance was the most appalling. It was as if he had emerged from the cave twenty years older; his voice was that of an old man; his face was furrowed with lines we had never seen before; his eyes were faded and glazed and sunk back into their sockets.

I felt shaky getting to my hands and knees and was unable to stand on my feet without Dave's help. I tumbled over with the first step I tried, hitting the ice with my shoulder to avoid falling onto my swollen hands. None of us had a sense of balance. Our legs were dried up and, along with our backs, were stiff from lying immobile for days We practiced walking, but it took ten or fifteen minutes of stretching and limbering up before we regained enough coordination to walk in a relatively straight line.

To be able to walk again was an achievement, but hardly a consolation, because even if the whiteout cleared, we didn't have nearly enough balance to climb down the hundreds of yards of steep ice that separated us from 17,200 feet. Yet waiting in the cave would be suicide, since one more day without food would certainly leave us without the strength to descend.

Dave grew nervous. Pirate leaned against a rock and mumbled to himself. Desperation made us begin to voice wild plans for escaping from the pass. We discussed the possibility of just Dave and I trying to make it out. Pirate said he'd wait by himself in the cave until we could get a rescue party to him; but of course assistance would not reach him for at least two days, and that would be too late. Once, feeling I was the strongest, I said I wanted to try it alone. I reasoned that if I made it down I could send in help, and if I didn't make it Dave and Pirate would still have a chance if the weather cleared.

How easy it might have been if I could have fully deceived myself. I knew my reasons for a solo descent were flimsily constructed excuses to conceal my desire to save Art Davidson above all else. I became afraid that my fear of our situation was stripping away my sentiments of loyalty to the others. I didn't want Dave or Pirate to see my ruthless self-centeredness. But then, wasn't this need to save myself a sense of self-preservation? And wasn't this healthy, even necessary?

As I began to feel panicky, my eyes glanced swiftly over the ice and rocks and at the whiteness all around us. Dave looked at me. Pirate appeared lost in his thoughts. I didn't know what to say. Despite the urgency of my desire to try it alone, that other sense of being unalterably bound to Dave and Pirate persisted. Maybe this inclination to stick it out with the others was only a reaction to loneliness, but perhaps it was a basic reaction I couldn't violate.

My fingers began to throb and my head felt light. I didn't seem to have control of my thoughts. I wanted to take off by myself, but I couldn't abandon Dave and Pirate. I had to save myself at any cost, but I wouldn't be alive now if it hadn't been for Dave and Pirate. What good was there in perishing together? If I had a better chance of making it alone, shouldn't I forget about Dave and Pirate and take off without them?

I felt I had to scream or run across the ice. To relieve my tension I looked at the clouds. I studied the different shades of grayness that walled us in. And it worked. My panic disappeared as quickly as it had rushed up.

Dave said we ought to hold off deciding what to do because the whiteout might clear. I nodded. Pirate looked at the hole in the ice that was our cave's entrance.

Clouds clung to the pass, filtering the sun's fight into a bleak variety of flat grays and whites. An eerie quietness had settled over the mountain; soundless and still, it seemed impossible that this was the same pass the wind had stormed through. The sky that had been terrifyingly alive hung around us lifelessly. The entire range, which had seemed to be some sort of living being during the days the wind had howled, now was only a frozen waste of ice and rock.

Hiding under the ice from all the fury, I'd felt closed in, but this day, standing outside in the stillness of the whiteout, I began to feel brief moments of claustrophobia, as if I were being smothered along with the mountain and all the peaks around us. Standing on our patch of ice it seemed as if the whiteout had cut us off from the world. The sky was gone, and we had only our little island of light in this immense grayness.

Pirate said we had to do something. We continued to stare into the cloud, hoping it would break open to let us descend. *Hoping*—we had come to understand it so well that it had lost much of its meaning; but none of its appeal. I decided that to hope was to ignore the reality of our situation in favor of a wishful belief that some stroke of luck would befall us. No one could come for us through this whiteout. I berated myself for ever hoping, and warned myself never to hope again. Faith was what I lacked. I needed faith that this whiteout, like any stretch of foul weather, would eventually end; and faith that we'd have the presence of mind and stamina to take advantage of that moment when it came. I told Dave we'd be lost if we stopped believing in ourselves; he looked puzzled and said, "Huh?"

Several minutes later I realized I was once again staring at the clouds, hoping they'd part.

As we grew weary of waiting for the whiteout to clear we searched among the rocks for food—a cache someone else might have left behind or some of our own supplies that had been blown away—but found nothing. We stood at the edge of the pass, looking down toward the 17,200-foot camp. Through the grayness I tried to picture Gregg, Shiro, John, and George camped in the cave, waiting patiently for a chance to look for us. Then I remembered they would have run out of food by now. But surely they hadn't left us.

For many minutes no one spoke. All our mountaineering experience told us that we should not descend into the whiteout because we would almost certainly lose our way, or else, weak and without a sense of balance, we would fall. At the same time, we were certain of what would be in store for us if we waited in the cave.

Hours had slipped by since we had first crawled out of the cave. Although the lateness of the hour was beginning to force us to make up our minds, every alternative still appeared futile. It seemed absurd to choose. I thought that if we ever decided there was no chance at all of our getting down, I'd use my last energies to wander up toward McKinley's north summit.

I told myself that was another desperate thought that ought to be discouraged. Our situation demanded thoughtfulness which we weren't certain we were capable of. The most frustrating part of having our minds affected by the altitude was our inability to know to what extent we were affected. Probably the duller we became, the less we realized we were dull at all.

At length it became apparent that our greatest chance lay in trying to find our way down the ice wall, instead of waiting for the whiteout to clear. Besides, we were disgusted with the cave; Pirate said crawling back into it would be the same as crawling into our grave. By descending we would at least be active, be trying. Dave said we'd better get our crampons on. Pirate said O.K., and I didn't say anything.

Dave, with Pirate lagging behind, headed back up the fifty yards or so to the cave, where we had left our crampons. I waited near the edge of the pass because Dave had thoughtfully offered to bring down my crampons and gear after he was set himself. As Pirate passed the scattered ruins of a large cache, I called after him to ask if he had checked it for food. He said that he and Dave had looked all through it without finding anything edible. Nonetheless, Pirate plowed again through the rubble of a shredded tarp, pieces of wooden crates which must have been airdropped, torn clothes, silverware, and all sorts of things we couldn't eat. I figured the cache was most likely one that Washburn had carefully prepared after one of his scientific expeditions, but twenty years of storms and curious climbers had left it a trash heap half buried in the ice. After a minute, Pirate stopped searching and looked at me without speaking. I asked if he had found anything.

"No." Very slowly he continued on up to get his crampons.

I stood in a daze, not wanting to do anything until someone came to take care of me. Staring at the cache, I remembered advice Shiro had once given me; since it was urging me to move, I tried to suppress the thought. Yet it nagged me: "When there is only one way to survive in the mountains, you must check every possibility to the very end in order to find the one that works." The cache was a possibility. Just possibly some food remained hidden toward the bottom of the rubbish; but the cache was forty feet away, forty feet uphill. I stood still, without the energy or desire to move. Shiro's words kept repeating themselves in my mind. I heard them in his soft accent: ". . . check every possibility to the very end." I resisted checking the cache; a waste of energy, I rationalized. Then, not realizing I had started, I was walking toward the cache. To get a grip on my ice axe I forced my fingers around the shaft, no longer caring whether my blisters broke—I was going to dig.

I whacked at the ice where it held the canvas tarp; my hands, revolting at the pain, dropped the axe. The tarp hadn't budged. I picked up the axe, and by the time I had swung a couple more times I was in a frenzy. I slashed and beat at the canvas frozen into the ice. I pried and yanked. Hitting with my axe as hard as I could, I must have struck a rock, because the axe's metal adze broke.

I became furious. I couldn't stop. I smashed at the pieces of wood, lashing out with my axe until I collapsed onto my knees. I was out of breath and dizzy, but as soon as my head began to clear I started swinging at the debris again. Still on my knees, I uncovered bits of rotten rope, pots, old socks, ladles, odd boots; and of all the absurd, useless luxuries there was even a colander.

I attacked the cache, driven by an obsession to reach the bottom of it. My hands throbbed with pain and my feet had become numb, but all that mattered was that I check every last inch of the trash. A rage drove me to see what was underneath. When I discovered another layer, I was careful not to destroy anything. I opened a box, but it was full of clothes.

I kicked some of the surface junk aside with my boots, then dug in again with my axe. Ice and splintered wood and strips of canvas were frozen around each other. I grabbed and yanked and kicked, and swung the axe, and eventually I reached another unopened box. I pried it open: more clothes on top, but underneath lay several cloth bags, small, white bags. Excited and exhausted, I felt my heart beating wildly as I fumbled to see what was in one of the bags. The drawstring came loose, and as I looked into the bag I'm certain I would have cried, if my body had had enough water to spare for tears.

Dried potatoes!

Farther inside the crate sat a box of raisins packaged in a wrapper that had gone out of style at least fifteen years ago! I found two more bags of potatoes and even uncovered a can of ham without holes in it!

We ate!

Dave enlarged the cave. Crouched on his knees the circulation to his legs was partly cut off. He mentioned that his feet were icy-cold below the arches, and mumbled about warming them on someone's stomach, but he didn't want to bother Pirate or me. I heard him ramble on to himself: "Oh, well, a couple toenails lost, nothing new. . . . It won't happen to you, Dave baby . . . don't sweat it. . . ."

Far into the night Dave brewed hot drinks and made quantities of raisin, ham, and potato stew. Life seemed easy again. Our cave was more comfortable and we had the security of knowing there would be something to eat the next day. We settled in, determined to hold out another week if necessary but hoping, as we had hoped for the last six nights, that we could descend in the morning.

⟩   ⟩   ⟩

I dreamed that a kindly man cut off my feet every time they grew too large. There would be several minutes of relief each time he sliced them off and set them on a shelf, but always my feet, glowing a bright chartreuse, would swell again to the size of basketballs and ache as if about to burst until they were cut off. I was lying in a small, dark cellar, and before long the shelves that lined the wails were filled with huge, luminous, green feet.

Dave woke me to say my tossing was keeping him awake. A sharp, pulsating ache made both my feet feel as if they were about to explode. They had become partly frozen while I had dug for the food. I wasn't sure whether they had thawed or frozen some more during the night. The only way to relieve the pain was to shift their position; sleeping, I had dreamed of each shift as a thoughtful slice of my friend's knife.

The wind was gone and the whiteout had disappeared. Soon we were all awake, eating, drinking, and wondering where we would meet Gregg, Shiro, and the others. Pirate tried to get us to laugh by saying they had probably scratched us off and flown on home. They must have descended to the 14,400-foot igloos for food, but I figured that they would be coming up to look for us and that we'd run into them on the wall below our cave or perhaps down at 17,200 feet. Dave, not quite so optimistic, said we wouldn't see them until we reached the igloos.

Two hours after waking we attempted to pull on our boots. Once I screamed out loud as Dave shoved and jammed my feet into my boots. Since Pirate's hands were as bad as mine, Dave had to help force his boots on too. When he got around to putting his own boots on, Dave had more trouble than he had with either Pirate or me. The ends of both his feet were swollen.

After crawling out of the cave, we bumped into each other and sprawled onto the ice as we tried to control the uncoordinated blocks of pain that were our feet. Every time one of our boots touched the ice a burning sensation shot up the calf. Pirate spotted a four-engine plane circling the summit. We were not just about to rush down onto the open ice toward 17,200 feet, where the plane could easily spot us. Before setting foot on the steep ice below the pass we had to learn to walk and climb on our injured feet. We stepped in place and practiced traversing a gentle slope. Unfortunately, walking down-hill was the most painful and difficult because all our weight jarred onto our frozen and half-frozen toes. Dave strapped on my crampons, then helped Pirate tighten his. Because his were the only hands that hadn't been frozen Dave also took the important anchor position at the end of the rope when we finally decided we were ready to start down.

The ice wall fell away from the pass at an angle of thirty to forty degrees. At sea level we could have almost played tag on ice no steeper than this; however, at eighteen thousand feet we had climbed this ice gingerly on the ascent, when our legs had been relatively strong and our balance keen. Now, as we wobbled on spindly, dried-up remnants of legs, each step was near the limit of our capability.

"Don't charge off, Pirate!" I felt I had to warn Pirate, who was leading, to go slowly even though he only crept out onto the ice wall. We tested each position of our feet before trusting our weight onto them.

Because the wind had stolen our packs we had our sleeping bags draped around our shoulders; they hung to our feet, sometimes snagging our crampons, but it was the only way we could carry the bags.

"Slower, Pirate!"

The only thing certain about each step was the pain it would send through our feet. Step after step Pirate led us across and down the ice. The rope tied us together with only a psychological protection; if one of us slipped, we would all peel off the wall. A belay was impossible. If we did come off there would be nothing we could do to arrest our fall until we crashed into the basin six hundred feet below.

Pirate stopped.

"Oh, God!" I whispered to myself. One of his crampons had loosened. We were caught on the steepest section of ice. Dave and I chopped out small ledges to relieve some of the strain on our ankles. Pirate's fingers had been too stiff to tie his crampon laces when we had started, but now they had to bind his crampon to his boot.

Dave called anxiously at Pirate to hurry up. My ankles felt on the verge of buckling. Pirate grappled with the stiff straps, cursing at the cold cutting into his fingers—he had to handle the metal crampon with bare fingers. He knew everything depended on him. Should he lose his balance while tugging at the frozen bindings, all our efforts to hold out during the storm would be for nothing.

Pirate straightened; he grabbed his ice axe. I sighed with relief and turned to see Dave grinning behind me.

"All right, you guys. . . . We're goin' down!"

Tense with caution, we placed one foot in front of the other. Each step was carefully considered. The large military plane which Pirate had noticed earlier swung out over the Kahiltna. Even if the plane located us, there was no way it could help us now. We didn't see Gregg, John, Shiro, and George climbing up toward us. Their absence began to worry me because I knew they'd be here to help us down the ice if they could possibly manage it.

"Slow down, Pirate!"

With the steepest ice behind us, Pirate quickened his pace. Actually, he was taking a step only every two or three seconds, but that seemed dangerously fast to me.

"You're gettin' us down, Pirate—you crazy honcho!"

Pirate paused to turn and holler, "Aaahaaaa. . . ."

The rough but level ice of the basin began passing beneath us. "We did it, we did it," I repeated to myself.

However, as the ice rose ever so slightly toward the rocks, our feet became so heavy that we were soon stopping to rest every seven or eight steps. The rocks appeared unfamiliar. When Dave motioned for Pirate to turn right, I said I thought we had to head for the rocks to the left. After discussing the difference of opinion for a moment, we decided that none of us were certain which particular outcrop of rocks the cave was next to. Tired as we were, it was discouraging to think we might go fifty or a hundred feet out of our way if we climbed toward the wrong rocks. We compromised by striking out in a line running directly between the two main rock outcroppings. Ten and then twenty yards of ice were covered; Pirate called out that he could see a bamboo pole sticking out of the ice. It looked to be about ten feet high. Since we had not brought a bamboo pole to this point, we figured a helicopter must have landed rescuers who had left the pole behind. But where were they now? Maybe the others had had an accident. Anyway, the cave had to be near the pole.

Weary and growing apprehensive, we slowly approached the pole. One moment it was hundreds of feet away, then we suddenly realized it was only ten feet away and wasn't a bamboo pole at all. It was simply a willow wand. Our eyes had fooled us. Somehow the altitude or our dehydration or perhaps even our lack of food had affected our sense of depth perception. It was particularly startling because each of us had been deceived in the same way.

We passed by the willow wand and approached the cave. Just before we peered into it, I was seized with a sudden fear that we might see bodies. They could have been trapped here and could have never made it down for more food. We looked in; to my relief the cave was deserted. In one corner a small pile of food was stacked against a stove. They must have descended thinking we'd never come down; yet on the slight chance that we would they had left us the most favored delicacies—sausage, cocoanut balls Gregg's wife had made, and some of the fruitcake my grandmother had baked for us.

While we ate, the circling plane spotted us. Then Sheldon's silver Cessna 180 appeared and flew low over the basin. We waved. He swung around, came in lower yet, and dropped a bag. I retrieved it. Bits of a smashed orange were scattered on the ice. I picked up a carefully wrapped kit but couldn't figure out what it should be used for. Although it was tempting to leave it where it had fallen, I decided the others might be able to determine what it was. I felt somewhat foolish when Pirate immediately recognized it as a radio; the altitude was affecting me more than I wanted to admit. Either our minds were too fuzzy to operate the radio or else it had been damaged when dropped, because we couldn't get it to send or receive.

Filled with food and a little water, we continued the descent. With extreme caution we inched our way down among the rocks along the ridge. We were climbing several times more slowly than we had ever ascended this section of the route. Reaching the fixed ropes, we lowered our bags in front of us to free our arms for handling the ropes.

Our feet suffered a cutting pain every time our boots hit the ice. It became almost unbearable for Pirate and me to grip the rope with our frostbitten hands. Once I slipped, and as I grabbed the rope to halt my fall I could feel the skin and blisters tearing across my fingers.

Near the end of the ropes we entered a cloud. Despite the whiteout, there could be no thought of waiting because we had to avoid bivouacking for another night. Since Dave had climbed this part of the route more often than Pirate or I, he took the lead. We climbed down deeper into the cloud. The tops of the high ridges on either side disappeared. Somewhere ahead in the grayness were two igloos and our friends; beyond the igloos lay an ice fall of enormous crevasses. Should we pass by the igloos, we would walk blindly over the edge of a crevasse. The grayness grew so thick that from my position in the middle of the rope I could see neither Dave nor Pirate.

Dave stopped, then started again. My knees and ankles seemed on the verge of collapsing. Slack rope on the snow in front of me indicated Dave had stopped again. We were lost.

Gray cloud and gray ice appeared the same; the glacier and the sky had become one wall of grayness. Since we couldn't see the slope where we set our feet, I began stumbling onto my hands with a crunching of stiff, swollen flesh.

I shouted into the grayness that I thought the igloos were to our right. The rope jerked me to a halt from behind; Pirate must have fallen onto the ice. I heard him yell that we should head more to the left. Dave said nothing. I lay flat on the ice myself, waiting for Pirate to pick himself up and retighten a loose crampon. After several minutes Dave called, "Let's go!"; with considerable effort I got to my feet, and we started staggering on through the whiteout. As we passed through the endless grayness, I began to think we had already gone beyond the igloos. I tried to pull my befuddled mind together to be ready to throw myself onto the ice in arrest position should Dave plunge into a crevasse. I still could not see him, and the rope disappeared in the grayness about ten feet in front of me. We might have passed within ten feet of the camp without spotting it. As the snow became deeper, I began wondering whether the igloos would be buried. Dave plodded on.

Blind, and uncertain that my legs could manage another step, I let the rope running to Dave pull me on.

"Waahoooo. . . ." A call in front of me—unable to see Dave, I wasn't sure it had been his voice.

"Igloos!" It was Dave's voice.

With luck or an astonishing instinct he had led us straight to the igloos.

Dave waited for Pirate and me to appear out of the whiteout so the three of us could share that first moment of greeting the others. Nearly delirious with relief and joy we shoveled the entrance of the main igloo free of some drifted snow, then pulled back the tarp which closed the igloo from the weather. We peered inside.

Darkness! The igloo was empty. We found the other igloo also deserted and dark. There wasn't even a note. Were we alone on the mountain? Where were they? None of us felt like voicing our disappointment that the others were gone, that they must have given up on us.

We attacked the food left in the largest igloo. Mashed potatoes, rice, jello, gorp, freeze-dried meat—never had food been so satisfying, but never before had our appetites been really insatiable. Long after we were full we continued to stuff food into our mouths—we had a compulsion to devour everything that was edible. It seemed irreverent to leave any food uneaten.

Despite the excitement of our feast, we ate quietly because we were weary and apprehensive about the fate of the other four.

"FIVE DAYS ON MOUNT HUNTINGTON"

AND

"MOMENTS OF DOUBT"

FROM
Moments of Doubt:
And other Mountaineering Writing of David Roberts
BY DAVID ROBERTS

TWO LINKED PIECES BY DAVID ROBERTS EXPLORE HIS EXPERIENCES on a successful but tragedy-marred expedition to Alaska's Mount Huntington in 1965, with the second, longer piece expanding the discussion to the larger issue of the risk of death faced by every active mountaineer. Roberts stands as one of the most articulate and thoughtful of writers in the field of mountain literature.

As he notes in his author's introduction to the first piece, "Five Days on Mount Huntington," Roberts wrote a number of articles about the Huntington expedition as he tried to come to grips with the death of his friend on the climb. Then, eight months after the climb, Roberts tore through the writing of his book on the expedition, *The Mountain of My Fear*, at a feverish pace— in nine days—in what he describes as an act of catharsis.

Some fourteen years later, Roberts returned with added perspective to the subject of fatal climbing accidents in his longer, more reflective discussion, "Moments of Doubt." Here he remains compelled, despite the horrors of the deaths he has witnessed, to return again and again to the mountains for the sheer happiness they provide

"Five Days on Mount Huntington" was first published in *Harvard Mountaineering*, 1967; "Moments of Doubt" originally appeared in *Outside* magazine, December 1980/January 1981. Both were republished in Roberts' collection of mountaineering writings titled *Moments of Doubt*, pages 3-10 and 195-209.

"FIVE DAYS ON MOUNT HUNTINGTON"

[Author's note: Before I decided to write a book about Mount Huntington in Alaska, I wrote four different articles about my expedition there for various journals. "Five Days" seems to me the best of the four, because it tends to tell the story most straightforwardly and because it deals only with the climax of the ascent. In the twenty years since the Huntington climb, I have never lived through a five-day span of comparable intensity.]

On July 29, 1965, it dawned perfectly clear again, the fifth such day in a row. In the small tent pitched on a three-foot ledge of ice beneath the huge granite overhang, Don Jensen and Ed Bernd prepared for an early start. They were tired from the strenuous pace of the last few days, but with the weather holding so remarkably, they knew they shouldn't waste an hour. By 7:30 A.M. they had begun climbing up the line of stirrups fixed on the overhang, the crux of the whole west face, which Matt Hale had skillfully led three days before. They were short on pitons and fixed ropes, but they were carrying the bivouac tent, in hopes of a chance to reach the summit of Mount Huntington. They knew that Matt and I would be bringing up equipment from our lower camp that day, but they couldn't afford to wait for it.

It took only a short while for both of them to top the overhang; but as soon as they had, Ed realized he'd forgotten his ice axe. A moment's pause—then they decided to go on without it. They alternated pitches, the leader using Don's axe, the second only a long ice piton. They were on a sixty-degree ice slope, patched with small rock outcroppings. They climbed well, chopping small steps, using only a belay piton at the top of each pitch. On the second, Don could place nothing better than a short soft-iron knife-blade, which he had to tie off. They left fixed ropes on the first three pitches, then saved their last one for the final cliff. Almost before they expected it, they were at the foot of it. Don took the lead. As Ed belayed, facing out, he could survey the throng of unnamed peaks to the south, and look almost straight down to the floor of the Tokositna Glacier, 5000 feet below his feet. Don started up the pitch boldly, swinging on his hands around a corner of the rough, solid granite, and placed a good piton, he used only two more above that, both for aid: the first, a shaky stirrup on a blank spot; the second, a hundred feet above Ed, a tiny knife-blade as a handhold by which he pulled himself up to the top of the cliff. Ed knew it was a magnificent lead, and he must have thrilled at Don's competence. In his turn he led up a steep snow fluting, and suddenly emerged on the bare, sweeping summit icefield. It rose, completely smooth, at a fifty-degree angle toward the mountain's summit. Quickly they climbed four pitches, but the ice was already starting to melt in the early afternoon sun. They stopped at the only rock outcrop in the whole expanse, and pitched the bivouac tent on a tiny ledge. There they sat, cooking a pot of soup on their laps, as the sun slanted toward the western horizon, toward Mounts Hunter and Foraker. As accustomed as they were by now to that sight, it must have seemed almost new this time, with the summit in reach for the first time in a month. After sunset they would start out for it, as soon as the snow had begun to freeze again.

Meanwhile, Matt and I had reached the high tent with supplies. We decided to go on above. Even if we couldn't catch up with Don and Ed, we thought we might safeguard the route for their descent. Matt noticed Ed's axe outside the tent. For a moment we were disturbed; then we decided he had simply forgotten it, so we packed it up to take with us.

Above the big overhang, we could follow the fixed ropes and the steps chopped in the ice. When I reached the top of the second pitch, I could see the anchor piton was poor. I tried to get a new one in, but there were no cracks. At last I clipped in to the eye of the bad piton—a mistake, for the fixed ropes were tied to the hero loop, not to the piton—and belayed Matt up. Matt led on. A few feet above me, he stopped to adjust his crampon. Suddenly he slipped, falling on top of me. Not very alarmed, I put up a hand to ward off his crampons and take the impact. I felt the snow ledge I was standing on break under my feet; then, abruptly, we were both falling. I was still holding Matt on belay; vaguely I realized the piton had probably pulled, but I couldn't understand why the fixed ropes weren't holding us. We gathered speed and began to bounce. Somehow I thought I was being hurt, without pain; and somehow, without fear, I anticipated the fatal plunge. But suddenly we stopped. Matt was still on top of me. Shakily we got to our feet. Now the fear came in little waves of panic. I said, almost hysterically, "We've got to get in a piton." We were standing on little knobs of rock in the middle of the clean, steep slope. Quickly I hammered in three or four pitons, none of them any good, and clipped us in. We were bruised, but not seriously hurt. However, Matt had lost one crampon and both his mittens. One of my crampons had been knocked off, but dangled from my ankle. My glasses had caught on the toe of my boot. Matt thought he had lost his axe, too, but we looked up and saw it planted in the ice where he had stopped to fix the crampon. We also saw the fixed ropes, still intact, even though the piton dangled near my feet. Then what had stopped our fall? Simultaneously we saw, almost unbelieving, that the climbing rope, dragging behind us, had snagged on one of the little knobs of rock, a rounded nubbin about the size of one's knuckle.

The discovery made us almost giddy, with a mixture of fear and astonishment at our luck. We discussed whether we should continue or descend. After a little while we decided to go on. Matt, with only one crampon, couldn't lead; but if I enlarged the right-foot steps for him, he could second. We felt very nervous as we climbed. I deliberately overprotected the route, putting in solid pitons wherever I could. We marveled at the pitches Don and Ed had led with so few pitons, but began to worry about them a little. We climbed the last cliff as the sun, low in the sky, turned the rock golden brown. The world seemed achingly beautiful, now that we had been reprieved to see it a while longer. The hard climbing seemed to stimulate us to a breathless exhilaration, the obverse face of the panic we had just felt.

As we emerged on the summit icefield, Ed saw us from their bivouac ledge. He let out a shout. Quickly we joined them, though the slope was in dangerously bad shape, and I had to use two rock pitons in the ice for anchors. Our reunion was poignant. We kidded Ed about leaving his axe; but when we told them about our near-accident, they seemed genuinely upset. Don was confident the summit could be reached that night. For weeks we had climbed, even camped, in separate pairs, meeting only as our ropes occasionally crossed while we switched leaders. Now we might climb toward the summit together; it would be a perfect finale.

Around 10 P.M. we roped together and started up, Don led in the almost pitch-dark; I came second; Matt followed me; and Ed brought up the rear. We were inexpressibly happy to be together. This silent climb in the night to the top of the mountain seemed a superb way to share our friendship. Our excitement was contagious. We were very tired, and yet the sky was full of stars, and the air was breathlessly still. Silhouetted in the constellation Cassiopeia, Don was leading; below me, Matt and Ed competently paced their movement to fit Don's.

Shortly after midnight we reached the summit ridge, Here we could walk continuously, but only with great care, for on one hand in the eerie darkness the drop was 5000 feet, 6000 feet on the other. Don could not be sure how large the cornices were that overlooked the Ruth Glacier; not, that is, until he stuck his foot through one. He pulled it back and retreated to my ice axe belay. He was near exhaustion from a long day of leading; I took over from him.

There remained only two vertical snow cliffs, precariously carved by a year's winds. I attacked them right on the cornice, reassured by the weight of the other three belaying me. The hollow snow required brutal efforts, and took almost the last of my strength. But finally I got up them both. Then it was only three easy pitches to the summit. The light was returning; in the northeast an orange rim of flame was sweeping the tundra. As we reached the very top, the sun rose.

We were extremely tired. We sat, listless, just below the summit, full of a dazed sense of well-being, but too tired for any celebration. Ed had brought a firecracker all the way to the top from some roadside stand in Wyoming; but we urged him not to set it off for fear it would knock the cornices loose.

It had taken us more than a month to climb Huntington's west face, a route some people had said was impossible. But people have always said things like that—our achievement had a much higher personal importance to us. It had been very difficult; the climbing had been spectacular; we had grown so discouraged that we almost abandoned the effort. But now this perfect finish, at dawn on a splendid day, together! I remember thinking even then that this was probably the best climb I could ever do, because things work out that well so rarely.

We talked to each other there, but the summit was for each of us a private experience. I do not know what Don, or Matt, or Ed felt. After an hour and a half, we started down. All the descent was anti-climactic. We wanted to hurry before the sun could melt the snow on the summit icefield. Below the bivouac tent we split again into two ropes of two. I realized how fatigued I was when I found it nearly impossible to swing out on rappel to retrieve some pitons. Finally, on the edge of exhaustion, we rappelled the overhang into our highest camp.

The four of us crowded into the two-man tent, pitched narrow to fit on its ledge of ice. There were still thirty-five pitches below us, sixteen to our other tent. At last we could relax, but we were terribly cramped and uncomfortable. We laughed and cheered and ate all the delicacies from our food box. We even managed to sleep a bit. But the weather was deteriorating, after five perfect days. In the late afternoon Ed suggested that he and I descend to the other tent that night. I agreed.

We were off by 9:40 P.M. A storm was evidently on its way in, and the air was relatively warm. The snow, consequently, was not in very good condition. As it grew dark, I occasionally shouted directions to Ed, who had been over these pitches only once, compared to my five times. I still felt tired, but Ed was in an exuberant mood. He said he felt he "could climb all night." We were being extra-cautious, it seemed, but this was easy going with the fixed ropes; it was even fun. We unroped to set up a rappel on the twenty-sixth pitch, a fine lead up a vertical inside corner that Don had made about two weeks before. Just before midnight on this last day of July, we chatted as Ed placed the carabiner and wound the rope around his body. We were talking about other rappels, about the first ones he had done at the Quincy Quarries back in Boston.

I said, "Just this pitch, and it's practically walking to camp."

"Yeah," he answered.

He leaned back. I heard an abrupt, jerking sound, and saw Ed's crampons spark the rock. Suddenly he was falling free below me. Without a word he fell, hit the ice fifty feet below, slid and bounced out of sight over a cliff. I shouted, but I doubt he even heard me. Suddenly he was gone. I knew he must have fallen 4000 feet, to the upper basin of the Tokositna, where no one had ever been.

I was alone. The night was empty. I shouted for Ed, but all that answered me was a mindless trickle of water near my face. I shouted for help to Don and Matt, then listened to more silence: they were too far above to hear me. I could not believe Ed was gone, and yet I could not believe anything else. I could feel the sense of shock wrapping me, like a blanket; I was seized with an urgency to do something. My first thought was to go down to look for Ed, but I put it out of my mind at once. For a moment I thought only of going up. Then it struck me that Ed was undeniably dead; therefore there was no emergency and I had to continue down.

I was without a rope, but I cut off a hank of fixed rope to tie in to the ropes below, and managed to climb down the vertical pitch. From there it was easy—but I went too fast, despite telling myself to slow down.

I reached the tent within twenty minutes after the accident. The sense of shock seemed to gather and hit me as I arrived. The tent was full of water (Matt and I had left the back door open!). Numbly I sponged it out and got in my sleeping bag. I took two sleeping pills. I could not figure out what had happened. Somehow the carabiner had come loose, for both it and the rope had disappeared with Ed. But no piton had pulled, no jerk had come on the fixed ropes. Out of all the mechanical explanations, all implausible, all irrelevant to our loss, emerged only the fact that it had happened. Ed was gone.

The pills and my tiredness put me to sleep. In the morning I woke with a dull sense of dread. The storm was continuing, and it had begun to snow. All that day I anticipated the arrival of Matt and Don, though I knew they would be taking their time. I became constantly nervous—what if something had happened to them, too? The minutes passed with agonizing slowness. I caught myself holding my breath, listening for a sound from them. When nightfall on August 1 came without their arrival, I was terribly disappointed. Again I took sleeping pills. Again I slept in a drugged stupor. The next day was the same; the same white-out and lightly falling snow. I grew afraid of the 3000-foot drop beyond the door of the tent. I tied myself in each time I had to go outside the tent. My balance seemed poor, my hearing painfully acute. I simply waited.

Meanwhile, Don and Matt had relaxed, slept well, eaten well. They had talked about the wonderful summit day while they waited for the weather to break clear again. At last, in the afternoon of August 2, they decided to pack up and descend. The pitches were in bad shape, and their heavy packs made for awkward climbing. In places the fixed ropes were coated with a solid sheath of ice.

They could see Ed's and my tracks below; and, though they could not see the tent itself, they could see that there were no tracks below it. This vaguely disturbed them, but they could think of no real cause for worry. Don noticed on the twenty-sixth pitch that some of the fixed rope had been cut off; this seemed very strange to him, but there were tracks below the pitch. . . . They were getting down with reasonable speed. Matt was going first. As he rounded a corner of the rock and looked down, all his fears dissolved: he saw the familiar orange tent and my head sticking out of it. He shouted a cheery hello, but I seemed not to have heard it in the wind. Don came in sight, then, and shouted another greeting. Again, I didn't answer. Matt was almost down to the tent. My silence seemed a bit peculiar, but surely—then he looked at the snow platform beside the tent, and saw that there was only one pack.

They took it bravely. They could understand the accident even less well than I. I had been afraid to tell them, but I leaned on them now, and they took the weight of my shock and helped me hold it.

We crowded together again and spent the night in the tent. The next day the storm increased. Around 7 P.M. we decided to complete the descent. We thought it should take about two more hours. It actually took eight.

The moment we got outside the tent, the whipping wind numbed us. We had a great deal of trouble chopping out the tent, and at last ripped out the corner of it. We had only one rope for the three of us, which made using the fixed ropes terribly clumsy. Matt had only one crampon, so he went in the middle. We tried placing him at various places along the rope, but none worked smoothly.

The conditions were hideous. A layer of new snow slid treacherously off the old ice. It grew dark quickly. We were shivering constantly, and had to shout at the tops of our voices to hear each other. Soon we couldn't even see the slope at our feet. We had to follow the ice-coated fixed ropes by feel, pulling them out of the crusted snow. I felt a continual dread of the sheer drop beneath us. We had three falls on the way down, but managed to catch each one with the fixed ropes.

It was the worst, most frightening climbing I have ever done. At last, in the early morning, we reached the last rappel. We slid down the ropes, out of the fierce gale to the blessedly flat, safe glacier below. Then we pulled own the rappel rope, cutting ourselves off for good from our route, from the summit, from the long, wonderful days of climbing, from Ed. We trudged back to our snow cave. Five days later Don Sheldon flew us out.

Thus an accident that made no sense, except in some trivial, mechanical way, robbed us suddenly of Ed, and of most of the joy of our accomplishment. Don, Matt, and I are left instead with a wilderness of emotions, with memories that blur too quickly of a friend who died too young. The shock and fear we lived with during the last days of our expedition all too easily now obscure the bright image of one perfect day—the summit day—when we seemed to work flawlessly together. Should we have found a safer way to become friends? Perhaps we could not. Perhaps the risk itself was what it took to bind us.

"MOMENTS OF DOUBT"

[Author's note: The most basic issue a mountaineer faces is the risk of death. In my case, the issue had an early immediacy, for by the time I was twenty-two I had witnessed three fatal climbing accidents. Not surprisingly, however, it took me fourteen years to face the issue in print.

"Moments of Doubt," which I sent in unsolicited, was my first piece published in *Outside*. I worked hard on it, and there is a certain gratification in the fact that, of all the articles I have written, this one has gained approval from the most readers.

The account here of Huntington overlaps with my earlier piece, "Five Days on Mount Huntington." For such repetition, I beg indulgence: the "plot" of the article seems to need it, and I am bemused to discover that I told the story of Ed Bernd's death somewhat differently the second time round, after fourteen years of remembering it.]

A day in early July, perfect for climbing. From the mesas above Boulder, Colorado, a heat-cutting breeze drove the smell of the pines up onto the great tilting slabs of the Flatirons.

It was 1961; I was eighteen, had been climbing about a year, Gabe even less. We were about six hundred feet up, three-quarters of the way to the summit of the First Flatiron. There wasn't a guidebook in those days; so we didn't know how difficult our route was supposed to be or who had previously done it. But it had gone all right, despite the scarcity of places to bang in our Austrian soft-iron pitons; sometimes we'd just wedge our bodies in a crack and yell "On belay!"

It was a joy to be climbing. Climbing was one of the best things—maybe the best thing—in life, given that one would never play shortstop for the Dodgers. There was a risk, as my parents and friends kept pointing out; but I knew the risk was worth it.

In fact, just that summer I had become ambitious. With a friend my age whom I'll call Jock, I'd climbed the east face of Longs Peak, illegally early in the season—no great deed for experts, but pretty good for eighteen-year-old kids. It was Jock's idea to train all summer and go up to the Tetons and do *the* route: the north face of the Grand. I'd never even seen the Tetons, but the idea of the route, hung with names like Petzoldt and Pownall and Unsoeld, sent chills through me

It was Gabe's lead now, maybe the last before the going got easier a few hundred feet below the top. He angled up and left, couldn't get any protection in, went out of sight around a corner. I waited. The rope didn't move. "What's going on?" I finally yelled. "Hang on," Gabe answered irritably, "I'm looking for a belay."

We'd been friends since grade school. When he was young he had been very shy; he'd been raised by his father only—why, I never thought to ask. Ever since I had met him, on the playground, running up the old wooden stairs to the fourth-grade classroom, he'd moved in a jerky, impulsive way. On our high school tennis team, he slashed at the ball with lurching stabs, and skidded across the asphalt like a kid trying to catch his own shadow. He climbed the same way, especially in recent months, impulsively going for a hard move well above his protection, worrying me, but getting away with it. In our first half-year of climbing, I'd usually been a little better than Gabe, just as he was always stuck a notch below me on the tennis team. But in the last couple of months—no denying it—he'd become better on rock than I was; he took the leads that I didn't like the looks of. He might have made a better partner for Jock on the Grand, except that Gabe's only mountain experience had been an altitude-sick crawl up the east side of Mount of the Holy Cross with me just a week before. He'd thrown up on the summit but said he loved the climb.

At eighteen it wasn't easy for me to see why Gabe had suddenly become good at climbing, or why it drove him as nothing else had. Just that April, three months earlier, his father had been killed in an auto accident during a blizzard in Texas. When Gabe returned to school, I mumbled my prepared condolence. He brushed it off and asked at once when we could go climbing. I was surprised. But I wanted to climb, too: the summer was approaching, Jock wasn't always available, and Gabe would go at the drop of a phone call.

Now, finally, came the "on belay" signal from out of sight to the left, and I started up. For the full 120 feet Gabe had been unable to get in any pitons; so as I climbed, the rope drooped in a long arc to my left. It began to tug me sideways, and when I yanked back at it, I noticed that it seemed snagged about fifty feet away, caught under one of the downward-pointing flakes so characteristic of the Flatirons. I flipped the rope angrily and tugged harder on it, then yelled to Gabe to pull from his end. Our efforts only jammed it in tighter. The first trickle of fear leaked into my well-being.

"What kind of belay do you have?" I asked the invisible Gabe.

"Not too good. I couldn't get anything in."

There were fifty feet of slab between me and the irksome flake, and those fifty feet were frighteningly smooth. I ought, I supposed, to climb over to the flake, even if it meant building up coils and coils of slack. But if I slipped, and Gabe with no anchor . . .

I yelled to Gabe what I was going to do. He assented.

I untied from the rope, gathered as many coils as I could, and threw the end violently down and across the slab, hoping to snap the jammed segment loose, or at least reduce Gabe's job to hauling the thing in with all his might. Then, with my palms starting to sweat, I climbed carefully up to a little ledge and sat down.

Gabe was now below me, out of sight, but close. "It's still jammed," he said, and my fear surged a little notch.

"Maybe we can set up a rappel," I suggested.

"No, I think I can climb back and get it."

"Are you sure?" Relief lowered the fear a notch. Gabe would do the dirty work, just as he was willing to lead the hard pitches.

"It doesn't look too bad."

I waited, sitting on my ledge, staring out over Boulder and the dead-straw plains that seemed to stretch all the way to Kansas. I wasn't sure we were doing the right thing. A few months earlier I'd soloed a rock called the Fist, high on Green Mountain above Boulder, in the midst of a snow storm, and sixty feet off the ground, as I was turning a slight overhang, my foot had come off, and one hand . . . but not the other. And adrenaline had carried me the rest of the way up. There was a risk, but you rose to it.

For Gabe, it was taking a long time. It was all the worse not being able to see him. I looked to my right and saw a flurry of birds playing with a column of air over near the Second Flatiron. Then Gabe's voice, triumphant: "I got it!"

"Way to go!" I yelled back. The fear diminished. If he'd been able to climb down to the snag, he could climb back up. I was glad I hadn't had to do it. Remembering his impatience, I instructed, "Coil it up." A week before, on Holy Cross, I'd been the leader.

"No, I'll just drape it around me. I can climb straight up to where you are."

The decision puzzled me. *Be careful,* I said in my head. But that was Gabe, impulsive, playing his hunches. Again the seconds crept. I had too little information, nothing to do but look for the birds and smell the pine sap. You could see Denver, smogless as yet, a squat aggregation of downtown buildings like some modern covered-wagon circle, defended against the emptiness of the Plains. There had been climbers over on the Third Flatiron earlier, but now I couldn't spot them. The red, gritty sandstone was warm to my palms.

"How's it going?" I yelled.

A pause. Then Gabe's voice, quick-syllabled as always, more tense than normal. "I just got past a hard place, but it's easier now."

He sounded so close, only fifteen feet below me, yet I hadn't seen him since his lead had taken him around the corner out of sight. I felt I could almost reach down and touch him.

Next, there was a soft but unmistakable sound, and my brain knew it without ever having heard it before. It was the sound of cloth rubbing against rock. Then Gabe's cry, a single blurt of knowledge: "Dave!"

I rose with a start to my feet, but hung on to a knob with one hand, gripping it desperately. "Gabe!" I yelled back; then, for the first time in half an hour, I saw him. He was much farther from me now, sliding and rolling, the rope wrapped in tangles about him like a badly made nest. "Grab something," I yelled, I could hear Gabe shouting, even as he receded from me, "No! Oh, no!"

I thought, there's always a chance. But Gabe began to bounce, just like rocks I had seen bouncing down mountain slopes, a longer bounce each time. The last was conclusive, for I saw him flung far from the rock's even surface to pirouette almost lazily in the air, then meet the unyielding slab once more, headfirst, before the sandstone threw him into the treetops.

What I did next is easy to remember, but it is hard to judge just how long it took. It seemed, in the miasma of adrenaline, to last either three minutes or more than an hour. I stood and I yelled for help. After several repetitions, voices from the Mesa Trail caught the breeze back to me. "We're coming!" someone shouted. "In the trees!" I yelled back. "Hurry!" I sat down and said to myself, now don't go screw it up yourself, you don't have a rope, sit here and wait for someone to come rescue you. They can come up the back and lower a rope from the top. As soon as I had given myself this good advice, I got up and started scrambling toward the summit, It wasn't too hard. Slow down, don't make a mistake, I lectured myself, but it felt as if I were running. From the summit I down-climbed the eighty feet on the backside; I'd been there before and had rappelled it. Forty feet up there was a hard move. *Don't blow it.* Then I was on the ground.

I ran down the scree-and-brush gully between the First and Second Flatirons, and got to the bottom a few minutes before the hikers. "Where is he?" a wild-eyed volunteer asked me. "In the trees?" I yelled back. "Somewhere right near here!"

Searching for something is usually an orderly process; it has its methodical pleasures, its calm reconstruction of the possible steps that led to the object getting lost. We searched instead like scavenging predators, crashing through deadfall and talus; and we couldn't find Gabe. Members of the Rocky Mountain Rescue Group began to arrive; they were calmer than the hiker I had first encountered. We searched and searched, and finally a voice called out, "Here he is."

Someone led me there. There were only solemn looks to confirm the obvious. I saw Gabe sprawled face down on the talus, his limbs in the wrong positions, the rope, coated with blood, still in a cocoon about him. The seat of his jeans had been ripped away, and one bare buttock was scraped raw, the way kids' knees used to look after a bad slide on a sidewalk. I wanted to go up and touch his body, but I couldn't. I sat down and cried.

Much later—but it was still afternoon, the sun and breeze still collaborating on a perfect July day—a policeman led me up the walk to my house. My mother came to the screen door and, grasping the situation at once, burst into tears. Gabe was late for a birthday party. Someone had called my house, mildly annoyed, to try to account for the delay. My father took on the task of calling them back. (More than a decade later he told me that it was the hardest thing he had ever done.)

In the newspapers the next day a hiker was quoted as saying that he knew something bad was going to happen, because he'd overheard Gabe and me "bickering," and good climbers didn't do that. Another man had watched the fall through binoculars. At my father's behest, I wrote down a detailed account of the accident.

About a week later Jock came by. He spent the appropriate minutes in sympathetic silence, then said, "The thing you've got to do is get right back on the rock." I didn't want to, but I went out with him. We top-roped a moderate climb only thirty feet high. My feet and hands shook uncontrollably, my heart seemed to be screaming, and Jock had to haul me up the last ten feet. "It's OK, it'll come back," he reassured.

I had one friend I could talk to, a touch-football buddy who thought climbing was crazy in the first place. With his support, in the presence of my parents' anguish, I managed at last to call up Jock and ask him to come by. We sat on my front porch. "Jock," I said, "I just can't go to the Grand. I'm too shook up. I'd be no good if I did go." He stared at me long and hard. Finally he stood up and walked away.

That fall I went to Harvard. I tried out for the tennis team, but when I found that the Mountaineering Club included veterans who had just climbed Waddington in the Coast Range and Mount Logan in the Yukon, it didn't take me long to single out my college heroes.

But I wasn't at all sure about climbing. On splendid fall afternoons at the Shawangunks, when the veterans dragged us neophytes up easy climbs, I sat on the belay ledges mired in ambivalence. I'd never been at a cliff where there were so many climbers, and whenever one of them on an adjoining route happened to yell—even if the message were nothing more alarming than "I think it goes up to the left there!"—I jerked with fright.

For reasons I am still not sure of, Gabe became a secret. Attached to the memory of our day on the First Flatiron was not only fear, but guilt and embarrassment. Guilt toward Gabe, of course, because I had not been the one who went to get the jammed rope. But the humiliation, born perhaps in that moment when the cop had led me up to my front door and my mother had burst into tears, lingered with me in the shape of a crime or moral error, like getting a girl pregnant.

Nevertheless, at Harvard I got deeply involved with the Mountaineering Club. By twenty I'd climbed McKinley with six Harvard friends via a new route, and that August I taught at Colorado Outward Bound School. With all of "Boone Patrol," including the senior instructor, a laconic British hard man named Clough, I was camped one night above timberline. We'd crawled under the willow bushes and strung out ponchos for shelter. In the middle of the night I dreamed that Gabe was falling away from me through endless reaches of black space. He was in a metal cage, spinning headlong, and I repeatedly screamed his name. I woke with a jolt, sat shivering for ten minutes, then crawled, dragging my bag, far from the others, and lay awake the rest of the night. As we blew the morning campfire back to life from the evening's ashes, Clough remarked, "Did you hear the screams? One of the poor lads must have had a nightmare."

By my senior year, though, I'd become hard myself. McKinley had seemed a lark compared to my second expedition—a forty-day failure with only one companion, Don Jensen, on the east ridge of Alaska's Mount Deborah. All through the following winter, with Don holed up in the Sierra Nevada, me trudging through a math major at Harvard, we plotted mountaineering revenge. By January we had focused on a route: the unclimbed west face of Mount Huntington, even harder, we thought, than Deborah. By March we'd agreed that Matt Hale, a junior and my regular climbing partner, would be our third, even though Matt had been on no previous expeditions. Matt was daunted by the ambition of the project, but slowly got caught up in it. Needing a fourth, we discussed an even more inexperienced club member, Ed Bernd, a sophomore who'd been climbing little more than a year and who'd not even been in big mountains.

Never in my life, before or since, have I found myself so committed to any project. I daydreamed about recipes for Logan bread and the number of ounces a certain piton weighed; at night I fell asleep with the seductive promises of belay ledges and crack systems whispering in my ear. School was a Platonic facade. The true Idea of my life lay in the Alaska Range.

At one point that spring I floated free from my obsession long enough to hear a voice in my head tell me, "You know, Dave, this is the kind of climb you could get killed on." I stopped and assessed my life, and consciously answered, "It's worth it. Worth the risk." I wasn't sure what I meant by that, but I knew its truth. I wanted Matt to feel the same way. I knew Don did.

On a March weekend Matt and I were leading an ice climbing trip in Huntington Ravine on Mount Washington. The Harvard Cabin was unusually full, which meant a scramble in the morning to get out first and claim the ice gully you wanted to lead. On Saturday I skipped breakfast to beat everybody else to Pinnacle Gully, then the prize of the ravine. It was a bitter, windy day, and though the gully didn't tax my skills unduly, twice sudden gusts almost blew me out of my steps. The second man on the rope, though a good rock climber, found the whole day unnerving and was glad to get back to the cabin.

That night we chatted with the other climbers. The two most experienced were Craig Merrihue, a grad student in astrophysics, said to be brilliant, with first ascents in the Andes and Karakoram behind him, and Dan Doody, a quiet, thoughtful filmmaker who'd gone to college in Wyoming and had recently been on the big American Everest expedition. Both men were interested in our Huntington plans, and it flattered Matt and me that they thought we were up to something serious. The younger climbers looked on us experts in awe; it was delicious to bask in their hero worship as we non-chalante it with Craig and Dan. Craig's lovely wife Sandy was part of our company. All three of them were planning to link up in a relaxing trip to the Hindu Kush the coming summer.

The next day the wind was still gusting fitfully. Matt and I were leading separate ropes of beginners up Odells Gully, putting in our teaching time after having had Saturday to do something hard. I felt lazy, a trifle vexed to be "wasting" a good day. Around noon we heard somebody calling from the ravine floor. We ignored the cries at first, but as a gust of wind came our way, I was pricked with alarm. "Somebody's yelling for help," I shouted to Matt. "Think they mean it?" A tiny figure far below seemed to be running up and down on the snow. My laziness burned away.

I tied off my second to wait on a big bucket of an ice step, then zipped down a rappel off a single poorly placed ice screw. Still in crampons, I ran down into the basin that formed the runout for all five gullies. The man I met, a weekend climber in his thirties who had been strolling up the ravine for a walk, was moaning. He had seen something that looked like "a bunch of rags" slide by out of the corner of his eye. He knew all at once that it was human bodies he had seen, and he could trace the line of fall up to Pinnacle Gully. He knew that Doody and Merrihue were climbing in Pinnacle. And Craig was a close friend of his. During the five minutes or so since the accident he had been unable to approach them, unable to do anything but yell for help and run aimlessly. I was the first to reach the bodies.

Gabe's I had not had to touch. But I was a trip leader now, an experienced mountaineer, the closest approximation in the circumstances to a rescue squad. I'd had first-aid training. Without a second's hesitation I knelt beside the bodies. Dan's was the worse injured, with a big chunk of his head torn open. His blood was still warm, but I was sure he was dead. I thought I could find a faint pulse in Craig's wrist, however, so I tried to stop the bleeding and started mouth-to-mouth resuscitation. Matt arrived and worked on Dan, and then others appeared and tried to help.

For an hour, I think, I put my lips against Craig's, held his nose shut, forced air into his lungs. His lips were going cold and blue, and there was a stagnant taste in the cavity his mouth had become, but I persisted, as did Matt and the others. Not since my father had last kissed me—was I ten?— had I put my lips to another man's. I remembered Dad's scratchy face, when he hadn't shaved, like Craig's now. We kept hoping, but I knew after five minutes that both men had been irretrievably damaged. There was too much blood. It had been a bad year for snow in the bottom of the ravine; big rocks stuck out everywhere. Three years earlier Don Jensen had been avalanched out of Damnation Gully; he fell 800 feet and only broke a shoulder blade. But that had been a good year for snow.

Yet we kept up our efforts. The need arose as much from an inability to imagine what else we might do—stand around in shock?—as from good first aid sense. At last we gave up, exhausted. I could read in Matt's clipped and efficient suggestions the dawning sense that a horrible thing had happened. But I also felt numb. The sense of tragedy flooded home only in one moment. I heard somebody say something like "She's coming," and somebody else say, "Keep her away." I looked up and saw Sandy, Craig's wife, arriving from the cabin, aware of something wrong, but in the instant before knowing that it was indeed Craig she was intercepted bodily by the climber who knew her best, and that was how she learned. I can picture her face in the instant of knowing, and I remember vividly my own revelation—that there was a depth of personal loss that I had never really known existed, of which I was now receiving my first glimpse.

But my memory has blocked out Sandy's reaction. Did she immediately burst into tears, like my mother? Did she try to force her way to Craig? Did we let her? I know I saw it happen, whatever it was, but my memory cannot retrieve it.

There followed long hours into the dark hauling the bodies with ropes back toward the cabin. There was the pacifying exhaustion and the stolid drive back to Cambridge. There was somebody telling me, "You did a fantastic job, all that anybody could have done," and that seeming maudlin—who wouldn't have done the same? There were, in subsequent weeks, the memorial service, long tape-recorded discussions of the puzzling circumstances of the accident (we had found Dan and Craig roped together, a bent ice screw loose on the rope between them), heated indictments of the cheap Swiss design of the screw. And even a couple of visits with Sandy and their five-year-old son.

But my strongest concern was not to let the accident interfere with my commitment to climb Huntington, now only three months away. The deaths had deeply shaken Matt; but we never directly discussed the matter. I never wrote my parents about what had taken place. We went ahead and invited Ed, the sophomore, to join our expedition. Though he had not been in the ravine with us, he too had been shaken. But I got the three of us talking logistics and gear, and thinking about a mountain in Alaska. In some smug private recess I told myself that I was in better training than Craig and Dan had been, and that was why I wouldn't get killed. If the wind had blown one of them out of his steps, well, I'd led Pinnacle the day before in the same wind and it hadn't blown me off. Almost, but it hadn't. Somehow I controlled my deepest feelings and kept the disturbance buried. I had no bad dreams about Doody and Merrihue, no sleepless nights, no sudden qualms about whether Huntington was worth the risk or not. By June I was as ready as I could be for the hardest climb of my life.

It took a month, but we climbed our route on Huntington. Pushing through the night of July 29–30, we traversed the knife-edged summit ridge and stood on top in the still hours of dawn. Only twelve hours before, Matt and I had come as close to being killed as it is possible to get away with in the mountains.

Matt, tugging on a loose crampon strap, had pulled himself off his steps; he landed on me, broke down the snow ledge I had kicked; under the strain our one bad anchor piton popped out. We fell, roped together and helpless, some seventy feet down a steep slope of ice above a 4500-foot drop. Then a miracle intervened; the rope snagged on a nubbin of rock, the size of one's knuckle, and held us both.

Such was our commitment to the climb that, even though we were bruised and Matt had lost a crampon, we pushed upward and managed to join Ed and Don for the summit dash.

At midnight, nineteen hours later, Ed and I stood on a ledge some fifteen hundred feet below. Our tents were too small for four people; so he and I had volunteered to push on to a lower camp, leaving Matt and Don to come down on the next good day. In the dim light we set up a rappel. There was a tangle of pitons, fixed ropes, and the knots tying them off, in the midst of which Ed was attaching a carabiner. I suggested an adjustment. Ed moved the carabiner, clipped our rope in, and started to get on rappel. "Just this pitch," I said, "and then it's practically walking to camp."

Ed leaned back on rappel. There was a scrape and sparks—his crampons scratching the rock, I later guessed. Suddenly he was flying backwards through the air, down the vertical pitch. He hit hard ice sixty feet below. Just as I had on the Flatiron, I yelled, "Grab something, Ed!" But it was evident that his fall was not going to end—not soon, anyway. He slid rapidly down the ice chute, then out of sight over a cliff. I heard him bouncing once or twice, then nothing. He had not uttered a word.

I shouted, first for Ed, then for Don and Matt above. Nothing but silence answered me. There was nothing I could do. I was as certain as I could be that Ed had fallen 4000 feet, to the lower arm of the Tokositna Glacier, inaccessible even from our base camp. He was surely dead.

I managed to get myself, without a rope, down the seven pitches to our empty tent. The next two days I spent alone—desperate for Matt's and Don's return, imagining them dead also, drugging myself with sleeping pills, trying to fathom what had gone wrong, seized one night in my sleep with a vision of Ed, broken and bloody, clawing his way up the wall to me, crying out, "Why didn't you come look for me?" At last Don and Matt arrived, and I had to tell them. Our final descent, in the midst of a raging blizzard, was the nastiest and scariest piece of climbing I have done, before or since.

From Talkeetna, a week later, I called Ed's parents. His father's stunned first words, crackly with long-distance static, were "Is this some kind of a joke?" After the call I went behind the bush pilot's hangar and cried my heart out— the first time in years that I had given way to tears.

A week later, with my parents' backing, I flew to Philadelphia to spend three days with Ed's parents. But not until the last few hours of my stay did we talk about Ed or climbing. Philadelphia was wretchedly hot and sticky. In the Bernds' small house my presence—sleeping on the living room sofa, an extra guest at meals—was a genuine intrusion. Unlike my parents, or Matt's, or Don's, Ed's had absolutely no comprehension of mountain climbing. It was some esoteric thing he had gotten into at Harvard; and of course Ed had completely downplayed, for their sake, the seriousness of our Alaska project.

At that age, given my feelings about climbing, I could hardly have been better shielded from any sense of guilt. But mixed in with my irritation and discomfort in the muggy apartment was an awareness—of a different sort from the glimpse of Sandy Merrihue—that I was in the presence of a grief so deep its features were opaque to me. It was the hope-destroying grief of parents, the grief of those who knew things could not keep going right, a grief that would, I sensed, diminish little over the years. It awed and frightened me, and disclosed to me an awareness of my own guilt. I began remembering other moments. In our first rest after the summit, as we had giddily replayed every detail of our triumph, Ed had said that yes, it had been great, but that he wasn't sure it had been worth it. I hadn't pressed him; his qualifying judgment had seemed the only sour note in a perfect party. It was so obvious to me that all the risks throughout the climb—even Matt's and my near-disaster—had been worth it to make the summit.

Now Ed's remark haunted me. He was, in most climbers' judgment, far too inexperienced for Huntington. We'd caught his occasional technical mistakes on the climb, a piton hammered in with the eye the wrong way, an ice axe left below a rock overhang. But he learned so well, was so naturally strong, complemented our intensity with a hearty capacity for fun and friendship. Still, at Harvard, there had been, I began to see, no way for him to turn down our invitation. Matt and I and the other veterans were his heroes, just as the Waddington seniors had been mine three years before. Now the inner circle was asking him to join. It seemed to us at the time an open invitation, free of any moral implications. Now I wondered.

I still didn't know what had gone wrong with the rappel, even though Ed had been standing a foot away from me. Had it been some technical error of his in clipping in? Or had the carabiner itself failed? There was no way of settling the question, especially without having been able to look for, much less find, his body.

At last Ed's family faced me. I gave a long, detailed account of the climb. I told them it was "the hardest thing yet done in Alaska," a great mountaineering accomplishment. It would attract the attention of climbers the world over. They looked at me with blank faces; my way of viewing Ed's death was incomprehensible. They were bent on finding a Christian meaning to the event. It occurred to them that maybe God had meant to save Ed from a worse death fighting in Vietnam. They were deeply stricken by our inability to retrieve his body. "My poor baby," Mrs. Bernd wailed at one point, "he must be so cold."

Their grief brought me close to tears again, but when I left it was with a sigh of relief. I went back to Denver, where I was starting graduate school. For the second time in my life I thought seriously about quitting climbing. At twenty-two I had been the firsthand witness of three fatal accidents, costing four lives. Mr. Bernd's laborious letters, edged with the leaden despair I had seen in his face, continued to remind me that the question "Is it worth the risk?" was not one any person could answer by consulting only himself.

Torn by my own ambivalence, studying Restoration comedy in a city where I had few friends, no longer part of a gang heading off each weekend to the Shawangunks, I laid off climbing most of the winter of 1965–66. By February I had made a private resolve to quit the business, at least for a few years.

One day a fellow showed up at my basement apartment, all the way down from Alaska. I'd never met him, but the name Art Davidson was familiar. He looked straight off skid row, with his tattered clothes and unmatched socks and tennis shoes with holes in them; and his wild red beard and white eyebrows lent a kind of rundown Irish aristocracy to his face. He lived, apparently, like a vagrant, subsisting on cottage cheese in the back of his old pickup truck (named Bucephalus after Alexander's horse), which he hid in parking lots each night on the outskirts of Anchorage. Art was crazy about Alaskan climbing. In the next year and a half he would go on five major expeditions—still the most intense spate of bit-range mountaineering I know of. In my apartment he kept talking in his soft, enthusiastic voice about the Cathedral Spires, a place he knew Don and I had had our eyes on. I humored him. I let him talk on, and then we went out for a few beers, and Art started reminding me about the pink granite and the trackless glaciers, and by the evening's end the charismatic bastard had me signed up.

We went to the Cathedral Spires in 1966, with three others. Art was at the zenith of his climbing career. Self-taught, technically erratic, he made up in compulsive zeal what he lacked in finesse. His drive alone got himself and Rick Millikan up the highest peak in the range, which we named Kichatna Spire. As for me, I wasn't the climber I'd been the year before, which had much to do with why I wasn't along with Art on the summit push. That year I'd fallen in love with the woman who would become my wife, and suddenly the old question about risk seemed vastly more complicated. In the blizzard-swept dusk, with two of the other guys up on the climb, I found myself worrying about *their* safety instead of mere logistics. I was as glad nothing had gone wrong by the end of the trip as I was that we'd collaborated on a fine first ascent.

Summer after summer I went back to Alaska, climbing hard, but not with the all-out commitment of 1965. Over the years quite a few of my climbing acquaintances were killed in the mountains, including five close friends. Each death was deeply unsettling, tempting me to doubt all over again the worth of the enterprise. For nine years I taught climbing to college students, and worrying about their safety became an occupational hazard. Ironically, the closest I came during those years to getting killed was not on some Alaskan wall, but on a beginner's climb at the Shawangunks, when I nearly fell head-first backwards out of a rappel—the result of a carabiner jamming in a crack, my own impatience, and the blasé glaze with which teaching a dangerous skill at a trivial level coats the risk. Had that botched rappel been my demise, no friends would have seen my end as meaningful: instead, a "stupid," "pointless," "who-would-have-thought?" kind of death.

Yet in the long run, trying to answer my own question "Is it worth it?" torn between thinking the question itself ridiculous and grasping for a formulaic answer, I come back to gut-level affirmation, however sentimental, however selfish. When I imagine my early twenties, it is not in terms of the hours spent in a quiet library studying Melville, or my first nervous pontifications before a freshman English class. I want to see Art Davidson again, shambling into my apartment in his threadbare trousers, spooning great dollops of cottage cheese past his flaming beard, filling the air with his baroque hypotheses, convincing me that the Cathedral Spires needed our visit. I want to remember what brand of beer I was drinking when that crazy vagabond in one stroke turned the cautious resolves of a lonely winter into one more summer's plot against the Alaskan wilderness.

Some of the worst moments of my life have taken place in the mountains. Not only the days alone in the tent on Huntington after Ed had vanished— quieter moments as well, embedded in uneventful expeditions. Trying to sleep the last few hours before a predawn start on a big climb, my mind stiff with dread, as I hugged my all-too-obviously fragile self with my own arms—until the scared kid inside my sleeping bag began to pray for bad weather and another day's reprieve. But nowhere else on earth, not even in the harbors of reciprocal love, have I felt pure happiness take hold of me and shake me like a puppy, compelling me, and the conspirators I had arrived there with, to stand on some perch of rock or snow, the uncertain struggle below us, and bawl our pagan vaunts to the very sky. It was worth it then.

PERMISSIONS

We gratefully acknowledge all those who gave permission for written material to appear in this book. We have made every effort to trace and contact copyright holders. If an error or omission is brought to our notice we will be pleased to remedy the situation in future editions of this book. For further information, please contact the publisher.

"Not a Private Affair," by Walt Unsworth, excerpted from *Everest The Mountaineering History*, © 2000 by Walt Unsworth. Reprinted by permission of the author.

"Makalu, Too. Wouldn't You?" excerpted from *Stone Palaces* by Geoffrey Childs, © 2000.

"Storm on Manaslu: A Classic Himalaya Expedition," by Reinhold Messner, excerpted from *To the Top of the World, Challenges in the Himalaya and Karakoramk*, © 1992 and 1999 by The Crowood Press Ltd.

Selection from *Nanda Devi: The Tragic Expedition*, by John Roskelley, © 2000.

Selection from *The Totem Pole*, by Paul Pritchard, © 1999. Reprinted by permission of Constable & Robinson, Ltd.

Selection from "Storm and Sorrow" and "The Edelweiss and the Cross" excerpted from *Storm and Sorrow in the High Pamirs*, by Robert W. Craig, © 1977, The Mountaineers Books. This book is now out of print.

"Lucky Joe," excerpted from *The Price of Adventure* by Hamish MacInnes, © 1987. Reprinted by permission of the author.

"The Fatal Accident on the Matterhorn," by Edward Whymper, excerpted from *Peaks, Passes, and Glaciers*, edited by Walt Unsworth, © 1981. Reprinted by permission of Walt Unsworth. Originally appeared in the *Alpine Journal* (London).

"Solo Winter Ascent: Fadden, 1936," by Dee Molenaar, excerpted from *The Challenge of Rainier*, © 1971 and 1973 by The Mountaineers, 1979 and 1987 by Dee Molenaar.

Selection from *Minus 148°: First Winter Ascent of Mt. McKinley* by Art Davidson, © 1969, 1986, 1999. Reprinted by permission of the author.

Selection from *Moments of Doubt* by David Roberts, © 1986.

ACKNOWLEDGMENTS

Extraordinary thanks to Bill Fortney, Geoffrey Nichols, Connie Pious, Deborah Easter, and Laura Drury.

❧   ❧   ❧

Climber and alpinist **Mark Synnott** is a master of big-wall climbs. He is re-nowned among the climbing community for his successful completion of major new routes in Baffin Island, the Karakoram Range, and Patagonia. In July 1999, with Alex Lowe and Jared Ogden, Synnott completed the first ascent of the northwest face of Great Trango Tower, one of the longest rock climbs ever completed. When he's not in the mountains, Mark is a freelance photo-journalist, motivational speaker, guide, and professional climber. He is a member of the North Face Climbing Team. A senior contributing editor to *Climbing Magazine*, Mark's work has appeared in many publications, includ-ing *National Geographic, Outside, Rock & Ice, Unlimited,* and *Sports Afield.* Mark lives in Jackson, New Hampshire with his wife and son.

Introductions to the individual selections in this anthology were written by **Donna DeShazo,** Seattle, who admits that her own climbing achievements fell short of the heights reached by the mountaineers whose work is extracted here. In her fifteen years as Director of The Mountaineers Books, however, she was privileged to meet and work with some of the finest climbers, writ-ers, and climber-writers in the genre, and developed an abiding love of moun-taineering literature.

THE MOUNTAINEERS, founded in 1906, is a nonprofit outdoor activity and conservation club, whose mission is "to explore, study, preserve, and enjoy the natural beauty of the outdoors. . . . " Based in Seattle, Washington, the club is now the third-largest such organization in the United States, with 15,000 members and five branches throughout Washington State.

The Mountaineers sponsors both classes and year-round outdoor activities in the Pacific Northwest, which include hiking, mountain climbing, ski-touring, snowshoeing, bicycling, camping, kayaking and canoeing, nature study, sailing, and adventure travel. The club's conservation division supports environmental causes through educational activities, sponsoring legislation, and presenting informational programs. All club activities are led by skilled, experienced volunteers, who are dedicated to promoting safe and responsible enjoyment and preservation of the outdoors.

If you would like to participate in these organized outdoor activities or the club's programs, consider a membership in The Mountaineers. For information and an application, write or call The Mountaineers, Club Headquarters, 300 Third Avenue West, Seattle, WA 98119; 206-284-6310.

The Mountaineers Books, an active, nonprofit publishing program of the club, produces guidebooks, instructional texts, historical works, natural history guides, and works on environmental conservation. All books produced by The Mountaineers Books fulfill the club's mission.

Send or call for our catalog of more than 500 outdoor titles:

The Mountaineers Books
1001 SW Klickitat Way, Suite 201
Seattle, WA 98134
800-553-4453
mbooks@mountaineers.org
www.mountaineersbooks.org

The Mountaineers Books is proud to be a corporate sponsor of Leave No Trace, whose mission is to promote and inspire responsible outdoor recreation through education, research, and partnerships. The Leave No Trace program is focused specifically on human-powered (nonmotorized) recreation.
Leave No Trace strives to educate visitors about the nature of their recreational impacts, as well as offer techniques to prevent and minimize such impacts. Leave No Trace is best understood as an educational and ethical program, not as a set of rules and regulations. For more information, visit *www.LNT.org,* or call 800-332-4100.